STUDY GUIDE

For Use With

Abnormal Psychology: Current Perspectives

Ninth Edition

by Lauren B. Alloy, John H. Riskind, and Margaret J. Manos

Prepared by
Michele Catone-Maitino
Hudson Valley Community College

McGraw
Hill

Boston   Burr Ridge, IL   Dubuque, IA   Madison, WI   New York   San Francisco   St. Louis
Bangkok   Bogotá   Caracas   Kuala Lumpur   Lisbon   London   Madrid   Mexico City
Milan   Montreal   New Delhi   Santiago   Seoul   Singapore   Sydney   Taipei   Toronto

Higher Education

Study Guide for use with Abnormal Psychology: Current Perspectives, Ninth Edition

Published by McGraw-Hill, an imprint of The McGraw-Hill Companies, Inc., 1221 Avenue of the Americas, New York, NY 10020. Copyright 2005 by The McGraw-Hill Companies, Inc., All rights reserved. Printed in the United States of America. Except as permited under the United Sates Copyright Act of 1976, no part of this publication may be reproduced or distributed in any form or by any means, or stored in a database or retrieval system, without the prior written permission of the publisher.

1 2 3 4 5 6 7 8 9 0   QPD/QPD   0 9 8 7 6 5 4

ISBN 0-07-245039-8

Vice president and Editor-in-chief: *Emily Barrosse*
Publisher: *Stephen Rutter*
Sponsoring editor: *John Wannamacher*
Director of development/Development editor: *Judith Kromm*
Editorial assistant: *Jane Acheson*
Marketing manager: *Melissa Caughlin*
Media producer: *Ginger Bunn*
Senior production supervisor: *Rich DeVitto*
Project manager: *Mel Valentín*
Compositor: *Noyes Composition and Graphics*
Typeface: *10/12 Times New Roman*
Printer: *Quebecor/Dubuque*

CONTENTS

CHAPTER 1
ABNORMAL BEHAVIOR: HISTORICAL PERSPECTIVES

LEARNING OBJECTIVES

By the time you have finished studying this chapter, you should be able to do the following:

1. List and describe four criteria for defining abnormality, and list four categories of behavior that most societies consider indicative of mental disorder. (2–4)

2. Describe how cultural and gender differences complicate the task of defining normal and abnormal behavior. (5–6)

3. List and describe the essential features of the medical model of abnormal behavior, and list the advantages and shortcomings of the medical model as presented in your text. (6–8)

4. List and define six perspectives that the text cites as alternatives to the medical model, and describe the kinds of mental health professionals employed within them. (6–8)

5. Cite the contributions of Hippocrates and Galen to the study of abnormal behavior, and contrast their views to those that prevailed in more ancient societies. (12)

6. Discuss how the cultural atmosphere of the Middle Ages influenced attitudes and actions toward the mentally ill during that period. (12)

7. Discuss the impact that witch hunting during the Renaissance had upon prevailing attitudes toward the mentally ill. (13)

8. List the contributions of Pussin, Pinel, Esquirol, Tuke, Rush, and Dix to the reform of mental health care in the eighteenth and nineteenth centuries. (14–18)

9. Define moral therapy, and discuss its place in the development of modern psychotherapy. (15–16)

10. Describe the social and historical factors that led to the rise and decline of large mental hospitals from the late nineteenth to the mid-twentieth centuries. (16–17)

11. Describe how the work of Wundt, Kraepelin, Krafft-Ebing, and Mesmer laid the foundation for the development of modern abnormal psychology. (20–22)

12. Cite the contributions of Liébeault, Bernheim, Charcot, Breuer, and Freud to the development of modern psychotherapy. (21–22)

13. Describe how African and Asian cultures differ from Western cultures in their understanding and treatment of mental disorders. (22–23)

14. List three assumptions your text uses in constructing a multiperspective approach to abnormal behavior, and discuss the benefits of such an orientation. (23–24)

15. Define prevention and discuss the differences between primary, secondary, and tertiary prevention. (10–11)

16. Define the historical and social factors that lead to the rise of the prevention movement. (17)

17. Define managed care and discuss the rise of managed behavioral health care. (19–20)

KEY TERMS

The following terms are in bold print in your text and are important to your understanding of the chapter. Look them up in the text and write down their definitions.

biogenic (6)
clinical psychologist (10)
community mental health centers (16)
community psychology (19)
deinstitutionalization (16)
exorcism (11)
free association (22)
general paresis (21)
humors (12)
hypnosis (21)
hysteria (21)
inpatient (16)
managed care (19)
medical model (6)
moral therapy (16)

neuroscience perspective (8)
norms (2)
outpatient (16)
prefrontal lobotomy (16)
prevention (9)
primary prevention (10)
psychiatric social worker (10)
psychiatrist (10)
psychoanalysis (22)
psychoanalyst (10)
psychogenic theory (21)
psychopathology (20)
secondary prevention (10)
syndrome (20)

IMPORTANT NAMES

Identify the following persons and their major contributions to abnormal psychology as discussed in this chapter.

Hippolyte-Marie Bernheim (21)
Josef Breuer (22)
Jean-Martin Charcot (21)
Vincenzo Chiarugi (14)
Dorothea Dix (15)
Jean Esquirol (14)
Sigmund Freud (22)
Galen (12)
Hippocrates (12)
Emil Kraepelin (20)

Richard Krafft-Ebing (21)
Ambrose-Auguste Liébeault (21)
Anton Mesmer (21)
Philippe Pinel (14)
Jean-Baptiste Pussin (14)
Benjamin Rush (15)
Thomas Szasz (7)
William Tuke (14)
Wilhelm Wundt (20)

GUIDED SELF-STUDY

1. Let's get an overview of the chapter before we begin. What topics will be discussed in this chapter? (Hint: Look at the outline on the first page of the chapter.)

Defining Abnormal Behavior

2. List some behaviors that you have observed that seemed abnormal to you.

   a.

   b.

   c.

3. List the four criteria for defining abnormal behavior presented in your text.

   a.

   b.

   c.

   d.

   Make up your own memory aid to remember these four criteria, or use the one given in the following Answers section (p. 13). (Note: Making up your own is more effective because you will have done mental exercise to create it.)

4. Identify the criterion that would be used to define each of the following situations as abnormal.

   a.   A three-year-old child who can read

   b.   A person who can't hold a job owing to chronic lateness

   c.   A man who has a wife and a girlfriend

   d.   A student who feels a little queasy just signing up for algebra

   e.   A woman who wrecks her new car while distracted by angry thoughts about her boss

5. Determine which criterion for abnormal you used for each of your examples in question two. Then, if there are any criteria you did not use, think up an example for those criteria as well. If you cannot, ask a classmate or your instructor so that you have a clear understanding of each of the criteria.

6. List some behaviors for which knowing the time period and culture would be critical in determining whether the behaviors would be considered abnormal.

7. Each of the following statements is associated with one of the criteria for defining abnormal behaviors. Select the associated criterion from the three choices listed below each statement.

   a.   Lack of an objective standard is especially problematical

   norm violation / statistical rarity / personal discomfort

   b.   Works fairly well in small, highly integrated societies

   statistical rarity / norm violation / maladaptive behavior

   c.   Favored by mental health professionals for its practicality

   personal discomfort / statistical rarity / maladaptive behavior

   d.   Its major weakness is that no values are considered

   statistical rarity / norm violation / maladaptive behavior

   e.   Very practical view—survival

   maladaptive behavior / statistical rarity / norm violation

   f.   Somebody has to be abnormal

   maladaptive behavior / personal discomfort / statistical rarity

8. Complete the following statements using these words: *harmful, erratic, variety, inappropriate, agreement, poor,* and *cultures.*

Even though the criteria for abnormality involve a (a)_____ of views, there is actually fairly clear

(b)_____ about what defines abnormal behavior even across different (c)_____. Maher and

Maher (1985) point out that in most societies four categories of behavior are seen as abnormal:

behavior that is (d)_____ to the self or to others without serving the interests of the individual; (e)

_____ reality contact—for example, beliefs that most people do not hold, or sensory perceptions of

things that most people do not perceive; emotional reactions (f)_____ to the person's situation; and

(g)_____ behavior—that is, behavior that shifts unpredictably.

Relating Abnormal Behavior to Groups

9. Fill in the blanks using the following terms: *major depression, Western, hallucination, norms, epidemiology, medical, women, Asian, religious,* and *moral.*

Gender and ethnicity must be considered when determining what is abnormal behavior in a specific individual because:

a. The number of people within the group having specific disorders is predictably different from the number

for that disorder in another group. That is to say, different populations have different _____. For

instance, _____ have more eating disorders than men. Also, eating disorders are _____

cultural phenomena, whereas koro is a phenomenon of some _____ cultures.

b. Different groups of people experience and express psychological disorders differently. The textbook's

example of Bill and Mr. Sinha points out that these two men probably had the same disorders. Mr. Sinha

thought he had masturbated too much as a teenager, which for him was a _____ and _____

issue. Bill saw his problem as a physical one and sought _____ intervention. The textbook

suggests that from these symptoms both men had what in the West is called _____ _____.

c. Different groups have different _____ about what is appropriate behavior. For example, some

cultures believe seeing the Virgin Mary is a religious experience, but an American diagnostician might think

this vision is a(n) _____.

Explaining Abnormal Behavior

10. After deciding which behaviors are abnormal, we now turn to trying to explain what causes such behavior. Use the following words or phrases to fill in these blanks about the causes of abnormal behaviors: *supernatural, naturalistic, body, relationships, disease.*

    The explanations used in this textbook are all (a)_____, which means they are explained as events

    of nature, such as disturbances in the physical human (b)_____ or in human (c)_____.

    (During ancient times and medieval times, (d)_____ explanations were common.) The

    medical model explained abnormal behavior as a (e) _____ process with symptoms caused by a

    malfunction in the body.

11. Thomas Szasz criticized the medical model vociferously, saying that mental illness, as the medical model

    viewed it, was a "myth." Szasz believed that mental illnesses were not illnesses in the medical sense.

    Instead, he called them problems in (a)_____, that were expressed as violations of moral,

    (b)_____,and (c)_____ norms.

12. _____ approaches explain disturbed behavior as mental processes caused by the person's interaction

    with the environment.

13. The psychological perspectives are theories based on intangible processes in the individual's mind interacting with the individual's environment. Each of the psychological perspectives focuses on different aspects of the mind to explain abnormal behavior. Draw lines to match the following perspectives with their central concern.

a.	psychoanalytic	disordered relationships
b.	behavioral	thinking
c.	cognitive	unconscious conflicts
d.	interpersonal	body chemistry
e.	sociocultural	social forces
f.	neuroscience	learning

14. How are the neuroscience perspective and the medical model alike, and how are they different?

Treating Abnormal Behavior

15. What two factors in a society determine how abnormal behavior will be treated?

16. List the three main concepts that define psychotherapy.

    a.

    b.

    c.

17. Define each of the four main types of mental health professional.

    a.   Psychiatrist:

    b.   Clinical psychologist:

    c.   Psychiatric social worker:

    d.   Psychoanalyst:

18. There are at least (a)_____ distinct forms of Western psychotherapies. The term (b)_____ refers to combining techniques from different approaches.

Preventing Abnormal Behavior

19. _____ is the process of keeping disorders from beginning in the first place.

20. Psychologists distinguish between primary, secondary, and tertiary prevention. Define and explain.

Ancient Societies: Deviance and the Supernatural

21. How did the ancient societies see abnormal behavior, and what type of therapy was probably used?

Greeks and the Rise of Science

22. What dramatic change effected by the ancient Greeks influenced the view of abnormal behavior?

23. List two accomplishments credited to Hippocrates.

    a.

    b.

24. _____ was the Greek physician, practicing in Rome, who showed that the body's arteries contained blood—not air, as was commonly thought.

Middle Ages and the Renaissance: Natural and Supernatural

25. Why is the fall of the Roman empire mentioned in this chapter?

By the way, when was the fall of the Roman empire?

26. In the Middle Ages and the Renaissance both (a)_____ and (b)_____ explanations were used to explain abnormal behavior. The Christian Church tended to encourage which explanation?

27. How did the witch hunts fit into the issue of abnormal behavior?

Eighteenth Century and After: Asylums

28. Where did science stand in the eighteenth and nineteenth centuries relative to the supernatural approach?

29. Before considering the asylum reformers, fill in the following blanks for a brief historical review of early institutionalized care of the psychologically disturbed.

In late Greek civilization, mental health (a)_____ were established for the care of the mentally ill. In Alexandria, temples of (b)_____ were set aside as asylums. In Arab countries, there were wards for the mentally ill within the general hospitals in the (c)_____ century. The first hospital set up exclusively for the insane was opened in Moslem Spain in the early (d)_____ century. After that, efforts to set up local community care for the mentally ill occured in many major cities.

30. List some of the conditions that existed in the care of the mentally ill that needed to be changed.

31. MORAL? or MORALE? That is the question! Write one of those words in each blank. Even though the therapy that the reformers advocated was called (a)_____ therapy, it did NOT address their (b)_____ behavior; its purpose was to raise their (c)_____.

32. If you were registered in the first psychiatry course in America, your teacher's name would have been

_____. (Anton Mesmer, Emil Kraepelin, Benjamin Rush, Ambrose Liébeault, or Wilhelm Wundt)

33. Dorothea Dix's efforts to help the mentally disturbed eventually led to a circumstance that she never intended. What was it?
   a. Mental illness was declared to be illegal.
   b. Mental hospitals developed into large impersonal places.
   c. Mental patients became subjects in the first psychological laboratory experiments.
   d. Hypnosis became the primary treatment for the mentally ill.

34. List four reasons for the decline of moral therapy.

   a.

   b.

   c.

   d.

35. During the late 1800s moral therapy was replaced by the practice of removing the mentally ill from the local communities and sending them off to institutions for _____ care, which was just warehousing them out of the sight of polite society.

36. List some of the problems that come with long-term institutional care of mental patients.

37. During the middle of the 1900s one of the efforts to manage uncontrollable patients was a crude brain surgery called a (a)_____ _____, which at best left the mental patient in a permanent

(b)_____ state. In the 1950s (c)_____ were discovered that were effective for calming formerly unmanageable patients. This change led to (d)_____ as hundreds of thousands of long-term

mental patients were released from the mental hospitals. In the year (e)_____ Congress passed the

Community Mental Health Centers Act to provide mental care within the patient's own community instead

of sending him/her off to some faraway institution.

38. Deinstitutionalization has contributed to a social phenomenon known as (a)_____, of whom

approximately one- (b)_____ are thought to be suffering from mental disorders.

Rise of the Prevention Movement

39. In (a)_____, an influential book, *Mental Health Manpower Trends*, written by (b)_____,

pioneered the idea that mental health should be accessible to everyone.

40. Define *community psychology*.

Foundations of Modern Abnormal Psychology

41. (a)_____ established the first psychological laboratory in the city of (b)_____ in the year

(c)_____. (d)_____ placed biogenic theory in the forefront of European psychiatric theory as

the medical model in his *Textbook of Psychiatry*. (e)_____ is also considered the founder of

experimental abnormal psychology. Another term for *abnormal psychology* is (f)_____.

42. Why is the diagnosis of syphilis included as part of one of the milestones in the development of abnormal
psychology?

43. What other mental and behavioral problems substantiated the medical model because they were found to
relate directly to specific brain pathologies?

44. What is the alternative to a biogenic cause? Explain what that term means.

45. Mesmer claimed he was trying to cure his patients by adjusting the (a)_____ in their bodies. His

technique was originally known as (b)_____ . From this work came Mesmer's great contribution to

abnormal psychology: the discovery of the power of (c)_____. Mesmer's technique was eventually

to be known as (d)_____.

46. What was the Nancy school of thought, and where did it stand on the disorder known as hysteria? Who
opposed the Nancy school?

47. The discovery that hysteria could be cured or induced by (a)_____ suggested that, in general,

(b)_____ factors could cause abnormal behavior.

48. Who eventually won in the debate between the Nancy school of thought and the Paris school of thought?

49. Assign the correct order (1–5) to the following events.

_____ Freud found that everyone could not be hypnotized.

_____ Freud became acquainted with Liébeault and Bernheim's ideas.

_____ Freud went to Paris to study with the French neurologist Charcot.

_____ Freud started using free association.

_____ Freud started to work with Breuer who was experimenting with the use of hypnosis.

Non-Western Approaches

50. What is the "West" in this chapter (and throughout this textbook)?

51. The African and Asian approaches to treating mental disturbances are quite different from traditional Western therapies. Why? (2 reasons)

a.

b.

52. The textbook's authors point out that although these cultures' therapeutic techniques appear quite different, they may actually share some of the same underlying mechanisms used in Western therapies.

a. What underlying mechanisms are similar in African and Western therapies?

b. What underlying mechanism is similar in Asian and some Western therapies?

A Multiperspective Approach

53. Fill in the key words in the three assumptions about human behavior that underlie the multiperspective approach.

a. Human behavior can be studied _____.

b. Abnormal behavior results from both _____ and _____ processes.

c. Each human being is _____.

Rise of Managed Behavioral Health Care

54. (a)_____ is an umbrella term for a variety of organizational structures, insurance benefits, and

regulations that both provide for and control the cost of health care procedures. The goal of managed care is

to control the (b)_____ of treatment, primarily by (c)_____ the use of services.

55. Discuss the influence managed care has had on mental health care.

HELPFUL HINTS

1. **Learn and understand well the six perspectives** listed in this chapter, and **save yourself trouble**. They are not going to go away. They are the ABCs of this course. A memory trick to recall the list of psychological perspectives is to use the first letter of the name of each perspective, which provides the acronym "**p**eanut **b**utter **c**hocolate **b**rownie **f**or **s**upper." I suggest that you reward yourself with a peanut butter chocolate brownie for supper when you can successfully list the six psychological perspectives from memory.

2. Since this chapter focuses on history, ask your instructor how much you are expected to know about specific dates and names.

3. Anytime you hear the word "behaviorism," translate it to "learning" until you become comfortable with behaviorism as a concept unto itself.

4. Translate the word "cognitive" to "thinking" until you become comfortable with the cognitive perspective.

5. Do not confuse the words "learning" and "thinking." These two words are not interchangable.

6. Be sure to distinguish among all the "psych"-something words. They all relate to the mind, but in a wide variety of ways. There are many of them: psychology, psychological, psychoanalytic, psychodynamic, psychogenic, psychometric, psychologist, psychiatrist, psychopathology, psychopharmacologist.

7. By the way, have you read "How to Use this Study Guide" found in the front of this workbook, right after the table of contents? If you haven't, you have already missed some more very important helpful hints.

8. Eclecticism and multimodal treatment are very similar concepts: They both involve the use of techniques from more than one perspective.

PRACTICE TEST

Use the following test questions to check your knowledge of the material in this chapter. You might want to write the answers on a separate sheet of paper so you can take the test more than once.

1. *Abnormal* in the statistical sense means that
   a. an individual has violated a social expectation.
   b. there are many people who share the same problem.
   c. the individual is in the minority in regard to that behavior.
   d. the individual lives up to only a few of the ideals of his/her society.

2. In an initial therapy session a client says, "I came here today because I am fed up with being depressed all the time. Life just doesn't seem worth living, and this has got to change." Which criterion of abnormality best applies to this client?
   a. statistical rarity
   b. norm violation
   c. maladaptive behavior
   d. personal discomfort

3. One possible explanation the text offers for the sex differences that show up in many psychopathologies is that
   a. women's greater hormonal variations make them more susceptible to mental imbalances.
   b. men are taught how to be stronger and therefore end up with fewer problems they can't handle.
   c. women are more open about their feelings and report their problems more often than men.
   d. men live more stressful lives and therefore generally experience more problems than women.

4. The term *biogenic* means
    a. incurable.
    b. neuroscience.
    c. organically caused.
    d. all people have it to some extent.

5. Which of the following perspectives on abnormal behavior assumes that problems result from a failure to learn appropriate ways of acting in the world?
    a. psychodynamic perspective
    b. sociocultural perspective
    c. behavioral perspective
    d. biological perspective

6. A researcher uses brain-imaging techniques to study schizophrenia. This method is consistent with which approach to abnormal behavior?
    a. psychodynamic
    b. behavioral
    c. cognitive
    d. biological

7. Which of the following mental health professionals will have an M.D. degree?
    a. psychiatric social worker
    b. clinical psychologist
    c. counselor
    d. psychiatrist

8. Although Hippocrates' belief that mental problems were caused by imbalances in things like blood, phlegm, and bile sounds rather silly today, his basic point, which is still true today, was that
    a. some people are naturally more physically fit than others.
    b. one cannot ignore the spiritual side of human nature in treating mental problems.
    c. improper digestion of food causes not only physical problems but mental problems as well.
    d. biochemistry can affect behavior and mental health.

9. When deviant behavior was believed to be caused by demonic possession, the accepted cure for forcing out the evil spirits was called
    a. isolation.
    b. moral therapy.
    c. exorcism.
    d. general paresis.

10. One of the most likely explanations for the witch hunts of the Renaissance was that they were designed to
    a. eliminate social, political, and religious nonconformists.
    b. prevent the spread of black plague.
    c. restore order after a period in which the Church encouraged too much superstitious behavior.
    d. create a secular state to oppose the power of the Church.

11. "I am often given credit for beginning the movement for the humane treatment of patients in asylums, but I was actually only continuing the work of an untrained layman who was my predecessor. Who am I?"
    a. Philippe Pinel
    b. Jean Esquirol
    c. Jean-Baptist Pussin
    d. Benjamin Rush

12. The nineteenth-century American educator who campaigned for humane treatment of the disturbed and who founded thirty-two mental hospitals was

    a.   Dorothea Dix.
    b.   Philippe Pinel.
    c.   William Tuke.
    d.   Sir Frances More.

13. Moral therapy was based on the idea that

    a.   mental problems were defects in moral character.
    b.   strict religious training is the best cure for mental disorder.
    c.   kind treatment, lowered stress, and a "morale"-raising environment would encourage a return to mental health.
    d.   the crowding found in large mental hospitals encouraged immoral behavior in patients.

14. Which of the following did NOT contribute to the decline of moral therapy?

    a.   prejudice against Irish immigrants
    b.   early successes of the medical model
    c.   understaffing and overcrowding of mental hospitals
    d.   the rise of the psychodynamic perspective on disorder

15. Which of the following was a major reason for the movement from large mental institutions to community-based care in the 1950s and 1960s?

    a.   the development of effective antipsychotic medications
    b.   the decline of moral therapy
    c.   the disproving of the medical model of disorder
    d.   an increased willingness on the part of taxpayers to pay for the training of more mental health professionals

16. Which of the following best summarizes the state of the community mental health system today?

    a.   It is an outmoded approach to treatment replaced early in this century by intensive institutional care.
    b.   It is a rapidly expanding alternative to custodial care and homelessness for the seriously disturbed.
    c.   It is inadequate to meet many community needs due to lack of funds and/or political support.
    d.   Recent advances in medical treatment of behavioral problems have made it largely unnecessary.

17. A distinct cluster of symptoms that describes a disorder is called a(n)

    a.   psychopathology.
    b.   prognosis.
    c.   syndrome.
    d.   etiology.

18. According to the text, the debate on psychological theory between the Paris and Nancy schools

    a.   led to the decline of the large mental hospital.
    b.   provided support for the medical model.
    c.   raised the possibility that apparently biological hysterical problems might be psychological in origin.
    d.   determined that hypnosis was an inadequate method of treatment.

19. During a session with your therapist, she asks you to relax and say whatever comes to mind. The therapist is using which of the following techniques?

    a.   hypnosis
    b.   free association
    c.   transference
    d.   meditation

20. Which of the following is NOT one of the assumptions that your textbook's authors use in their multiperspective approach?
    a. Human behavior can be studied scientifically.
    b. The scientific study of psychology rules out subjective speculation about mental processes.
    c. Abnormal behavior is the product of both psychological and biological processes.
    d. Each human being is unique.

ANSWERS

Guided Self-Study (p. 2)

1. Defining, explaining, and treating abnormal behavior and a history of how abnormal behavior has been dealt with over the centuries.

2. Some examples: talking aloud to one's self, wearing bizarre clothing, biting fingernails down to nubs, falling asleep at a rock concert, cheating on one's mate, screaming at a newborn baby, driving a hundred miles per hour, watching the execution of a criminal.

3. Norm violation (2)
   Statistical rarity (3)
   Personal discomfort (3)
   Maladaptive behavior (3)
   (Memory trick to recall these four criteria: MNoPqR)

4. a. Statistical rarity (3)
   b. Maladaptive behavior (3)
   c. Norm violation (2)
   d. Personal discomfort (3)
   e. Maladaptive behavior (3)

   It is possible that there may be some debate over the correctness of one or more of these answers. For example, situation "e" may also be listed as "personal discomfort" because she is experiencing distress over her boss's treatment of her. However, the best answer would probably be "maladaptive behavior" because her reaction to the situation has now contributed to more problems, hassle, expense, and perhaps loss of transportation.

5. Which criterion you used depends on the reasoning behind what you said. For example, biting fingernails down to nubs could fit any one of the criteria depending on what reason you gave: Norm violation, if you said society says one should not bite nails to the quick. Statistical rarity, if you said because very few people engage in nail biting. Personal discomfort, if you said the person who does it is very unhappy about it. Maladaptive behavior, if you said he/she can't get a job or a date because of it.

6. Examples might be women wearing slacks, deliberately inflicting pain on one's body, breastfeeding infants in public places, or a man or woman who has three spouses at one time.

7. a. personal discomfort (3)
   b. norm violation (2)
   c. maladaptive behavior (3)
   d. statistical rarity (3)
   e. maladaptive behavior (3)
   f. statistical rarity (3)

8. a. variety
   b. agreement
   c. cultures
   d. harmful
   e. poor
   f. inappropriate
   g. erratic

9. a. epidemiology, women, Western, Asian
   b. religious and moral, medical, major depression
   c. norms, hallucination

10. a. naturalistic
    b. body
    c. relationships
    d. supernatural
    e. disease (6–8)

11. a. living
    b. legal
    c. social (6–8)

12. psychological (8)

13. psychoanalytic-unconscious conflicts; behavioral-learning; cognitive-thinking; interpersonal-disordered relationships; sociocultural-social forces; neuroscience-body chemistry (8)

14. Both are biologically based, but the neuroscience perspective does not insist on biology being the only factor (8–9).

15. The structure of the society and the assumed causes of the abnormal behavior (9)

16. a. relatively formal relationship
    b. with a trained professional
    c. to address psychological and behavioral problems (10)

17. a. Medical doctor (only profession that can prescribe drugs)
    b. Ph.D. or Psy.D.—four to six years graduate level training and a one-year clinical internship
    c. Master's degree in social work with special training in psychological counseling
    d. Training in the Freudian approach to psychology. Most are psychiatrists, but that is not an absolute requirement. (10)

18. a. 1000
    b. eclectic (10)

19. Prevention (10)

20. Primary prevention is concerned with preventing mental disorders from developing. Secondary prevention focuses on reducing the risk for a particular mental disorder. Tertiary prevention involves doing therapy or treatment. (100)

21. Abnormal behavior was the result of supernatural influences, and exorcism was used to eliminate evil spirits from the mentally ill person. Exorcisms ranged in treatment from physical torture that may sometimes have caused death to rest and community prayers. (11)

22. They began to consider mental disorder as a natural process. (11)

23. a. careful observation (11)
    b. biogenic explanation (11)

24. Galen (12)

25. The fall of Rome marked a change in the way mental disorder was viewed; Greek and Roman rationalism was replaced with a more supernatural approach (12); fifth century A.D. (12)

26. a. supernatural (12)
    b. natural (12)
       The Christian Church tended toward supernatural explanations. (12)

27. Witch hunting likely comprised mainly economic and political maneuverings to eliminate rivals. Records indicate that some mentally ill individuals were persecuted by witch hunters, but the majority of the mentally ill were of little interest to them. (13)

28. Science was beginning to edge out the supernatural. (12–17)

29. a. retreats (13)
    b. Saturn (13)
    c. eighth (14)
    d. fifteenth (14)

30. barbarous treatments thought to be therapeutic for abnormal behavior, and horrid living conditions (15–16)

31. a. moral (15)
    b. moral (15)
    c. morale (15)

32. Benjamin Rush (15)

33. "b" is correct. Dorothea Dix worked to establish mental hospitals to care for the mentally ill so that they would not be placed in jails and poorhouses. However, as these hospitals grew larger, more impersonal, and costly, the principles of moral therapy that emphasized humane treatment were lost. (15–16)

34. a. Not enough people were trained in moral therapy methods. (16)
    b. Second-generation moral therapy advocates were not as influential as the original developers of moral therapy methods. (16)
    c. Prejudice and ethnic discrimination against groups being treated at taxpayers' expense. (16)
    d. Rise of medical model. (16)

35. custodial (16)

36. Social stigma, damage to self-esteem, loss of reality contact and norms of a normal community life, emphasizing the "sick" role, which perpetuates the need to be hospitalized. (16)

37. a. prefrontal lobotomy (16)
    b. vegetative (16)
    c. medications [phenothiazines] (16)
    d. deinstitutionalization (16)
    e. 1963 (16)

38. a. homelessness
    b. fourth (17)

39. 1959, George Albee (17)

40. Community psychology is an area of psychology that focuses on the community rather than an individual. (19)

41. a. William Wundt (20)   d. Emil Kraepelin (20–21)
    b. Leipzig, Germany (20)   e. Kraepelin (20–21)
    c. 1879 (20)   f. *psychopathology* (20)

42. A sign of advanced syphilis can be a mental syndrome called *general paresis*. The discovery by Krafft-Ebing that general paresis is the result of the physical disease syphilis was dramatic evidence to support the medical model's position that disease processes cause mental illnesses. (21)

43. senile psychoses, toxic psychoses, cerebral arteriosclerosis, mental retardation (21)

44. *psychogenic*, which means caused by psychological stress (21)

45. a. magnetism (21)
    b. mesmerism (21)
    c. suggestion (21)
    d. hypnosis (21)

46. The Nancy school, which started with Liébeault and Bernheim, believed hysteria had psychogenic causes instead of a biogenic one. Opposition came from the Paris school—Charcot and his followers. (21–22)

47. a. hypnosis (21)
    b. psychological (22)

48. The Nancy school of thought won out, and even Charcot was won over. (21–22)

49. 4, 2, 1, 5, and 3 (22–23)

50. The United States and Europe (23)

51. a. Their treatments are more closely connected to religion.
    b. They place less emphasis on the individual and more on the group. (22–23)

52. a. African techniques seem to use suggestion, reassurance, manipulation of the environment, emotional venting, and group therapy, which are techniques seen in various Western therapies.
    b. Asian techniques use meditation and self-reflection, which emphasize self-awareness, not unlike the insight therapies in Western culture. (22–23)

53. a. scientifically
    b. psychological, biological
    c. unique (23–24)

54. a. managed care
    b. cost
    c. restricting (19)

55. Managed care originated to assist in regulation of cost and limitation of services. As a result care has been compromised, and decisions, adequacy of treatment, and practitioner-client confidentiality have been questioned. (19–20)

Practice Test (p. 10)

1. a. No, social expectations come under the heading of norm violation.
   b. Just the opposite—rarity is the issue with statistical abnormality.
   c. Correct!
   d. This is dealing with the issue of social norms again.

2. a. No, this person is not concerned about how rare his behavior is, only how it feels.
   b. No. Here again, the issue is internal experience, not social acceptance.
   c. This is a little closer since misery may make one less efficient, but the focus is still feelings.
   d. Right!

3. a. Hormone variations are involved in things like PMS, but generally this is not the case.
   b. Actually, having to act strong all the time can get in the way of dealing with problems.
   c. Yes!
   d. The first part of this statement is unsupported and the second part has it just backward.

4. a. *Genic* means "origins" (as in Genesis), so cure is not the issue.
   b. Close, since *neuro-* and *bio-*"go together, but remember what *-genic* means.
   c. Right!
   d. Not really. Just because something is biologically caused, it is not necessarily universal.

5. a. No. Freud assumed that most behavior comes from built-in motives or attempts to control them.
   b. Close, but this perspective focuses on other things besides learning, such as labeling.
   c. Correct!
   d. No. The biological perspective looks more at the "hardware" than at the process of learning itself.

6. a. No. Psychodynamic theorists deal more with abstract processes of mind than with the brain.
   b. Sorry. Behaviorists see the brain as a sort of "black box" and concentrate on behavior.
   c. No. Cognitive types focus on the thinking process more than on the brain that thinks.
   d. Right!

7. a. No. Remember what "M.D." stands for: "medical doctor."
   b. No. Psychologists have an academic degree, not a medical one.
   c. Like psychologists, these folks have an academic background.
   d. Correct!

8. a. This is true, but it is not related to Hippocrates' ideas about the causes of illness.
   b. This is also important, but remember that Hippocrates was talking about bodily fluids here!
   c. No. The idea is much more basic than that.
   d. Yes! At its core, this is what Hippocrates was thinking about.

9. a. This question is just a test of your vocabulary. *Isolation* means solitary confinement.
   b. The term *moral* might trip you up, but this comes later in the history section.
   c. Right!
   d. No. This is the old term for the effects of untreated syphilis.

10. a. Correct!
    b. Some fanatics may have thought witches caused illness, but this was not the main motive.
    c. No. The Church did not encourage spiritual experimentation at all.
    d. No way. Secular power apart from the Church was actively discouraged.

11. a. Correct!
    b. Esquirol was Pinel's successor.
    c. Pussin was the untrained layman.
    d. Rush was an American reformer.

12. a. Yes!
    b. Pinel was a French reformer.
    c. Tuke was an English reformer.
    d. More was a medieval Englishman.

13. a. No. "Moral" is used a bit differently here. It does not just refer to ethical behavior.
    b. Wrong again. In fact, strict control was avoided in moral therapy practice.
    c. Right!
    d. No. You were fooled by the conventional meaning of "moral" as it is used today.

14. a. No, this was a big factor. People did not want to pay for the treatment of "undesirables."
    b. Again, this was a big factor because moral therapy depended on environmental influences.
    c. Once more, this was a large influence in the decline of care associated with moral therapy.
    d. Right! Freud's ideas were largely independent of what was going on in large institutions.

15. a. Yes!
    b. No. Moral therapy was long gone by then.
    c. No. In fact, the development of certain drugs boosted the prestige of the medical model.
    d. Unfortunately, just the opposite.

16. a. No, it is relatively recent and replaced institutional care.
    b. No. It is not rapidly expanding, although it could offer some hope for these people if it were.
    c. Correct!
    d. No. The kind of medical advance that makes community care necessary has not yet arrived.

17. a. Another vocabulary tester. Psychopathology is just another term for mental illness.
    b. No. Prognosis is the prediction of future outcomes.
    c. Yes!
    d. No. Etiology refers to causes of a disorder.

18. a. No. Large mental hospitals were becoming more common then.
    b. Actually, it tended to threaten the medical or biological approach.
    c. Right!
    d. Actually, hypnosis was the process that looked quite promising for proving psychogenesis.

19. a. No. Remember, saying whatever comes to mind means you're *free* to say what you want.
    b. Yes!
    c. No. This means transferring issues from your life into the relationship with your therapist.
    d. No. This is process for clearing the mind and is unrelated to psychoanalysis.

20. a. No, this is a major assumption that makes scientific psychology possible.
    b. Correct! Just because it tries to be scientific does not mean that speculation is out of bounds.
    c. Again, this is a key assumption.
    d. Once more, a key assumption.

CHAPTER 2
DIAGNOSIS AND ASSESSMENT

LEARNING OBJECTIVES

By the time you have finished studying this chapter, you should be able to do the following:

1. Define *psychological assessment*, and list two goals of the assessment process. (26–27)

2. Define *psychiatric diagnosis*, list four criticisms of diagnosis, and explain why diagnosis is used in spite of these criticisms. (28–30)

3. List and describe the five axes of diagnosis used in *DSM-IV-TR*, and compare this diagnostic approach to the dimensional system of classifying mental disorders. (30–32)

4. Discuss the current revisions and need for change in the *DSM-IV-TR*. (31–32)

5. Define the concept of reliability in assessment, and describe three kinds of reliability discussed in the text. (32–34)

6. Define the concept of validity in assessment, and describe two types of validity mentioned in the text. (34–35)

7. Summarize the text's discussion of problems in assessment and what can be done about them. (35–37)

8. Discuss how the interview is used as an assessment tool, and summarize its advantages and disadvantages. (37–38)

9. List four currently used intelligence tests, and review the controversial aspects of using intelligence scores in psychological assessment. (38–41)

10. List and briefly describe four personality tests (two projective and two self-report) discussed in the text, and discuss the pros and cons associated with each. (41–45)

11. List and describe two psychological tests for the detection of organic impairment. (47–48)

12. Describe five types of psychophysiological measures and their advantages. (48–52)

13. Indicate how measures of physiological functions are used in psychological assessment. (48–49)

14. Indiate how measures of brain structure and function are used in assessment. (48–49)

15. Discuss the advantages and disadvantages of using observation in natural settings as an assessment tool. (49–50)

16. Explain how cultural bias can make accurate assessment and diagnosis difficult. (50–52)

KEY TERMS

The following terms are in bold print in your text and are important to your understanding of the chapter. Look them up in the text and write down their definitions.

categorical classification (30)

comorbidity (34)

descriptive validity (34)

diagnosis (38)

dimensional classification (30)

DSM-IV-TR (28)

electroencephalogram (EEG) (48)

electromyogram (EMG) (49)

galvanic skin response (49)

intelligence quotient (IQ) (39)

intelligence tests (38)

interjudge reliability (33)

internal consistency (33)

interview (37)

mental status exam (MSE) (37)
mini mental status exam (MMS) (37)
Minnesota Multiphasic Personality
   Inventory-2 (MMPI-2) (45)
person variables (50)
polygraph (49)
predictive validity (34)
projective personality tests (41)
psychological assessment (26)
psychological test (38)
psychometric approach (38)

reliability (32)
responses sets (46)
Rorschach Psychodiagnostic Inkblot
   Test (41)
self-report personality inventories (45)
situational variables (49)
test-retest reliability (33)
Thematic Apperception Test (TAT) (42)
traits (38)
validity (34)

IMPORTANT NAMES

Identify the following persons and their major contributions to abnormal psychology as discussed in this chapter.

Alfred Binet (39)

Howard Gardner (40)

D. L. Rosenhan (30)

David Wechsler (39)

GUIDED SELF-STUDY

1. What is the big picture for this chapter?

2. Psychological assessment involves a mental health professional collecting, (a)_____, and

    (b)_____ information about a person in order to (c)_____ the complex array of

    (d)_____ that constitutes the person's life.

3. Psychological assessment (a) *is / is not* a new invention. Each assessment system is based on a theory about

    human (b)_____ These can vary across (c)_____ and periods in history. Modern Western

    assessment techniques are based on theories that are (d)_____-genic and/

    or (e)_____-genic.

Why Assessment?

4. The two goals of psychological assessment are (a)_____ and (b)_____.

5. Psychological assessments are used to collect information for the scientific purpose of increasing

    (a)_____ of human behavior and/or in (b)_____- making for the future of that specific

    individual.

Diagnosis of Mental Disorders

6. All sciences classify. Mental health professionals classify mental disorders according to patterns of behavior, (a)_____, and (b)_____. The first person to develop a comprehensive classification system for serious mental disorders was (c)_____. He did this in the late (d)_____ century.

7. In l952 the APA (which stands for (a)_____ _____ _____ published its own variation on the system known as the *DSM* (which stands for (b)_____ _____

_____ _____ _____ _____ _____) There have been several revisions, and the current one, (c)_____, was published in (d)_____.

8. The World Health Organization (WHO) publishes its own classification known as the *ICD*, which stands for the (a)_____ _____ _____ _____. (b) How does the *ICD* compare to the *DSM-IV-TR*?

9. Place the following four steps of the diagnostic process in the proper order:

_____ Write down the diagnosis in the file.

_____ Speculate what the different possible diagnoses might be.

_____ See if the patient has at least the minimum number criteria to quality for that diagnosis.

_____ Determine which criteria the patient demonstrates in the possible diagnostic options.

10. The assessment process results in a diagnosis that describes the person's problem and gives a prediction for the future. This is known as the patient's/client's _____.

11. Having a standardized diagnostic system defines a vocabulary for clear (a)_____. (b) List the people who use the *DSM-IV-TR* as their standardized diagnostic system. (Name at least four groups.)

12. Indicate whether each of the following phrases is a *justification* or a *criticism* of diagnosis.

a. _____ Abnormal as qualitatively different from normal

b. _____ Artificial clarity

c. _____ Grouping people for research studies

d. _____ Illusion of explanation

e. _____ Standardize terms for communications

f. _____ Tied to the medical model

g. _____ Reduces the focus on the individuality

13. a. What was D. L. Rosenhan's experiment about?

    b. What were the results?

    c. What was the point of this research?

    d. Who was "fooled," and who was not?

14. Early editions of *DSM* had brief, vague descriptions of disorders. But now, each diagnosis has the following information associated with it. Draw a line from each feature to its definition.

    a. Essential features   Define the disorder

    b. Associated features   Distinguish from other disorders

    c. Diagnostic criteria   Must be present

    d. Differential diagnosis   Usually present

15. Another important feature in *DSM-IV* is the five standard informational items that make up each diagnosis. These five areas of the individual's functioning are called the _____ of diagnosis.

16. Name the five axes in order.

    I.

    II.

    III.

    IV.

    V.

17. Here are descriptions of the five axes. Identify them by their numbers.

    a. _____   Accompanied long-term disorders; not a clinical syndrome

    b. _____   Measure of coping or adjustment

    c. _____   Medical conditions

    d. _____   Diagnostic label for serious current psychological problem

    e. _____   Current social, occupational and environmental stressors

18. Fill in the blanks using the following terms: *reliability, neurosis, cause, behavioral descriptions,* and *validity*.

    Another important concept which was introduced in 1980 in *DSM-III* was the idea of unspecified

    (a)_____, which means there are no assumptions made about the causes of mental disorders. The

    1980 edition deleted the use of the term (b)_____, which is a Freudian term (psychoanalytic) that

    implies unconscious conflicts as the cause. Thus, disorders are now categorized by (c)_____. The

    goal of this change was to increase (d)_____ and (e)_____.

19. Define the following terms in your own words.

    a.   Reliability:

    b.   Validity:

20. Here are the descriptions of three different kinds of reliability in psychological assessment tools. Write the name of each next to its description.

    a.   _____ Each part within a measuring instrument measures the same thing.

    b.   _____ Measuring instrument gives the same result each time it is used.

    c.   _____ Measuring instrument gives the same result regardless of who uses it.

21. When the *DSM* categories were broad and general, people "fit" into categories easily (perhaps too easily), and they often fit into too many categories for the diagnosis to be meaningful. With increased precision and specificity, that problem has been reduced; however, now more people are being diagnosed as "disorder not otherwise specified," which means

    _____.

22. The two kinds of validity are (a)_____ and (b)_____.

23. If a test measures what it is supposed to we are testing _____.

24. Fill in the following blanks with the correct term: *reliability* or *validity*. One can have (a)_____

    without (b)_____, but one cannot have (c)_____ without (d)_____.

25. (a)_____ is the term used for an individual who meets the diagnostic criteria for more than one Axis I diagnosis. Recent research reveals that it is (b) *more / less* common to have two or more disorders than to have just one. This brings up the theoretical question of whether these are independently coexisting disorders or whether one is secondary to the other.

26. List some of the problems associated with assessment that affect the reliability and validity of assessment tools.

    a.

    b.

    c.

    d.

27. With reference to practical considerations, the diagnostician may want a diagnosis that is serious enough that

    (a)_____ will pay and harmless enough not to (b)_____ the individual. Two popular

    disorders that fit both of these specifications are (c)_____ disorder and (d)_____ disorder.

Methods of Assessment

28. List four categories of assessment methods discussed in this chapter.

    a.

    b.

    c.

    d.

    We recommend that you construct a memory trick so that you can recall these categories with little effort.

29. List four categories of psychological tests and two examples for each category.

    a.

    b.

    c.

    d.

30. Match the phrases with the following assessment techniques: *Interview, Psychological testing, Laboratory testing,* and *Observation in natural settings.*

    a. _____ may get at truths that people with problems can't or won't report.

    b. _____ is a standard procedure of presentation of a series of stimuli.

    c. _____ tends to provide workable answers to behavioral problems.

    d. _____ can pinpoint the occurrence of stress reactions in an individual.

    e. _____ is the oldest method of assessment.

    f. _____ uses the psychometric approach as its dominant method.

    g. _____ is the most commonly used method.

    h. _____ requires tremendous investment of time.

    i. _____ is the primary means of diagnosing organicity.

    j. _____ involves watching events unfold without interference.

    k. _____ can be structured or unstructured.

    l. _____ may involve a polygraph (lie detector).

31. Tell which category of psychological test or specific assessment tool is most accurately described by the following terms: *Bender Visual-Motor Gestalt Test, Intelligence tests, MMPI-2, Projective tests, Psychological tests for organicity,* and *Rorschach.*

    a. _____ are routinely used and may have major impact on a person's life.

    b. _____ try to tap unconscious motives.

    c. _____ is the most widely used self-report personality inventory.

    d. _____ allow participants the greatest freedom in expressing themselves.

    e. _____ is the most famous of the projective tests.

    f. _____ were the first kind of psychological test to be widely used.

g. _____ are used to distinguish biogenic from psychogenic cases.

h. _____ requires drawing of nine simple designs.

i. _____ uses ten inkblots.

32. The following terms are commonly heard in connection with assessment of individuals with abnormal behaviors. Tell what each term means literally, what it assesses, and to what category of assessment technique it belongs.

a. CT:

b. WAIS-R:

c. Bender-Gestalt:

d. MMPI:

e. PET:

f. WISC-III:

g. Stanford-Binet:

h. MRI:

i. Rorschach:

j. EEG:

k. Halstead-Reitan Battery:

l TAT:

m. IQ:

n. MSE:

o. MMS:

p. ATQ-R:

q. MMPI-2:

r. GSR:

Cultural Bias in Assessment

33. In Chapter One, differences in cultures led to differences in how mental distress is experienced and expressed.

That difference can lead to cultural (a)_____ in the area of psychological assessment. It is

problematic if it leads to a diagnosis that does not provide the most beneficial outcome for the client/patient.

The text discusses two problem areas in cross-cultural assessment situations: One is if the mental health

professional does not know the (b)_____ for that individual's culture. A second problem exists

when the mental health professional is not fluent in the individual's native (c)_____.

34. Research suggests that culture-based bias on the part of the clinician could result in diagnoses that show
    a. more pathology in the individual than is really there.
    b. less pathology in the individual than is really there.
    c. either of the above
    d. none of the above

PRACTICE TEST

Use the following test questions to check your knowledge of the material in this chapter. You might want to write the answers on a separate sheet of paper so you can take the test more than once.

1. Psychological assessment is the process of

    a. collecting, organizing and interpreting information about a person.
    b. placing the person's problem into a system of classification.
    c. deciding whether a research subject should be placed in an experimental group or a control group.
    d. analyzing the outcome of a research program.

2. The prediction about the likely outcome of a disorder is referred to as a(n)

    a. diagnosis.
    b. etiology.
    c. prognosis.
    d. assessment.

3. Rhonda says, "I'm afraid of riding in elevators because I have claustrophobia." Her statement would support which criticism of psychiatric diagnosis?

    a. Diagnosis implies that abnormal behavior is qualitatively different from normal behavior.
    b. Diagnosis fails to provide a language for communicating about abnormal behavior.
    c. Diagnosis provides an illusion of explanation.
    d. Diagnosis fails to classify behavior adequately.

4. Information on Axis II of the *DSM-IV-TR* indicates

    a. a personality disorder or mental retardation.
    b. a relevant medical condition.
    c. the person's most recent level of functioning.
    d. any recent stressors that contributed to the psychological problem.

5. If different parts of a test yield the same results, the test is said to demonstrate

    a. test-retest reliability.
    b. inter-judge reliability.
    c. internal consistency.
    d. predictive validity.

6. Consistency is associated with _____; meaningfulness is associated with _____.

    a. validity, coverage
    b. reliability, validity
    c. validity, reliability
    d. reliability, standardization

7. James smokes marijuana daily and is almost always "stoned." He has lost several jobs because of his marijuana smoking. In addition, James experiences hallucinations, delusions, and incoherent thinking—the cardinal signs of paranoid schizophrenia. James illustrates the diagnostic problem called

    a. pathognomic symptoms.
    b. pathological bias.
    c. comorbidity.
    d. neurosis.

8. The tendency among many clinicians to look for what is wrong with a client instead of what is healthy is called

    a. actuarial judgment.
    b. a decision rule.
    c. pathological bias.
    d. epidemiology.

9. In an initial psychotherapy session, a psychologist spends an hour observing the female client's dress and facial expressions while asking questions about her family, educational, and work experiences. Which form of assessment technique is this therapist using at the moment?

    a. Naturalistic observation
    b. Projective personality testing
    c. Self-report personality testing
    d. Interview

10. Which of the following is a quick and widely used screening test for dementia?

    a. WPPSI
    b. CAT
    c. MCMI
    d. MMS

11. A child is given a standardized test that measures verbal ability as well as problem-solving ability that does not depend on verbal skills. We can be pretty sure the child is being tested with

    a. a projective intelligence test.
    b. a Wechsler intelligence test.
    c. the TAT or CAT.
    d. the MMPI-2.

12. A fourth-grader is tested with an IQ test, and he shows below-average intelligence on verbal ability and mathematical-logical reasoning. Solely on the basis of these test results, someone concludes that the child cannot be successful in life. According to Howard Gardner, why is this an erroneous conclusion?

    a. IQ tests are not designed to measure verbal ability.
    b. IQ tests are not designed to measure mathematical-logical reasoning.
    c. Other capacities such as interpersonal and musical abilities determine people's success in life.
    d. Verbal ability and mathematical-logical reasoning are not true forms of intelligence.

13. Some people enjoy looking at clouds and figuring out what the cloud shapes remind them of. This is similar to which psychological test?

    a. TAT
    b. Wechsler Intelligence Scale
    c. MMPI-2
    d. Rorschach ink blots

14. Which of the following is an accurate criticism of projective tests of personality?

    a. They have poor interjudge reliability, but they show high validity.
    b. They involve too many complicated and subjective inferences.
    c. They have validity that is too high.
    d. They prevent subjects from expressing themselves freely.

15. Sabrina takes a personality test that asks her to agree or disagree with over five hundred statements such as, "I forgive people easily" and "I often got into trouble when I was younger." We can assume that Sabrina is taking the _____ test.

    a. MMPI-2
    b. Rorschach
    c. Bender Visual-Motor Gestalt
    d. Thematic Apperception

16. Bill took an MMPI-2, and his results show a moderately high score on the depression scale. Lacking any additional information, the best way to interpret this is to say that

    a. Bill should be given a diagnosis of depression.
    b. Bill is immature, suggestible, and demanding.
    c. Bill is seriously disturbed.
    d. Bill answered many questions the same way depressed people do.

17. Imogene is taking a self-report personality test. She wants people to like her and so she simply responds with answers she thinks people want to hear. Her test is being distorted by a(n)

    a. acquiescence set.
    b. straight set.
    c. positive transfer.
    d. social desirability set.

18. Which of the following asks a subject to reproduce nine simple designs with paper and pencil in order to check for organic impairment?

    a. MMPI-II
    b. Halstead-Reitan Neurophysiological Battery
    c. Bender Visual-Motor Gestalt Test
    d. Mini Mental Status Exam

19. You are in a crowded store, and the person next to you pushes you to get out the door. If you say to yourself, "That guy must be really nasty!" you are attributing his behavior to a _____ variable.

    a. situational
    b. personal
    c. functional
    d. structural

20. Suppose two individuals, one from suburbia and the other from the inner city, showed the same pattern of aggressive and paranoid behaviors. In diagnosing these two persons, a clinician should

    a. give them the same diagnosis in order to be objective about the behaviors.
    b. give them different diagnoses if the diagnosis will determine if insurance pays for the treatment.
    c. consider whether the behaviors are more or less reasonable given the client's environment.
    d. base the diagnosis on ethnic background rather than on living environment.

ANSWERS

Guided Self-Study (p. 20)

1. The outline at the beginning of the chapter is always the place to start. In this chapter the summary paragraph of the introduction on page 28 gives an overview of assessment issues in very simple words: Assessment—what it aims to do, how well it succeeds, and why it fails. Then methods of assessment and problems of cultural bias in assessment are discussed. (27)

2. a. organizing
   b. interpreting
   c. understand
   d. behaviors (27)

3. a. is not
   b. behavior
   c. cultures
   d. biogenic
   e. psychogenic (27)

4. a. description
   b. prediction (27)

5. a. understanding
   b. decision (27)

6. a. thought
   b. emotion
   c. Kraepelin
   d. nineteenth (28)

7. a. American Psychiatric Association
   b. Diagnostic and Statistical Manual of Mental Disorders
   c. *DSM-IV-TR*
   d. 2000 (28)

8. a. International Classification of Diseases
   b. *DSM-IV-TR* and *ICD-10* (tenth edition) are consistent with each other. (28)

9. 4, 1, 3, and 2 (28)

10. prognosis (28)

11. a. communication
    b. scientific reseachers, government agencies, insurance companies, and mental health professionals (28)

12. a. criticism   e. justification
    b. criticism   f. criticism
    c. justification   g. criticism (28–29)
    d. criticism

13. a. Rosenhan planted fake patients in a mental hospital and waited for them to be discovered.
    b. While discharged after varying periods of time, they were never discovered to be faking their problems.
    c. Rosenhan wanted to find out if mental health professionals could recognize "normality" when they saw it.
    d. The staff were fooled, but the other mental patients were not fooled. (30)

14. a. Essential features define the disorder.
    b. Associated features are usually present in the disorder.
    c. Diagnostic criteria are features that must be present for a diagnosis to be made.
    d. Differential diagnosis helps distinguish one disorder from another. (31)

15. axes (32)

16. I.   Clinical syndrome
    II. Personality disorders or mental retardation (children and adolescents)
    III. General medical disorders
    IV. Psychosocial and environmental problems
    V.   Global assessment of functioning (32)

17. a. Axis II
    b. Axis V
    c. Axis III
    d. Axis I
    e. Axis IV (32)

18. a. cause
    b. neurosis
    c. behavioral descriptions
    d. reliability
    e. validity (32–33)

19. a. consistency, stability, doing the same thing over and over (33)
    b. measures what it says it measures (34)

20. a. internal consistency
    b. test-retest reliability
    c. interjudge reliability (33)

21. those people do not fit anywhere in the well-defined categories (34)

22. a. descriptive validity (34)
    b. predictive validity (35)

23. validity (34)

24. a. reliability
    b. validity
    c. validity
    d. reliability (32–35)

25. a. comorbidity
    b. more (34)

26. a. The test giver's personal demeanor may influence the person's behavior. (35)
    b. Assessments that require interpretation by the diagnostician may be influenced by the diagnostician's perspective. (36)
    c. Practical considerations influence the diagnoses: What disorders does this person's insurance cover? And who is going to have access to this information? (36)
    d. Some clinicians simply do not follow the rules of diagnosis. (37)

27. a. insurance
    b. stigmatize
    c. anxiety
    d. adjustment (37)

28. a. the interview
    b. psychological tests
    c. laboratory tests
    d. observation in natural settings (37)

29. a. intelligence tests (Stanford-Binet and the Wechslers) (38–39)
    b. projective personality tests (Rorschach and TAT) (41–45)
    c. self-report personality inventories (MMPI-2 and MCMI-III) (45–47)
    d. psychological tests for organic impairment (Bender-Gestalt and Halstead-Reitan) (47–49)

30. a. Observation in natural settings (49–50)
    b. Psychological testing (38)
    c. Observation in natural settings (49–50)
    d. Laboratory testing (49–50)
    e. Interview (37)
    f. Psychological testing (38)
    g. Interview (37)
    h. Observation in natural settings (49–50)
    i. Laboratory testing (49–50)
    j. Observation in natural settings (49–50)
    k. Interview (37)
    l. Laboratory testing (49–50)

31. a. Intelligence tests (38–41)
    b. Projective tests (41–45)
    c. MMPI-2 (45–47)
    d. Projective tests (41–45)
    e. Rorschach (41)
    f. Intelligence tests (38–41)
    g. Psychological tests for organicity (47–49)
    h. Bender Visual-Motor Gestalt Test (48)
    i. Rorschach (41)

32. a. CT is computerized tomography; it X-rays the brain; it is a laboratory test. (48)
    b. WAIS-R stands for Wechsler Adult Intelligence Scale-Revised; it is a psychological test for the measurement of intelligence. (38-41)
    c. Bender-Gestalt is Bender Visual-Motor Gestalt Test, a psychological test to detect organic impairment. (48)
    d. MMPI stands for Minnesota Multiphasic Personality Inventory; it self-report psychological test for assessing personality. (45–47)
    e. PET stands for positron emission tomography; it is a laboratory test that gives a picture of neural activity in the brain. (48)
    f. WISC-III stands for Wechsler Intelligence Scale for Children (third edition); it is a psychological test for the measurement of intelligence. (39)
    g. Stanford-Binet is a psychological test for the measurement of intelligence. (39)
    h. MRI stands for magnetic resonance imaging; it is a laboratory test that gives a detailed picture of internal brain structures. (48)
    i. Rorschach is a projective psychological test using inkblots to assess personality. (41)
    j. EEG stands for electroencephalogram; it is a laboratory test that measures electrical activity in the brain by means of scalp electrodes. (48)
    k. Halstead-Reitan Battery is a psychological test for pinpointing organicity (damage in the brain). (48)
    l. TAT stands for Thematic Apperception Test; it is a projective psychological test that assesses personality with ambiguous pictures. (42)
    m. IQ stands for intelligence quotient; it is a measure of intellectual ability. (39)
    n. MSE stands for mental status exam; it is a process of looking for signs of mental disorder through questioning and observation. (37)
    o. MMS stands for mini mental status exam; it is the short form of the MSE used to screen for dementia. (37)
    p. ATQ-R is the Automatic Thoughts Questionnaire-Revised, a self-report psychological test for assessing cognitive distortions. (47)
    q. MMPI-2 is the revised (second edition) of the self-report psychological test MMPI. See answer d. (47)
    r. GSR is Galvanic Skin Response. It is a laboratory test of the activation of the autonomic nervous system. (49)

33. a. bias (51–52)
    b. norms (51–52)
    c. language (51–52)

34. "c" is correct; either more or less pathology than is actually present (51–52)

Practice test (p. 28)

1. a. Correct!
   b. No, this is diagnosis.
   c. No, this is a completely different subject and would probably be done randomly anyway.
   d. To analyze is to assess, but in this chapter the term specifically refers to evaluating a person's problem,

2. a. No. Diagnosis is the classification of the problem.
   b. Sorry, etiology refers to causes.
   c. Yes!
   d. No. Assessment involves both description and prediction, but prognosis is more specific in this case.

3. a. No. She is simply describing her situation, not comparing herself to non-claustrophobics.
   b. No. She is communicating about it just fine. She is just going in circles with her words.
   c. Correct! Labeling something is not explaining it, just describing it.
   d. Incorrect. Classification is what diagnosis is all about.

4. a. Correct!
   b. No. This would be Axis III.
   c. Sorry. This would be Axis V.
   d. Incorrect. This would be Axis IV.

5.   a.   No. Remember we are looking *within* the test here.
      b.   No. Once again, it is the test's performance within itself that is the issue here.
      c.   Yes!
      d.   A consistency problem will result in a validity problem, but internal consistency is the main issue here.

6.   a.   No. Consistency is related to reliability and meaningfulness asks the question, "Is it valid?"
      b.   Right!
      c.   No. Just the other way around.
      d.   Half right, but standardization, although important, is a more of a procedural issue.

7.   a.   Incorrect. Pathognomic symptoms are symptoms that are not found in any other problem
      b.   No. This is the tendency to see pathology rather than health.
      c.   Yes! In other words, James has more than one problem.
      d.   Sorry. Neurosis is a term for the less severe disorders that do not impair reality contact. If anything, James is psychotic.

8.   a.   No. This is the use of statistics to predict outcomes and decide treatment.
      b.   No. This is the criterion by which a decision is made.
      c.   You got it!
      d.   Sorry. This is the study of the distribution of a disorder in a population.

9.   a.   Tempting, but incorrect. The therapist's office is far from a natural setting for the client.
      b.   No. This would involve a test such as the TAT.
      c.   No. This would involve a test such as the MMPI-2.
      d.   Right!

10.   a.   Sorry. This is an intelligence test for preschoolers.
      b.   No, this is a projective personality test for children.
      c.   Incorrect. This is a self-report personality test.
      d.   Correct!

11.   a.   Nonsense answer; there is no such thing.
      b.   Yes, indeed! These tests look at both verbal and performance issues.
      c.   No. These are projective personality tests.
      d.   No. This is also a personality test. When you see the word *ability,* what is measured is usually related to intelligence.

12.   a.   No, in fact they are designed to measure that very thing.
      b.   No, they are designed to measure this ability too.
      c.   Yes! Gardner believes these are important issues that are ignored in many tests.
      d.   Sorry, but these are important components in intelligence.

13.   a.   Incorrect. The TAT is projective, but the stimuli are a lot less abstract than cloud shapes.
      b.   No. An intelligence test is a lot more specific and has right and wrong answers.
      c.   No. Close, but this a self-report personality test with requiring yes-no answers.
      d.   Correct!

14.   a.   No. If you recall, you cannot have high validity if the test is unreliable.
      b.   Right!
      c.   Sorry, but you can't have too much validity.
      d.   Incorrect. In fact, these tests allow more self-expression than most others.

15.   a.   Correct!
      b.   No. The Rorschach is the inkblot test.
      c.   No. This is a drawing test designed to get at neurological problems.
      d.   Sorry. This is the TAT, and it is a projective test.

16. a. No. Basing a diagnosis on one test result is a bad idea.
    b. Not really. Drawing conclusions about personality based on one test is also a bad idea.
    c. No. Again, not enough information is available, and serious disturbance is way too sweeping a conclusion.
    d. Yes! Given the information we have, this is the best we can do right now.

17. a. No. This means she cannot disagree with the statements in front of her.
    b. This is a nonsense answer—no such thing, unless you are playing tennis.
    c. Incorrect. This is a concept out of memory and learning research.
    d. Correct!

18. a. No, this is a personality test.
    b. Close, but no cigar. This is an organic impairment test, but not the one we are looking for.
    c. Yes!
    d. No. This is designed to determine how in touch with the here-and-now a person is.

19. a. No. Nastiness is not a property of the situation, it is a property of a person.
    b. Right!
    c. No. This is not a type of variable your text talks about in connection with attributions.
    d. Incorrect. Again, your text does not talk about this as an attributional factor.

20. a. No. Objectivity is important, but behavior means different things in different situations.
    b. No. This is unethical, but unfortunately, not unheard of.
    c. Correct!
    d. Incorrect. Stereotyping people is a poor idea no matter what the motive, since it is not fair to the individual.

CHAPTER 3
RESEARCH METHODS IN ABNORMAL PSYCHOLOGY

LEARNING OBJECTIVES

By the time you have finished studying this chapter, you should be able to do the following:

1. List and define four objectives of the scientific method. (55–57)

2. List three conditions that must be met before cause and effect can be established. (56)

3. Distinguish between internal and external validity, and describe the means by which each is obtained. (56–57)

4. Describe the case study method of research and discuss its advantages and limitations. (58)

5. Describe the process of designing an experiment, from hypothesis formation through the development of operational definitions and the establishment of independent and dependent variables. (57–59)

6. Distinguish between experimental and control groups, and describe three kinds of control techniques that are applied to factors influencing the outcome of an experiment. (58–62)

7. Explain how expectations on the part of experimenters and subjects can influence the outcome of an experiment, and describe measures that are commonly taken to minimize these expectations. (59–61)

8. Discuss the role of statistical analysis and inference in scientific research. (61–62)

9. Describe and explain the necessary ethical components in research. (62–64)

10. Describe correlational research designs, tell what one can and cannot conclude from correlations, and why. (64–66)

11. Define longitudinal studies, including high-risk designs, and discuss their advantages and shortcomings. (66)

12. Define epidemiological studies, and describe the difference between incidence and prevalence. (66–67)

13. Define clinical trials and analogue experiments and give an example of each. (67–68)

14. Describe single case experimentation, give examples of two variations of this research design, and tell how it differs from a traditional case study. (69–72)

KEY TERMS

The following terms are in bold print in your text and are important to your understanding of the chapter. Look them up in the text and write down their definitions.

ABAB design (70)
analogue experiment (68)
behavior high-risk design (66)
case-control design (64)
case study (58)
clinical significance (62)
clinical trials (67)
clinicians (57)
confounding (56)
control (56)
control groups (63)

control techniques (59)
correlation coefficient (65)
correlational research (64)
covariation of events (56)
demand characteristics (59)
dependent variable (58)
description (55)
double-blind (59)
elimination of plausible alternative causes (56)
epidemiology (66)
experimenter effects (59)

external validity (56)
generalizability (56)
genetic high-risk design (66)
high-risk design (66)
hypothesis (57)
incidence (66)
independent variable (58)
informed consent (62)
internal validity (56)
longitudinal studies (66)
multiple-baseline design (70)
null hypothesis (61)
operational definitions (58)

placebo (59)
prediction (56)
prevalence (66)
prospective studies (66)
random assignment (59)
random sample (57)
replicate (57)
representativeness (56)
single-case experiment (70)
statistical inference (61)
third-variable problem (65)
time-order relationship (56)
understanding (56)

IMPORTANT NAME

Identify the following person and his major contribution to abnormal psychology as discussed in this chapter.

Sarnoff Mednick (66)

GUIDED SELF-STUDY

1. First, can you name the topic of this chapter in two words?

   If you did not know the two words and had to look them up, say them to yourself a couple of times, write them three times, and create a memory aid. All of this is to underscore the importance of always knowing the name of the chapter you are studying!

2. What are the two topics discussed under research methods in this chapter?

   a.

   b.

3. What is the difference between research methods and research designs?

4. What is difference between research designs and experimental designs?

5. Complete the blanks for the scientific method using the following terms: *control, description, prediction,* and *skeptical.*

   The scientific method has a doubting attitude called a (a)_____ attitude and four objectives, which

   are (b)_____, (c)_____, (d)_____, and understanding.

6. Place a check in front of each of the following activities that you have ever done.

   ____ Bought a different shampoo and tried it out on your hair

   ____ Tried a different gasoline in your vehicle to see if it would give you better mileage

   ____ Tried a different gas to see if it would get rid of the "pinging" in your car's engine

   ____ Bought a pair of good running shoes to see if they would help your legs ache less

   ____ Eaten breakfast in the morning instead of just your usual cup of black coffee to see if eating would give you more energy

___ Driven several different routes to school to check for the quickest one

___ Thrown away that bowl of furry-green-something in the refrigerator to see if it was the source of that horrible stench

___ Tried sitting in a different area of the bus to see if you liked the ride any better there than in your "usual" place

___ Changed deodorants, looking for one that would make it through the day

If you have ever engaged in any of these activities, you were doing informal experimentation. You came up with a hypothesis, that is, whatever your idea was that you wanted to check out. Then you proceeded to engage in some activity and watched for the results.

7. Using the scientific method, we can state the underlying cause of a phenomenon only after three conditions have been met. The conditions are

   a.

   b.

   c.

8. Two more concerns that are very important to the scientific method are reliability and validity. These terms are used in scientific terminology the same way we use them in everyday conversation. Write a definition in your own words for each of these terms.

   a. Reliability:

   b. Validity:

9. _____ means two or more causal factors are acting simultaneously to affect the outcome.

10. _____ means having the research free of confounding factors.

11. _____ means being able to extend research findings to others beyond the subjects in that particular study.

12. _____ means the extent to which research findings can be generalized to different populations, settings, and conditions.

13. Generalizability depends on the _____ of the sample.

14. When doing research that is to be generalized, the test group (sample) must be representative of the entire group (population) to which the results will be generalized. The text says a random sample of the population is needed to be able to generalize the research findings. The text points out that one must "carefully" choose the random sample. How can one carefully choose something that is supposed to be random?

15. Which of the following methods is most likely to result in a random sample for a memory experiment?
    a. Use the first twenty people that walk in to volunteer.
    b. Put all possible names in a hat and pull out twenty of them.
    c. Pick all the people who most want to participate in the experiment.
    d. Use the people who remembered to bring in their completed questionnaires.

16. What was the flaw in Brady's "executive monkey" research?

17. Brady's flaw was discovered because other researchers failed to _____ Brady's findings.

18. Samples of (a)_____ are samples that are readily available for researchers to use. However, these samples may not actually be (b)_____ samples of the population in question. The factor that caused them to all be readily available may be a selection factor in itself; therefore, the results could not be (c)_____ to those who did not have that factor, and the study would not have (d)_____ validity.

19. Now for the actual process of conducting science. List three key elements (i.e., the three steps in an experiment) that indicate adherence to the scientific method.

    a.

    b.

    c.

20. When you turn in your research proposal, your instructor glances at it, then looks at you and says, "Your hypothesis is falsifiable." Is this a *compliment* or a *criticism*?

21. An operational definition is specified by
    a. a set of objective criteria.
    b. two or more scientific terms.
    c. statistics based on the null hypothesis.
    d. expectations of demand characteristics.

22. Which of the following is a good operational definition for "tall?"
    a. people who never have trouble reaching top shelves
    b. people who are measured to be at least six feet in height
    c. people who describe themselves as tall
    d. people who are judged by others to be tall

23. The three ways factors (variables) are dealt with in research are

    a.

    b.

    c.

24. When a variable is "held constant," which of the following is true?
    a. None of the subjects are allowed to have it.
    b. A placebo is required.
    c. It is the same for all subjects.
    d. All subjects must have it in varying degrees.

25. To deal with factors that are uncontrollable, researchers (a)_____ them through (b)_____ assignment.

26. Manipulated factors is to (a)_____ as measure factor is to (b)_____

27. For the following research examples, list the independent variable and the dependent variable.

   a. Children with schizophrenic parents are being compared with children of nonschizophrenics on IQ tests.

   b. Music aptitude is being compared in left-handers and right-handers.

   c. The effects of different teaching methods on student performance.

   INDEPENDENT VARIABLE   DEPENDENT VARIABLE

   a.

   b.

   c.

28. We may like our friends to try to make us happy, but *we do not want our subjects in our experiment to "try" to do anything!* However, human subjects in experiments develop ideas about what is going on and how they should act. Another name for these expectations that they may inadvertently start to display is (a)_____ characteristics. Also, you as experimenter may inadvertently see events the way you expect them to turn out. This would be an (b)_____ effect. To avoid both of these biases, a (c)_____ _____ procedure can be used whereby neither the subjects nor the experimenter knows who is in what group. Explain this procedure.

29. In experiments in which some subjects get the treatment and some do not, a _____ control group must be used to make those who got nothing think they got something.

30. The hypothesis stated in a negative form (assuming that the independent variable has no effect) is called the (a)_____ hypothesis. If there is a difference between the groups that statistical analysis tells us could have happened by chance with a likelihood of only (b)_____, we reject the null hypothesis and call the results statistically significant. In other words, (c)_____ times out of a hundred we risk being wrong. We risk saying that the independent variable did have an effect when it really did not. See the Helpful Hints (p. 42) for more on this.

31. Since conclusions about a whole population are drawn from data coming from a sample of that population, those conclusions must be based on statistical _____.

32. Professional researchers would like to hear which of the following statements about their research?
    a. Your work does not need to be duplicated.
    b. Your work is so good that it will never be duplicated.
    c. I duplicated your work, but my findings are different from yours.
    d. I duplicated your work and found exactly the same results that you did.

Research Designs

33. The second topic in this chapter about research methods is specific research designs. Different designs are used for different purposes. Your textbook likened the researcher's selection of a particular design to a carpenter selecting which of the following?
    a. kind of wood to use
    b. tool to work with
    c. color of paint for the finish
    d. assistant to hire

34. List the four types of research designs that this textbook discusses. And here's my usual recommendation: Make up a memory trick so that they can be recalled with ease.

    a.

    b.

    c.

    d.

35. What is the name of the research design where a researcher manipulates an independent variable and measures a dependent variable?

36. How can research be done on "bad things?" Researchers can't abuse children and brainwash people for the sake of research. So how can they collect information on "bad things?"

Correlational Research

37. Complete these blanks, using each of the following terms: *+1.0, -1.0, decrease, decreases, direction, increase, increases, zero*

    The poorest correlation is (a)_____. This means there really is no correlation at all. The highest

    possible correlation is (b)_____ or (c)_____. These mean a perfect correlation exists. The

    pluses or minuses tell only the (d)_____ of the correlation (i.e., direct or inverse) not the absolute

    degree of it. In a positive correlation, the two variables either (e)_____ together or (f)_____

    together. In a negative correlation, one of the variables (g)_____ while the other (h)_____.

38. Which correlation in each of the following pairs is the strongest?
    a. -0.5 or +0.2
    b. +0.4 or +0.3
    c. -1.0 or +0.9

39. List possible third variables that could be responsible for the situations below:

   a. Every time you are around one particular relative you get a severe headache. Otherwise you don't get many headaches. Erroneous causality conclusion: That relative is so irritating that he/she actually causes you to be physically ill. Possible third factor:

   b. You study the most for your most difficult class, but you continue to make unsatisfactory grades on the tests. It even seems the harder you study, the worse your grade is. Erroneous causality conclusion: Don't study; it only confuses you. Or, you are not bright enough, or the tests must be unfair. Possible third factor:

   c. Your cat has developed a rash when it started eating leaves off the bush in the back yard. Erroneous causality conclusion: The bush caused the rash. Possible third factor:

Single Case Study

40. What is the difference between the case study and the single-case experiment?

41. Choose the term below that is associated with each phrase. Some are used more than once.

   ABAB   *Epidemiology*
   Analogue experiment   *Essential characteristic*
   Baseline   *High-risk design*
   Case study   *Longitudinal study*
   Case-control design   *Multiple baseline*
   Correlational study   *Single case experiment*
   Demand characteristic   *Double-blind experiment*

   a. _____ is also called a prospective study.

   b. _____ meets only the covariation requirement in trying to explain causes.

   c. _____ is a research method that has many variables that are not controlled.

   d. _____ is an experiment that imitates real life.

   e. _____ is useful in encouraging clinical innovation.

   f. _____ is very useful for description and prediction.

   g. _____ involve tight control that may gain internal validity at the cost of external validity.

   h. _____ can provide the feel of what it is like to live with a particular disorder.

   i. _____ permits causality inferences.

   j. _____ has the possibility of the "third variable" problem.

   k. _____ is a correlational study that lasts over years.

   l. _____ is used to avoid removing a positive effect.

   m. _____ is interested in "incidence" and "prevalence."

   o. _____ uses subjects that are more likely to have a disorder.

   p. _____ tests return to baseline when treatment is removed to demonstrate effect.

   q. _____ involves undesirable behaviors from subjects.

r. _____ involve common factors that define a population.

s. _____ is the behavior measure before intervention.

t. _____ correlates behavior of those with a certain disorder and those without it.

r. _____ neither subject or experimenters know what treatment is being administered.

42. What research designs are likely to be the most applicable to the following circumstances? Explain your choice.

a. Access to records of a man (but not the man himself) who has broken his neck three times because he is certain that he can fly

b. Puppies who need paper training

c. Impact of parental divorce on children's emotional maturation according to age of child at time of divorce.

HELPFUL HINTS

1. To keep independent variables and dependent variables separate, try some of these memory tricks if you can't come up with one yourself. (As always, ones you create yourself will be best for you.) To remember which variable is manipulated: The independent variable is manipulated (moved around) because independent people go where they want to go. Dependent variables have to be watched (measured) just like dependent creatures (babies and pets). The independent variable controls the "poor little helpless" dependent variable.

2. The first time I encountered the list of objectives for the scientific method, I thought someone had gotten them out of order. I thought "understand" should be before "predict" and "control." I was to learn later that there are many phenomena we can predict and exert some control over, but we still don't understand why they are happening. For example, in the 1950s some drugs were found to reduce symptoms in some mental patients. No one knew why they worked, but they did. So "predict" and "control" often come long before "understand." (59)

3. Find out from your instructor if you need to know the specific details of research examples in the text or if you need to understand just the general concept that the research examples typify.

4. Even if your interests are not in doing research, you need to understand the basics of research methods and designs so that you can understand research findings. For example, you need to know that correlational studies CANNOT prove causality. In communications media, correlations are sometimes reported with the implication that there is a cause-and-effect relationship between the two factors; as an informed listener, you should see the error in such an implication.

5. Beware of two words that look very similar: *pro*spective (p. 66) and *per*spective.

6. Participants in this chapter are people or animals being used in experiments. The participant in an experiment is never the "topic" of the research.

7. The concept of the null hypothesis is really not that complicated. Yes, the researcher really does believe he/she is studying something real; otherwise, there would be no reason to do the experiment. But to avoid getting carried away with his/her enthusiasm and coming to a falsely optimistic conclusion about the study, the researcher uses the null hypothesis in evaluating his/her data and assumes that nothing of significance is happening until the data show otherwise. This is very much like the idea of "innocent until proven guilty" in a criminal court. The prosecutor really does believe the defendant is guilty, but the deck is stacked in the defendant's favor to avoid sending an innocent person to jail. In research, the deck is stacked to avoid the conclusion of cause and effect when there really isn't any. Also, the statistics must be done from this negative perspective (i.e., that there is no difference) because statisticians can figure the probability of outcomes when there actually is no difference. They cannot figure the probability of a particular outcome if there is a difference between the two groups.

8. There are two "randoms" in this chapter: random sample of a population and random assignment of the subjects from the sample to the different groups in the experiment. In other words, the random sample will be randomly assigned in the experiment.

PRACTICE TEST

Use the following test questions to check your knowledge of the material in this chapter. You may want to write the answers on a separate sheet of paper so you can take the test more than once.

1. When scientists say they are interested in description, this means they are interested in
   a. explaining the causes of behavior.
   b. developing strategies to change a behavior for the better.
   c. defining and classifying events.
   d. eliminating alternative causes for an event.

2. Covariation of events, a time-order relationship, and the elimination of other plausible alternative causes are the three conditions for
   a. proving a correlation.
   b. establishing causality.
   c. removing experimenter bias.
   d. demonstrating statistical significance.

3. Before a person with multiple personality disorder develops the first symptoms, there is often a history of physical abuse. We cannot, however, say that abuse causes multiple personality disorder unless we can
   a. reverse the time-order relationship to see what happens under those conditions.
   b. actually witness the abuse.
   c. find a way to confound abuse and personality.
   d. eliminate plausible alternative explanations.

4. In selecting subjects for research, I try to be sure that all subgroups of the population are present in my sample in the proportion found in the larger population. I am trying to get a _____ sample for my research.
   a. correlated
   b. representative
   c. idiographic
   d. null

5. Which of the following research methods would be most appropriate in studying an extremely rare disorder?
   a. the epidemiological study
   b. the case study method
   c. the natural groups design
   d. the analogue experiment

6. Which of the following is a real drawback to the case study approach?
   a. The experimenter is not dealing with real-life people.
   b. Case studies deal only with common and fairly uninteresting problems.
   c. Case study results can be applied only to the "average" person.
   d. Cause-and-effect conclusions can rarely be drawn safely.

7. Which of the following is the best operational definition of "hunger?"
   a. a spoken desire for food
   b. willingness to eat when food is available
   c. going without food for twenty-four hours
   d. eating until you are full

8. Grandma manipulates the amount of sugar in her holiday cookies to determine its effect on the taste of the cookies. The sugar is the _____ variable.
   a. contingent
   b. separation
   c. independent
   d. dependent

9. Why is random assignment of subjects to the various groups in an experiment an important thing to do?
   a. This spreads uncontrolled variables around and minimizes their effect on the results.
   b. This keeps subjects from learning too much about the purpose of the study.
   c. It can sometimes eliminate the need for statistical analysis.
   d. It is a way to avoid the necessity of a control group.

10. When neither the subjects nor the researcher having direct contact with the subjects knows who is in the experimental group and who is in the control group, the study is said to involve a _____ procedure.
    a. double-blind
    b. inferential
    c. null hypothesis
    d. case study

11. I design an experiment in which one group of subjects receives a new medication and a second group receives a sugar pill. Neither the technician who administers the pills nor the subjects receiving them know who is getting what. This is an experiment involving a _____ control group and a _____ procedure.
    a. null; random groups
    b. randomized; double-blind
    c. placebo; double-blind
    d. placebo; demand characteristic

12. In scientific experimentation, when the null hypothesis is rejected it can be concluded that the
    a. independent variable probably had an effect.
    b. dependent variable had no effect.
    c. independent variable had no effect.
    d. dependent variable probably had an effect.

13. I am interested in the relationship between education level and the likelihood of criminal behavior, so I randomly select people, note the level of education achieved, and then relate that to the number of criminal convictions each has had. This is an example of
    a. the case study method.
    b. a correlational research design.
    c. an analogue experiment.
    d. an epidemiological study.

14. What is the "third-variable problem" in correlational design?
    a. the possibility that an unknown variable may be influencing the two correlated variables
    b. the inability to deal with more than two variables at the same time
    c. the tendency to try to manipulate too many variables without adequate statistical control
    d. the problem of needing a third experimenter in double-blind experiments

15. Which of the following correlation coefficients demonstrates the strongest relationship?
    a. +0.10
    b. +0.80
    c. -0.15
    d. -0.95

16. Of the things necessary to discuss cause and effect, a longitudinal study is specifically designed to get a better handle on
    a. covariation of events.
    b. time-order relationships.
    c. elimination of alternative explanations.
    d. internal validity.

17. Mental retardation was found to occur in one of every twenty-five people in a particular ethnic group. This is a report of
    a. statistical frequency.
    b. epidemiological significance.
    c. prevalence.
    d. incidence.

18. Use of animal subjects instead of human subjects, use of controlled laboratory conditions instead of the real world, and the use of college students instead of a more random sample from the population are all characteristics of the
    a. epidemiological study.
    b. analogue experiment.
    c. ABAB design.
    d. multiple-baseline design.

19. The "A" in an ABAB design refers to
    a. control groups.
    b. treatment conditions.
    c. baseline conditions.
    d. placebo conditions.

20. What is the major problem with single-subject research designs?
    a. the necessity of doing without a control condition
    b. the correlational nature of the study
    c. the inability to demonstrate a time-order relationship
    d. the low level of external validity

ANSWERS

Guided Self-Study (p. 36)

1. Research methods! Make sure you *do not* interchange the words *methods* and *designs*. (54)

2. a. characteristics of the scientific method
   b. research designs (64)

3. *Research methods* is an inclusive term that refers to a variety of different matters that are of concern in research (the scientific method). *Research designs* is an exclusive term that refers to the specific way the research is approached. Research designs is a subcategory of the topic research methods. (64)

4. Research designs are all those methods that collect information using the scientific method. There are four research designs discussed in this chapter. The experimental designs are only those specific research designs that use manipulation of an independent variable to see if the dependent variable changes. Experimental designs are a subcategory of research designs (67).

5. a. skeptical (55)
   b. description (55)
   c. prediction (56)
   d. control (56)

6. No right or wrong here; these are your own.

7. a. covariation of events. (56)
   b. time-order relationship. (56)
   c. elimination of plausible alternative causes. (56)

8. a. dependable and consistent (56)
   b. is really what it says it is (56)

9. Confounding (56)

10. Internal validity (56)

11. Generalizability (56)

12. External validity (56)

13. representativeness (56)

14. The required carefulness is about how to select in order to insure randomness. Each person must have an equal chance of being selected. (57)

15. "b" is the method to provide a random selection. All subjects are available for selection and in no particular order. (57)

16. Brady failed to use random assignment of subjects to the groups. (57)

17. replicate (57)

18. a. convenience (57)
    b. random (57)
    c. generalized (56)
    d. external (56)

19. a. Develop a hypothesis. (57)
    b. Formulate operational definitions. (58)
    c. Establish methods of control. (58–59)

20. This is a compliment. A well-formulated hypothesis is scientifically useful if it has testability (can be tested). Ultimately, if a hypothesis cannot be tested for a yes or no answer (falsifiability), the hypothesis has no scientific usefulness. (57)

21. "a" (58)

22. "b" (58)

23. a. manipulate and measure results (58–60)
    b. balancing (58–60)
    c. hold them constant (58–60)

24. "c" (59)

25. a. balance
    b. random (59)

26. a. independent
    b. dependent (58)

27. independent variable
    a. having or not having schizophrenic parents
    b. handedness
    c. before and after etiquette class
    dependent variable
    a. IQ test scores
    b. musical aptitude test scores
    c. social perception ratings (59–60)

28. a. demand (59–60)
    b. experimenter (59–60)
    c. double-blind (60–61)
    In a double-blind experiment, the person who sets up circumstances (assigns subjects to test groups) is not the one who interacts with the participants. (60–61)

29. placebo (59)

30. a. null
    b. 5 percent
    c. 5 (64)

31. inference (61)

32. "d" (57)

33. "b" (64)

34. a. correlational research (64)
    b. epidemiological studies (66–67)
    c. experimental designs (67–68)
    d. single-case experiment (69–70)

35. experimental designs (67–68)

36. The researchers can use natural group research (also called correlational research design). They study the differences between groups of people who have had the bad experience during their lives and groups of people who have not had that specific bad experience. (64–66)

37. a. zero   e. increase
    b. +1.0   f. decrease
    c. -1.0   g. increases
    d. direction   h. decreases (64–66)

38. a. -0.5
    b. +0.4
    c. -1.0 (64-66)
    Remember, the sign has nothing to do with the absolute value; it only tells if the correlation is direct or inverse (together or opposite).

39. a. The relative has on some chemical (cologne, hair spray) to which you are allergic.
    b. Anxiety is most likely the third variable here. You may be so anxious about the course that your anxiety impairs your thinking skills while studying and/or while taking the test. Actually you may not be studying as much as you think, because anxious thoughts fill much of your study time.
    c. The cat has some dietary deficiency that is causing the rash and causing the cat to eat the leaves from that bush.

40. The case study is a research design which depends on intensive description and intellectual analysis of a single individual. One needs only thorough records for this approach. The single-case experiment gathers information by manipulating an independent variable (usually a treatment technique) in the subject to see how his/her behavior (the dependent variable) changes. The single-case experiment is not under the topic of experimental designs because it focuses on only one subject. The other experimental designs are all based on multiple subjects (69–70).

41. a. Longitudinal study (66)
    b. Correlational study (64)
    c. Case study (58)
    d. Analogue experiment (68)
    e. Case study (58)
    f. Correlational study (64)
    g. Analogue experiments (68)
    h. Case study (58)
    i. Analogue experiments (68)
    j. Correlational study (64)
    k. Longitudinal study (66)
    l. Multiple baseline (70)
    m. Epidemiology (66)
    o. High-risk design (66)
    p. ABAB (70)
    q. Demand characteristic (59)
    r. Essential characteristics (59)
    s. Baseline (70)
    t. Case-control design (64)
    u. Double-blind experiment (60)

42. a. Case study, because your access is only to the records of this "weird bird," and it is a fairly safe bet that he is one of a kind. (69–70)
    b. Multiple baseline, because whatever progress you make you want to keep. (70–71)
    c. Natural group design, because you have to take the subjects as they come without doing any unethical manipulation. (64)

Practice Test (p. 43)

1. a. No. Explanations deal with causes; descriptions simple tell what it there.
   b. No. Change may be an ultimate goal, but this is not description.
   c. Correct!
   d. Sorry. This is related to alternative "a."

2. a. No. Correlations examine only covariation.
   b. Yes!
   c. No. These three concepts deal with the circumstances being studied, not the person doing the work.
   d. Incorrect. Statistical significance deals with the likelihood that an event happened by chance.

3. a. Nonsense alternative. Like it or not, we cannot make time run backward.
   b. No. Reliable documentation can often substitute for actual witnessing of an event.
   c. Nonsense alternative. Confounding is not something we want to do; rather we want to avoid it.
   d. Correct!

4. a. No. Variables can be correlated, but this is not a term used for assembling a sample.
   b. Yes!
   c. Fine-sounding word, but it is not in the text (pertains to individual persons).
   d. Sorry. Hypotheses can be null, but not samples (null means zero, or nothing).

5. a. No. Epidemiology (populations studies) will tell you only that the problem is rare!
   b. Right!
   c. No. The word group here should tell you that with a rare problem this is impractical.
   d. With a rare problem, it is important that you look at the real thing, not an imitation.

6. a. No. Just the opposite. Case studies are about as real-life as you can get.
   b. Again, just the opposite can be true. See question 5.
   c. No. since case studies deal with individuals, they can be extremely non-average.
   d. You got it!

7. a. Spoken desires (subjective reports) are what operational definitions are designed to avoid.
   b. No, this could be an example of an eating habit, not true hunger—too subjective.
   c. Yes! This is concrete and reproduceable.
   d. Sorry. Once again, this is a very subjective state of affairs.

8. a. No. The text describes no variable by this name.
   b. No again. There is no such variable.
   c. Correct!
   d. No. This is the one you measure, not manipulate.

9. a. Correct!
    b. Not really. If secrecy is important, something like a double-blind approach is needed.
    c. No. Statistical analysis is always required.
    d. Incorrect. In fact, the control group is going to be one of the groups subjects are randomly assigned to.

10. a. Correct!
    b. No, this term applies to the statistical analysis of data, not to the collection of it.
    c. Incorrect. The null hypothesis is used in evaluating the experiment, not in conducting it.
    d. No. This is a contradiction. You can't have groups in a case study (one-person study).

11. a. No. Null is a form of hypothesis, and most experiments involve randomly assigned groups.
    b. Half right. But the idea of a randomized control group says nothing special here.
    c. Yes!
    d. Again, half right. Demand characteristics are unwanted response patterns that a subject gives, possibly as a result of expectations.

12. a. Correct!
    b. No. Dependent variables don't *have* effects; they *represent* the effects.
    c. No. This would be the case if one *failed* to reject the null hypothesis.
    d. Sorry. Same problem as with "b" above.

13. a. No. Multiple subjects are used here and the key word is relationship.
    b. Right!
    c. Sorry. No experiment here at all, because nothing is being manipulated, just measured.
    d. No. Epidemiological studies simply spell out rates of occurrence, not relationships.

14. a. Correct!
    b. No. Multiple variables can be dealt with, but you have to know about them first.
    c. Not really. Many variables can be manipulated, and while a lack of adequate statistical methods may make the results incomprehensible, it does not introduce unknown variables, which is what a "third" variable is.
    d. No. Variables and experimenters are totally different things.

15. a. No. Strength of a correlation increases the farther you get from zero, in either direction.
    b. Sorry. This one is pretty far from zero, but is there another one even farther away?
    c. No. Pretty close to zero here, several others are better.
    d. Correct!

16. a. No. Think of the term "*long*itudinal" as implying a *long* time.
    b. Yes!
    c. Incorrect. Alternative explanations can only be eliminated by controlling and manipulating the possibilities in an experiment.
    d. No. This is not one of the requirements listed for determining cause and effect.

17. a. This is a general kind of answer that does not relate to the specific terms used in the text.
    b. Nonsense answer. There is no such thing.
    c. Yes!
    d. No. Incidence requires a specified time span.

18. a. No. Epidemiological studies examine incidence and prevalence in populations.
    b. Right! Think of the term "analogy."
    c. No. All of the situations given in the question represent substitutions for real things of interest. ABAB designs study the real thing.
    d. Sorry. This is another example of a design that studies the actual topic of interest.

19.   a.   No. ABAB is a single subject design, so there are no control groups.
      b.   No. "A" comes before "B" so it refers to whatever you do first. What do you have to do before treatment?
      c.   Right! Aside from the logic of first and second, there is no good reason to use the letters "A" and "B" to refer to baseline and treatment. "B" and "T" make more sense, but that's the way it is.
      d.   No. If a placebo were involved, the multiple-baseline approach would be more appropriate.

20.   a.   No, the subject acts as his/her own control.
      b.   No, single-subject designs are experiments, not correlational studies.
      c.   Actually, they do this quite well, with either successive treatments or sequences of baseline and treatment conditions.
      d.   Yes! One subject does not a sample, much less a population, make.

CHAPTER 4
THE BEHAVIORAL, COGNITIVE, AND SOCIOCULTURAL PERSPECTIVES

LEARNING OBJECTIVES

By the time you have finished studying this chapter, you should be able to do the following:

1. Define and briefly describe the field of Behaviorism. (75–77)

2. Briefly describe the background of behavioral psychology. (76–78)

3. Identify the basic mechanisms of learning. (78–80)

4. Discuss abnormal behavior as a product of learning. (79–81)

5. List major contributors to the field of behaviorism. (76–77)

6. Identify essential elements to each contributor's perspective. (76–77)

7. List criticisms of behavioral psychology. (87–88)

8. Define and briefly describe the field of cognitive psychology. (88–89)

9. Briefly describe the background of the cognitive approach to treatment. (88–89)

10. Define cognitive behaviorism. (89–90)

11. Discuss abnormal behavior as a product of faulty cognitions. (90)

12. Discuss and evaluate the cognitive approach to treatment. (94–98)

13. Identify the essential elements to each contributor's perspective. (97–98)

14. List criticisms of the cognitive perspective. (97)

15. Define and briefly describe the sociocultural perspective. (98–99)

16. List social-situational influences on behavior. (98–99)

17. Identify factors of mental illness and social ills. (99)

18. List reasons for the stigma attached with mental illness and labeling. (99)

19. Identify sociocultural factors to those identified as mentally ill. (99–101)

20. Identify and describe the sociocultural factors to access treatment. (101)

21. Discuss prevention as a social issue. (101–102)

KEY TERMS

The following terms are in bold print in your text and are important to your understanding of the chapter. Look them up in the text and write down their definitions.

attribution (92)
behavior therapy (83)
behavioral experiment (95)
behavioral perspective (75)
cognition (88)
cognitive appraisal (90)
cognitive behaviorism (89)

cognitive case conceptualization (95)
cognitive distortion (90)
cognitive perspective (88)
cognitive reflex (76)
cognitive restructuring (95)
conditioned reflexes (76)
conditioned reinforcers (79)

conditioned response (78)

conditioned stimulus (78)

contingency (79)

contingency management (85)

decatastrophizing (95)

derived stimulus relations (82)

discrimination (80)

disorder-specific bias (91)

exposure (84)

extinction (80)

generalization (80)

hierarchy of fears (84)

hypothesis testing (95)

law of effect (77)

learning (76)

negative reinforcement (79)

operant conditioning (79)

positive reinforcement (79)

primary reinforcer (79)

punishment (79)

radical behaviorism (77)

rational-emotive therapy (94)

reinforcement (79)

respondent conditioning (78)

rules (81)

schema (93)

selective attention (93)

shaping (80)

sociocultural perspective (98)

Socratic questioning (95)

stigma (99)

stimulus equivalence (81)

systematic desensitization (84)

three-term contingency (80)

unconditioned response (78)

unconditioned stimulus (78)

vulnerability-stress model (91)

IMPORTANT NAMES

Identify the following persons and their major contributions to abnormal psychology as discussed in this chapter.

Albert Bandura (93)

Aaron Beck (88)

Albert Ellis (89)

Michael Mahoney (95)

Donald Meichenbaum (94)

Ivan Pavlov (76)

B. F. Skinner (77)

Edward Lee Thorndike (77)

John B. Watson (76)

GUIDED SELF-STUDY

The Behavioral Perspective

1. Ivan Pavlov described the principle of (a)_____. Classical conditioning consists of the following

   components: The (b)_____ is a stimulus that produces a response without prior learning—an

   unlearned response called the (c)_____ response; a previously neutral stimulus that eventually

   elicits the conditioned response is called the (d)_____; it elicits a learned response called the

   (e)_____ response.

2. In B. F. Skinner's approach, _____, every thing a person does, says, and feels constitutes
   behavior—even if the unobservable can be subjected to experimental analysis.

3. A form of learning in which consequences of behavior lead to changes in the probability of the behavior is
   called _____.

4. Skinner suggests that our world is full of reinforcers. The (a)_____ is one to which we respond
   instinctively, without learning. (b)_____, also called secondary reinforcers, are stimuli to which we
   have learned to respond through their association with primary reinforcers.

5. Shaping is defined as the process of
   a. reinforcing every avoidance response an organism makes.
   b. reinforcing successive approximations of the target behavior.
   c. directing an organism toward a specific stimulus target.
   d. changing a primary reinforcer into a secondary reinforcer.

6. The classical conditioning process by which a conditioned response automatically spreads is called
   a. extinction.
   b. generalization.
   c. spontaneous recovery.
   d. discrimination.

7. _____ occurs when a baby learns to get cranky when approached by all men with dark hair, because once a dark haired man yelled and made her cry.
   a. Generalization
   b. Spontaneous recovery
   c. Extinction
   d. Discrimination

8. The Millers are unhappy with their latest grades of their teenage son. In response, they have taken away their son's privileges to drive. The Millers are using what type of punishment?
   a. positive punishment
   b. negative reinforcement
   c. positive reinforcement
   d. negative punishment

9. Which of the following learning methods is the one that makes reference to the person using the behavior as an instrument to obtain the consequence?
   a. classical conditioning
   b. observational learning
   c. latent learning
   d. operant conditioning

10. Learning is more effiecient in operant conditioning if the reward is _____ and not _____.
    a. delayed, immediate
    b. negative, positive
    c. immediate, delayed
    d. positive, negative

11. Briefly discuss Pavlov's theory.

12. Briefly discuss Watson's theory.

13. Briefly discuss Skinner's theory.

14. Explain what kind of problem would be treated with systematic desensitization?

The Cognitive Perspective

15. The interest in cognitive processes, such as (a)_____, _____, and _____

    _____, has been around a long time. However, not until the decade of the (b)_____ did the

    cognitive perspective enter abnormal psychology. Cognition is an important part of abnormal psychology for

    two reasons: (c)_____, and (d)_____.

16. In a psychology course, cognition equals thinking, and behaviorism equals learning; *never* be imprecise with

    these terms! They also come together in the line of thought called *cognitive behaviorism*. Early behaviorists

    as a group were interested in studying only observable events. They talked only about (a)_____ and

    response. However, some psychologists then said that although thoughts are not observable behaviors, they

    are significant factors in behaviors. Theorists who focused on thinking use the (b)_____ perspective.

    So when a group of psychologists talked about thoughts (cognition) operating within the principles of basic

    learning theory (behaviorists), they were called (c)_____ _____.

17. The general term that cognitive theorists use to describe the evaluation process that occurs between stimulus
    and response is based on memories, beliefs, and expectations, and accounts for the wide differences in
    individual behavior is
    a. defensive attribution.
    b. schematic aberration.
    c. latent processing.
    d. cognitive appraisal.

18. Define *attribution*.

19. Ideas so deeply entrenched that a person is not even aware that they lead to unhappiness and dysfunction is
    referred to Beck as
    a. dysfunctional attitudes.
    b. automatic thoughts.
    c. false cognitions.
    d. irrational beliefs.

20. "I must be liked by virtually everyone, otherwise I am worthless." This statement, in Ellis's terms, is an
    example of a(n)
    a. faulty cognition.
    b. dysfunctional attitude.
    c. irrational belief.
    d. activating experience.

21. Cognitive theorists say the most powerful reinforcement comes from (a)_____ the person, which is

    reinforcement that comes from the things we (b)_____ _____ _____ about our

    own behavior.

22. Write the name of the correct theorist(s) in the blank preceding each concept. The theorists are *Ellis, Beck, Meichenbaum, Mahoney,* and *Bandura*.

a. _____ Developed self-instructional training

b. _____ Looks for cognitive distortions

c. _____ Irrational beliefs

d. _____ Self-talk—the things people say to themselves before, during, and after their actions

e. _____ Outcome expectancies

f. _____ Developed rational-emotive therapy

g. _____ Efficacy expectancies

h. _____ Magnification

i. _____ Overgeneralization

j. _____ Selective abstraction

k. _____ Developed constructivist cognitive therapy

l. _____ Aims at helping the client understand and change his worldview, called a narrative

m. _____ Two most influential cognitive behaviorists

n _____ Has an "ABC"system

o. _____ Says depressed people have a "negative triad"

23. (a)_____ _____is an area of cognitive research that considers how the mind takes in, stores, and uses information. This area of study has made a distinction between two types of processing that the mind does: controlled processing and automatic processing. List some of your own behaviors that that fit into each of these categories.

b. Automatic processing:

c. Controlled processing:

24. Although some people object to the human mind being compared with a computer, why might the computer also complain about the analogy?

25. Why is selective attention a critical function of our cognitive abilities?

26. Name the two organizing structures proposed in cognitive theory.

27. Give your schema for a fast food restaurant.

28. Which schemas are of most interest to abnormal psychology?

29. a. _____ is the broad general term for cognitive approaches to therapy.

 b. _____ is the oldest cognitive therapy.

 c. _____ is Beck's term for the thinking pattern found in depression.

 d. _____ is considering the possible reality of our worst fears actually happening.

 e. _____ is correcting of inaccurate cause-and-effect thinking.

 f. _____ is checking out assumptions in the real world.

 g. _____ is the basic concept in the cognitive explanation for transference.

30. List the therapist associated with each of the follow types of cognitive therapy:

 a. _____ is known for self-instructional training.

 b. _____ is known for rational-emotive therapy.

 c. _____ is known for constructivist cognitive therapy.

31. List four criticisms of the cognitive perspective.

32. List three contributions attributed to cognitive therapy.

33. Match the theorist with the concept.

 1. Pavlov ___.   a   operant conditioning

 2. Skinner ___.   b.   classical conditioning

 3. Watson ___.   c.   separation-individuation

 4. Thorndike ___.   d.   law of effect

 5. Beck ___.   e.   irrational beliefs

 6. Ellis ___.   f.   cognitive distortions

The Sociocultural Perspective

34. Define the sociocultural perspective.

35. Some researchers believe that powerful "situational forces" lead ordinary people to act in extreme ways. This was evidenced by Philip Zimbardo's prison study. Explain why this study was influential to the sociocultural perspective?

HELPFUL HINTS

1. The word "thinking" can be substituted for the word "cognitive" until you become comfortable with the term. This should help you understand the cognitive perspective.

2. The word "learning" can be substituted for the word "behaviorism" until you become comfortable with behaviorism as a concept.

3. As each perspective is discussed, try to focus only on that one perspective. I often tell my class to put on their "cognitive glasses" and view the world only from that perspective. Then switch to your "behavioral glasses."

4. Arrange major contributors according to their perspective. You should be able to identify the perspective as well as its major contributors and independent theories.

PRACTICE TEST

1. Reinforcers that are innately reinforcing, such as food and water, are called
   a. primary reinforcers.
   b. secondary reinforcers.
   c. extinguished reinforcers.
   d. tertiary reinforcers.

2. Learning that results from the consequences of behaviors is called
   a. extinguished conditioning.
   b. operant conditioning.
   c. classical conditioning.
   d. positive conditioning

3. B. F. Skinner is identified as a
   a. behavioral theorist.
   b. cognitive theorist.
   c. sociocultural theorist.
   d. psychodynamic theorist.

4. Dysfunctional thoughts that produce maladaptive behavior are considered characteristic of _____ theory.
   a. classical
   b. cognitive
   c. sociocultural
   d. behavioral

5. Systematic desensitization involves three steps:
   a. gradual conditioning, response, and extinction.
   b. fear, reaction, and extinction.
   c. relaxation training, heirachy of fears, and desensitization.
   d. relaxation training, conditioning, and desensitization.

6. Parents who throw their toddler, who is dreadfully fearful of the water, into a swimming pool may be using which technique?
   a. flooding
   b. systematic desensitization
   c. graded exposure response
   d. prevention

7. Another word for learning is _____.
   a. thinking
   b. behaviorism
   c. cognition
   d. maturation

8. _____ was an American psychologist who is credited with founding the behavioral movement.
   a. John B. Watson
   b. Ivan Pavlov
   c. Edward Lee Thorndike
   d. Rosalie Rayner

9. Sociocultural theorists believe that we often underestimate the power of situational forces.
   Examples are
   a. genetically influenced mental illness.
   b. poverty and racism.
   c. medical conditions.
   d. schizophrenia.

10. Poverty is a significant risk factor for the possibility of psychopathology. Why?
    a. compromised immune systems
    b. more stress and less resources and social supports
    c. less education in impoverished areas
    d. lack of insight to illness

11. The goal of primary prevention is
    a. modifying existing risk factors so that they do not lead to disorders.
    b. treating disorders as quickly as possible.
    c. using the medical model to reduce symptoms.
    d. eliminating the cause of a disorder.

12. To prevent or eradicate the kinds of social ills that place people at risk, cognitive theorists believe that many abnormal behavior patterns, such as anxiety disorders and depression, can be viewed as the result of
    a. dysfunctional or inappropriate automatic processing.
    b. depleted levels of serotonin.
    c. these behaviors being socially learned.
    d. unconscious determinants.

13. Micheal Mahoney, a constructivist cognitive theorist, suggests that self-exploration should be an important part of therapy. Techniques he would suggest consist of
    a. poems, journals and speaking "streams of consciousness."
    b. dream analysis.
    c. understanding childhood memories.
    d. rational emotive therapy.

ANSWERS

Guided Self-Study (P. 52)

1. a. classical conditioning
   b. unconditioned stimulus
   c. unconditioned response
   d. conditioned stimulus
   e. conditioned response (78)

2. radical behavioralism (77)

3. operant conditioning (79)

4. a. primary reinforcer
   b. Conditioned reinforcers (79)

5. "b" (80)

6. "b" (80)

7. "a" (80)

8. "d" (80)

9. "d" (79)

10. "c" (79)

11. Pavlov's theory: Belief that many of our automatic emotional reactions are acquired through *classical conditioning* (salivating dog experiment) (76)

12. Watson's theory: Founder of behaviorism (Little Albert study) (76)

13. Skinner's theory: Principles of *operant conditioning* (Skinner box experiment) (77)

14. Systematic desensitization can be used to treat anxiety disorders as well as phobias. (84)

15. a. memory, reasoning, problem solving
    b. 1970s
    c. Many abnormal disorders involve serious cognitive disturbances.
    d. Certain cognitive patterns may actually cause some disorders instead of just being secondary symptoms (88).

16. a. stimulus
    b. cognitive
    c. cognitive behaviorists (88–89)

17. "d" (90)

18. An attribution is a belief you have about what caused an event, particularly a person's behavior. Two examples:

    Tom does that because he is an all-purpose idiot! (global, stable, internal)
    Tom did that because he was under too much pressure from his boss. (specific, unstable, external) (92)

19. "b" (89)

20. "c" (90)

21. a. within
    b. say to ourselves (88)

22. a. Meichenbaum
    b. Beck (88)
    c. Ellis (89)
    d. Meichenbaum
    e. Bandura (93)
    f. Ellis (89)
    g. Bandura (93)
    h. Beck (88)

    i. Beck (88)
    j. Beck (88)
    k. Mahoney
    l. Mahoney
    m. Ellis and Beck (88, 89)
    n. Ellis (89)
    o. Beck (88)

23. a. Information processing (93)
    b. Automatic processing behaviors: driving in routine conditions, flipping the TV controller during commercials, dialing familiar phone numbers, searching for the car keys that you chronically lose (93)
    c. Controlled processing behaviors: learning to drive a car, ordering food from a restaurant's menu whose cuisine is unknown to you, deciding how you are going to tell your family that for the first time you are not coming home at all during vacation (93)

24. The computer might want to point out that it stores all information that it receives and stores it accurately. The human mind picks and chooses among which data bits it will store. The human mind also has serious problems with accuracy; it may store data bits to say what it wants them to say instead of recording them accurately. (93)

25. We could not possibly process all the data that comes into our sensory channels. Selective attention directs the cognitive focus to those bits of data that are relevant for survival. For example, that little strange feeling about your ankle, your brain writes off as probably your pant leg. Your brain does not even mention it to you. However, when you are told someone has let a pet snake loose in the library for "fun," your brain tells you to check out that little feeling about your ankle. (93)

26. schemas and beliefs (93–94)

27. Fast food restaurants: order at a central counter or drive-through, a standard menu, carry your own tray, no table cloths or table service, inexpensive fare (93–94)

28. Self-schemas, because they are who we think we are—our self-concepts, our identities (94)

29. a. Cognitive restructuring (95)
    b. Rational-emotive (94)   e. Reattribution training (95)
    c. Negative triad (95)   f. Hypothesis testing (95)
    d. Decatastrophizing (95)   g. Schema (93)

30. a. Donald Meichenbaum (94)
    b. Albert Ellis (89)
    c. Michael J. Mahoney (95)

31. a. It depends on inference.
    b. Life is not entirely cognitive (rational).
    c. Changing one's way of thinking may not always be the best solution to a problem.
    d. The underlying therapeutic mechanism of cognitive therapy is still unproven. (97)

32. a. It focuses on operationalized variables in an empirical approach while working with intangible processes (thoughts and emotions).
    b. It is a very practical approach, described precisely in manuals so that an individual can use the techniques without the intervention of a therapist.
    c. Manuals also include methods to assess the effectiveness of the techniques so that that large-scale outcome studies may be done. (94–97)

33. 1. b (76)   4. d (77)
    2. a (77)   5. f (88)
    3. c (76)   6. e (89)

34. The sociocultural perspective studies abnormality in an environmental context. (98)

35. The findings of the Zimbardo study demonstrate that even experts underestimate the power of situational forces. (98–99)

Practice Test (p. 57)

1. a. Correct!
   b. An example of a secondary reinforcer is money.
   c. No. No such term.
   d. No. Wrong guess.

2. a. No. No such term.
   b. Correct!
   c. No, classical conditioning does not involve consequences.
   d. No. No such term.

3. a. Correct!
   b. No, cognition implies thinking.
   c. No, sociocultural theory takes into account society and culture.
   d. No, psychodynamic theory focuses on unconscious determinants.

4. a. No. Classical conditioning is a term associated with Pavlov's theory.
   b. Correct!
   c. Sociocultural Theory has its own theory.
   d. Think of learning.

5. a. No, not correct.
   b. No, extinction is a component to operant conditioning.
   c. Correct!
   d. Wrong guess.

6. a. Correct! Immersing the child into its fear.
   b. This would be a gradual process.
   c. No, wrong term.
   d. No, wrong term. Look these other terms up.

7. a. No, another word for thinking is cognition.
   b. Correct!
   c. No, another word for cognition is thinking.
   d. No, maturation is growth.

8. a. Correct!
   b. No. Pavlov, classical conditioning.
   c. No. Thorndike, law of effect.
   d. No. Rosalie Rayner assisted with Little Albert study.

9. a. No. This is not a situational force.
   b. Correct!
   c. No. These are not situational forces.
   d. No. This is not a situational force.

10. a. No, not necessarily.
    b. Correct!
    c. No, not necessarily.
    d. No, not necessarily connected.

11. a. No. This is secondary prevention.
    b. No. Treatment is included in tertiary prevention.
    c. Incorrect, medically based.
    d. Correct!

12. a. Correct!
    b. No. Biological theory.
    c. No. Behavioral theory.
    d. No. Psychoanalytical theory.

13. a. Correct!
    b. No. Freudian.
    c. No, could be many theories.
    d. No, Ellis developed this theory.

CHAPTER 5
THE PSYCHODYNAMIC, HUMANISTIC-EXISTENTIAL, AND INTERPERSONAL PERSPECTIVES

LEARNING OBJECTIVES

By the time you have finished studying this chapter, you should be able to do the following:

1. List three basic principles held in common by all psychodynamic theorists. (105–108)

2. Describe the three levels of consciousness proposed by Freud. (107–108)

3. Describe the functions of the id, ego, and superego. (107–108)

4. Define anxiety as Freud viewed it, and list and describe defense mechanisms. (108–110)

5. List and describe the four stages of personality development in Freudian theory. (110–111)

6. Identify post-Freudian "descendants" and their contributions to psychodynamic theory. (111–117)

7. Define the elements of psychoanalysis, and identify differences to modern psychodynamic therapy. (117–120)

8. List four criticisms of psychodynamic theory. (120–122)

9. Define and discuss the two humanistic-existential schools of thought. (123)

10. Discuss the reasons for the rise of the humanistic-existential movement. (123–124)

11. Discuss the work of Carl Rogers and Abraham Maslow, founders of the contemporary humanistic-existential perspective. (124–126)

12. Define Maslow's heirachy of needs and drive toward self-actualization. (125–126)

13. Define Carl Roger's humanistic perspective as it relates to positive regard. (124–125)

14. Define the emphasis of the interpersonal perspective. (127)

15. Understand the focus and primary mechanisms of IPT (interpersonal therapy). (127)

16. Identify the advantages to integrating theoretical perspectives. (127–128)

KEY TERMS

The following terms are in bold print in your text and are important to your understanding of the chapter. Look them up in the text and write down their definitions.

alienation (126)	humanistic-existential perspective (123)
anal stage (110)	id (107)
anxiety (108)	interpersonal perspective (127)
castration anxiety (111)	interpretation (106)
client-centered therapy (125)	latency (111)
conditions of worth (125)	libido (107)
defense mechanism (108)	neuroses (111)
depth hypothesis (106)	object relations (115)
ego (107)	Oedipus complex (111)
Electra complex (111)	oral stage (110)
genital stage (111)	phallic stage (110)
hierachy of needs (125)	phenomenological approach (123)

positive psychology (124)
psychoanalysis (106)
psychodynamic perspective (105)
psychosexual development (110)
psychosis (111)

self-actualization (124)
structural hypothesis (107)
superego (108)
unconscious (106)
valuing process (124)

IMPORTANT NAMES

Identify the following persons and their major contributions to abnormal psychology as discussed in this chapter.

Alfred Adler (113)
Mary Ainsworth (116)
John Bowlby (116)
Erik Erikson (114)
Sigmund Freud (106)
Heinz Hartmann (114)

Karen Horney (113)
Carl Gustav Jung (113)
Melanie Klein (115)
Heinz Kohut (116)
Margaret Mahler (115)
Harry Stack Sullivan (113)

GUIDED SELF-STUDY

The Psychodynamic Perspective

1. There is one man's name that I could mention that every one of you would probably recognize at once as a person in the field of psychology. Can you guess that name? Even more important, can you spell it?

2. If I had said his name, what would have been the first thing that popped into your mind?

3. Use the following terms to fill in the blanks: *psychodynamic, psychoanalysis,* and *psychoanalytic.*

   (a)_____ is the name of Freud's theory; however, the whole line of thought that has developed out

   of his work is called the (b)_____ perspective. Freud is called the father of (c)_____ theory;

   however, many theorists have since altered some of Freud's theory and developed their own theories to add

   to this perspective. So, Freud's (d)_____ theory is an example of (e)_____ theory, but all

   (f)_____ theory is not (g)_____ theory.

4. While the psychodynamic perspective on psychology may be interpreted in different ways by different psychologists, almost everyone who takes this point of view would agree on three basic ideas. Match these phrases to their explanations: *unconscious, early childhood,* and *psychic determinism.*

   a. _____   Behavior is not freely chosen by the individual

   b. _____   Individuals are unaware of most of their psychological
                               processes

   c. _____   The most important time of psychological development

5. Use the following terms to identify the Freudian concepts below: *depth hypothesis, unconscious, perceptual conscious, latent, content,* and *manifest content.*

   a. _____   The key concept of psychoanalysis—Freud's most important
                               contribution to psychology

   b. _____   The range of things you are aware of now

c. _____ Things you are not aware of and cannot recall even if you try

d. _____ According to Freud the most important level for mental processing

e. _____ The overt plot of a dream

f. _____ The deep, symbolic meaning of the dream

6. Use the three elements of Freud's structural hypothesis—*id*, *ego*, and *superego*—to complete the following statements.

a. _____ Is entirely unconscious

b. _____ Emerges around the age of six months

c. _____ Is preoccupied with issues of morality

d. _____ Is the most conscious of the three

e. _____ Operates on the reality principle

f. _____ Emerges around the age of five to six years

g. _____ Uses a standard called the "ego ideal"

h. _____ Is present at birth

i. _____ Uses defense mechanisms to ward off anxiety

7. Use the following terms to complete the statements: *anxiety, id, ego, superego*, and *defense mechanisms*.

The personality structure that organizes the conscious life of the person is the (a)_____. When this

personality structure is threatened by reality, or by impulses from the (b)_____, or by demands from

the (c)_____, the result is (d)_____ The ego uses ego (e)_____ _____ to

distort reality to reduce unbearable anxiety.

8. Write the name of the proper defense mechanism next to its definition:

rationalization   *sublimation*   *displacement*
intellectualization   *denial*   *isolation*
regression   *repression*   *identification*
reaction formation   *projection*   *undoing*

a. _____ Transforms unacceptable impulses into more socially appropriate forms

b. _____ Moves emotional reactions from an original object to a safer object

c. _____ Cuts emotional responses off from the events that cause them

d. _____ The refusal to acknowledge the existence of a source of anxiety

e. _____ The most fundamental defense mechanism—it pushes unacceptable material into the unconscious

f. _____ Attributes one's own unacceptable impulses to other people

g. _____ Finds socially acceptable reasons for doing what is unacceptable

h. _____ Replaces an emotional experience with a cognitive understanding

i. _____ Takes one back to a time of life when issues were more easily dealt with

j. _____ Handles unacceptable feelings by changing them into their opposites

k. _____   Is ritual behavior to erase the effect of an unacceptable impulse

9. In Freud's view, personality develops during early childhood in stages. List Freud's four stages and one period of psychosexual development in the correct order:

10. Use the stages you listed in the previous question as answers in the following blanks.

    a. The focus of the _____ stage of development is mature sexual relationships.

    b. The focus of the _____ stage is the functions of bodily elimination.

    c. The focus of the _____ stage is mouth behavior.

    d. The focus of the _____ stage is the sexual organs.

11. The Oedipus complex is a crucial event in the (a)_____ stage. During this stage, boys experience

    (b)_____ _____, while girls experience (c)_____ _____

Complete the next three questions using these terms: *id, neuroses, superego, psychoses,* and *balance.*

12. In Freud's theory, the normal personality may have ongoing conflicts among the id, the ego, the superego, and the real world, but to remain normal the ego must be able to maintain a dynamic _____ among these forces.

13. In the abnormal personality, psychic energy is divided unevenly, and the id or superego may gain disproportionate power. When the (a)_____ is dominant, the result may be an amoral, impulsive individual. When the (b)_____ dominates, excessive guilt or suspiciousness may be the result.

14. In the less severe forms of abnormality, an individual may be troubled and inefficient in living but still retain reality contact. These types of problems are called (a)_____. In more severe disorders, reality contact may be lost because of overwhelming conflict and the breakdown of defenses. These problems are called (b)_____.

15. List three positions post-Freudian theorists have taken that depart substantially from Freud.

    a.

    b.

    c.

16. Write the name of the appropriate post-Freudian thinker in front of each identifying phrase. The names are *Jung, Adler, Sullivan, Hartmann, Erikson, Mahler, Horney,* and *Kohut.*

    a. _____   coined the term "inferiority complex."

    b. _____   proposed eight stages of development.

    c. _____   pioneered the treatment of severe disorders.

d. _____ was a major founder of "ego psychology."

e. _____ emphasized object relations theory.

f. _____ stressed of separation-individuation from the mother.

g. _____ believed that parents give children calmness and greatness.

h. _____ developed the concept of collective unconscious.

i. _____ emphasized a striving for superiority.

j. _____ developed the concept of narcissistic personality disorder.

k. _____ identified psychosocial, not psychosexual stages.

l. _____ proposed "basic" anxiety.

m. _____ was an early female psychoanalytic thinker.

n. _____ said penis envy wasn't the issue, but status and power envy were.

o. _____ formulated attachment theory.

p. _____ focused on the mother's sensitivity to child's signals.

17. The goal of Freudian therapy was to make the unconscious (a)_____. The patient could then work through the material and resolve conflicts, which would lower anxiety and reduce his excessive use of self-defeating (b)_____.

18. What are the four techniques Freudian therapists use to discover what is in the unconscious?

19. How does modern psychodynamic therapy differ from traditional Freudian psychoanalysis? (three ways)

20. Psychodynamic theory is criticized on a number of grounds, and it is credited with a number of contributions to psychology. Identify each of the following as a *credit* or a *criticism*.

a. _____ Demythologized mental illness

b. _____ Does not lend itself to straightforward experimental testing

c. _____ Stimulated advances in therapy

d. _____ Interpretations of the unconscious are subjective

e. _____ Based on unrepresentative, culturally biased sample

f. _____ Focused twentieth-century thinking on the "inner" world

g. _____ A reductive interpretation of life

The Humanistic-Existential Perspective

21. The (a)_____ perspective is an outgrowth of the reaction to the (b)_____ perspective. Two theorists, (c)_____ and (d)_____, laid the foundation for the humanistic-existential perspective.

22. Define the phenomenological approach.

23. Maslow proposed five levels of needs, each of which must be satisfied before a person can proceed to the next level:

    Level 1 _____

    Level 2 _____

    Level 3 _____

    Level 4 _____

    Level 5 _____

24. The views of existential psychologists emphasize the difficulty of living authentically in the (a)_____

    world. The result is inauthenticity and a denial of the true self. This "spiritual death" is referred to by

    existentialists as (b)_____.

25. In contrast to the relatively pessimistic view adopted by psychodynamic theorists, humanistic theorists put

    forward an emphatic _____ vision of the human being.

26. Humanist and existentialist see a fundamental distinction between the (a)_____ sciences and the

    (b)_____ sciences.

27. List four scientists known for their contributions to the psychodynamic perspective.

28. Maslow proposed five levels of needs. Identify each level within the hierarchy of needs.

    a. _____   Physical comfort
    b. _____   Close friendships
    c. _____   Stable environment
    d. _____   Openly free and expressive
    e. _____   Survival instinct
    f. _____   Need to be respected by others
    g. _____   Maximum potential for growth

29. Client-centered therapy was developed by _____.

30. Rogers suggests that _____, respect and approval, with no conditions of worth be used in client-centered therapy.

31. The concept in which humanists and existentialists see the individual as a work in progress throughout life

    is referred to as human potential and _____.

Interpersonal Perspectives

32. The interpersonal perspective is actually not just one but (a)_____ approaches. They all emphasize

    the importance of (b)_____ (c)_____ was one of the first theorists to systematically develop

    an interpersonal approach to psychiatric disorders. IPT (which stands for (d)_____) was originally

    conceived for the treatment of (e)_____.

33. Name the contributors to the interpersonal perspective.

34. What psychiatric disorders are associated with marital difficulties and inadequate social supports?

HELPFUL HINTS

1. Be alert when learning the specific psychological definitions of textbook terms. Psychological terms have sometimes been adopted for general conversational use. Their conversational usages are sometimes quite different from their technical definitions. Don't just glance at a vocabulary word, recognize it, and move on to the next term. Read the definition closely to see if that definition is consistent with the usage with which you are familiar. For instance, "his/her ego is bigger than it needs to be" does not relate to the way Freud used the term "ego."

2. Do not let your personal opinions of the different perspectives impair your learning. Frequently, I have students who totally reject "all that sexuality" in psychoanalytic theory. (Freud would say that was massive denial.) Because of this attitude, these students may not seriously study Freud's theory. Skipping over Freud's theory does not punish Freud; it only undermines the student's grade. Freudian theory is not going to go away. It is one of the major psychological theories.

3. Note that there are two ego defense mechanisms that are very similar in spelling: repression and regression. Don't confuse them.

4. Freud uses four stages of psychosexual development. The latency period is termed a *period*, not a *stage*. So, when you learn Freud's four psychosexual stages in order, what you really have to know are Freud's four stages and one period in order. If you are asked how many psychosexual stages Freud theorized, the answer is "four" even though you had to learn five terms to cover psychosexual development.

5. Now that we have learned about several theories, try to keep your theories and theorists straight. Make a grid for yourself, and list theories and place theorists underneath each heading. Remember: Humanists are more "humane;" therefore, they focus on the person and the potential of the self. Try to find commonalities among the theorists that are easy for you to recall.

PRACTICE TEST

Use the following test questions to check your knowledge of the material in this chapter. You may want to write the answers on a separate sheet of paper so you can take the test more than once.

1. The psychodynamic perspective is a school of thought in which
   a. the assumption that biological similarities between people in families or communities determine much of the individual's behavior.
   b. the tendency to look outside of the individual for explanations for behavior.
   c. a pronounced focus on free will and self-determination in explaining both normal and abnormal behavior.
   d. a pronounced focus on psychic determinism and unconscious determinants.

2. The founder of the psychodynamic school of psychology was
   a. B. F. Skinner.
   b. Edward L. Thorndike.
   c. Ivan Pavlov.
   d. Sigmund Freud.

3. According to Freud, the true unconscious meaning of a dream is its _____ content.
   a. manifest
   b. subliminal.
   c. underlying.
   d. latent.

4. A seven-year-old resumes bedwetting and using a pacifer shortly after his parents adopt a new toddler. He is probably using which defense mechanism?
   a. denial
   b. repression
   c. regression
   d. projection

5. When Tim was a child, he had painful dental work performed. Each visit filled him with fear. As an adult, Tim seems to always forget his dental appointments. He is reminded after a message is left on his answering machine. Tim may be using which defense mechanism?
   a. regression
   b. repression
   c. projection
   d. displacement

6. According to Freud, an adult who chain smokes cigarettes for the need to have something in his or her mouth may
   a. have had unsatisfied oral needs that led to dependency in adulthood.
   b. be indulging in sexual gratification.
   c. exhibiting classical conditioning.
   d. have entered the phallic stage early.

7. According to Freudian theory, who of the following is id-driven?
   a. a rapist
   b. a hungry baby
   c. a conscientious student
   d. both A and B

8. Which of the following is true?
   a. The id operates on what Freud calls the pleasure principle.
   b. The ego is sexual and aggressive.
   c. The ego is equivalent to what we call "conscience."
   d. The superego operates on the reality principle.

9. Freud's primary route to the unconscious was _____, whereby the client simply verbalizes whatever thoughts come to mind, in whatever order they occur, taking care not to censor them either for logic or for propriety.
   a. transference
   b. free will
   c. free asssociation
   d. generalization

10. The concept of self-actualization refers to
   a. the need to fulfill one's own unique maximum potential.
   b. having your fundamental needs met.
   c. the process one goes through during therapy.
   d. the need to feel competent and respected.

11. In contrast to the relatively pessimistic views of human potential adopted by psychodynamic theorists, humanists believe
   a. that one's self is determined by the unconscious determinants.
   b. that the environment helps shape each individual.
   c. that if people are allowed to develop freely, without undue constraints, they will become rational, socialized, and constructive beings who are motivated to fulfill their capabilities.
   d. that the psychodynamic perspective does not emphasize the necessary focus of unconscious conflict with healthy development.

12. Of the humanists with optimistic vision, who have been the two most influential?
   a. Freud and Jung
   b. Jung and Horney
   c. Jung and Watson
   d. Rogers and Maslow

13. Which of the following is a contribution of the interpersonal perspective?
   a. It has produced some effective treatment strategies, namely IPT.
   b. It has concentrated interest on the effects of early sexual abuse.
   c. It has removed the stigma associated with being a mental patient.
   d. It has proven the essential correctness of the medical model.

14. _____ is known as a post-Freudian, psychodynamic thinker but is also known as a father of the interpersonal school of psychotherapy.
   a. Rogers
   b. Maslow
   c. Sullivan
   d. Jung

15. Existential theorists believe
   a. it is important to appreciate fully each moment as it occurs.
   b. that fundamental flaws in human nature are the cause of psychological disorders.
   c. that unconscious factors are the basis of human behavior and existence.
   d. that human existence represents a continual struggle between good and evil.

16. Which theorist conceptualized a pyramidlike structure called the *hierarchy of needs* specifying the order in which human needs must be fulfilled?

  a. Mahler
  b. Maslow
  c. Rogers
  d. Jung

17. Each of Freud's psychosexual stages centers on

  a. the mother-infant bond.
  b. one of the body's erogenous zones.
  c. crises in childhood.
  d. development of adequate defense mechanisms.

18. Which of the following is criticism that has been leveled at psychodynamic therapy?

  a. It demands a degree of scientific objectivity that is not easy to come by in complex relationships.
  b. It tries to cover too much ground in that it lays all the blame for mental disorder on family relationships.
  c. Many of its promoters reject attempts to evaluate their claims and techniques empirically.
  d. It emphasizes that most of our behavior is operated unconsciously; therefore, motives are unknown to us.

19. Which of the following statements best characterizes current thinking regarding the theoretical perspective that should be assumed by a clinician?

  a. Clinicians typically adopt one perspective and treat all individuals alike.
  b. Most clinicians tend to identify with one perspective but borrow from others when appropriate.
  c. Most clinicians view the psychodynamic perspective as outdated; therefore, they use the humanistic perspective.
  d. Most clinicians use the medical perspective of psychological disorders.

20. To counteract the conditions of worth a person experienced in childhood, Rogers believed that the client should be treated with

  a. sympathy.
  b. unconditional positive regard.
  c. courtesy.
  d. dream analysis.

ANSWERS

Guided Self-Study (p. 64)

1. Freud (105–106)

2. Sex (if you are typical)

3. a. Psychoanalysis
   b. psychodynamic
   c. psychodynamic
   d. psychoanalytic
   e. psychodynamic
   f. psychodynamic
   g. psychoanalytic (105–106)

4. a. psychic determinism
   b. unconscious
   c. early childhood (106)

5. a. depth hypothesis
   b. perceptual conscious
   c. unconscious
   d. unconscious
   e. manifest content
   f. latent content (106)

6. a. id (107)
   b. ego (107)
   c. superego (107–108)
   d. ego (107)
   e. ego (107)

   f. superego (107–108)
   g. superego (107–108)
   h. id (107)
   i. ego (107)

7. a. ego
   b. id
   c. superego
   d. anxiety (108–109)
   e. defense mechanisms (108)

8. a. sublimation (110)
   b. displacement (109)
   c. isolation (109)
   d. denial (109)
   e. repression (108)
   f. projection (109)

   g. rationalization (109)
   h. intellectualization (110)
   i. regression (110)
   j. reaction formation (110)
   k. undoing (110)

9. oral stage, anal stage, phallic stage, latency period, genital stage (110–111)

10. a. genital
    b. anal
    c. oral
    d. phallic (110)

11. a. phallic
    b. castration anxiety
    c. penis envy (111)

12. balance (111)

13. a. id
    b. superego (107–108)

14. a. neuroses
    b. psychoses (100)

15. a. emphasis on the ego
    b. emphasis on social relationships
    c. extension of the developmental period (100)

16. a. Adler (113)
    b. Erikson (114–115)
    c. Sullivan (113)
    d. Hartmann (114)
    e. Mahler (115–116)
    f. Mahler (115–116)
    g. Kohut (116)
    h. Jung (113)

    i. Adler (113)
    j. Kohut (116)
    k. Erikson (114–115)
    l. Horney (113–114)
    m. Horney (113–114)
    n. Horney (113–114)
    o. Bowlby (116)
    p. Ainsworth (116)

17. a. conscious
    b. ego defense mechanisms (108)

18. Free association and the analysis of dreams, resistance, and transference (117–118)

19. a. Therapist's behavior: face-to-face with patient and more active (verbally interacting with the patient and advising the patient)
    b. Focus: more on current personal relationships and a little less on distant past
    c. Form of therapy: briefer and less intensive (119)

20. a, c, and f are contributions; b, d, e, and g are criticisms (120–122)

21. a. humanistic-existential
    b. psychodynamic
    c. Rogers
    d. Maslow (125)

22. Listening with maximum empathy to everything that patients communicate about their experiences (123)

23. Level 1—biological needs
    Level 2—safety needs
    Level 3—belongingness and warmth
    Level 4—esteem
    Level 5—self-actualization (125–126)

24. a. modern
    b. alienation (126)

25. positive (123)

26. a. natural
    b. human (126)

27. Any four of the following: Freud, Klein, Erikson, Mahler, Kohut, Bowlby, and Ainsworth (111–116)

28. a. level 1
    b. level 3
    c. level 2
    d. level 5
    e. level 1
    f. level 4
    g. level 5 (125–126)

29. Rogers (124–125)

30. unconditional positive regard (125)

31. uniqueness (123)

32. a. several
    b. interpersonal relationships
    c. Stack
    d. interpersonal therapy
    e. depression (127)

33. Stack Sullivan, Klerman (127)

34. substance abuse, depression, and panic disorder (127)

Practice Test (p. 70)

1. a. No. Look at the names of the perspectives—there's no hint of biological involvement there.
   b. No.
   c. No.
   d. Correct!

2. a. Sorry. This is one of those "either you know it or you don't" questions—not much context.
   b. No.
   c. No. Did you know Pavlov wasn't even a psychologist? He was a physiologist who gave the real founder of behaviorism his ideas.
   d. Correct!

3. a. No, wrong term.
   b. No, wrong term.
   c. No, not a clinical term.
   d. Correct! (unconscious understory)

4. a. Sorry. This would be refusal to believe or see the truth. That would be an assumption of the biologists.
   b. No, this would be to unconsciously forget.
   c. Correct!
   d. Wrong, this would be to place ones's own negative attributes onto others.

5. a. No, this is to revert back.
   b. Correct!
   c. No. Wrong defense mechanism.
   d. Incorrect. Review defense mechanisms.

6. a Correct!
   b. Incorrect.
   c. Incorrect.
   d. No, not so.

7. a. No, not just this answer.
   b. No, not just this answer.
   c. No.
   d. Correct, both A and B!

8. a. Correct!
   b. Wrong. The id is sexual and aggressive.
   c. No. The superego is considered the "conscience."
   d. No. The ego operates on the reality principle.

9. a. Sorry. Wrong term.
   b. No.
   c. Correct!
   d. No, not a component of psychodynamic therapy.

10. a. Exactly!
    b. No. However, this is a basic need.
    c. No.
    d. No. However, this is a need that Maslow defines

11. a. No. This thought would be psychodynamic.
    b. No. This thought would be sociocultural.
    c. Correct!
    d. Incorrect. The psychodynamic perspective does emphasize unconscious conflict.

12. a. No.
    b. No.
    c. No, Jung is a post-Freudian.
    d. Correct!

13. a. Correct.
    b. Incorrect. This would be of more interest to the Freudians.
    c. Incorrect.
    d. No.

14. a. No.
    b. No.
    c. Correct!
    d. No.

15. a. Correct!
    b. No, unrelated to existential.
    c. No, psychodynamic.
    d. Incorrect.

16. a. No.
    b. Correct!
    c. No. However, Rogers is a humanist.
    d. No.

17. a. No. Freud may be concerned about the mother-child relationship, but not all stages center on this.
    b. Yes!
    c. Sorry. Erikson is concerned with psychosocial crises.
    d. No.

18. a. No, actually a lack of scientific rigor is part of the problem.
    b. Not really. In fact, it is sometimes criticized for being too limited in its scope.
    c. Correct.
    d. Incorrect.

19. a. Incorrect. All clients are unique, therefore treatment varies.
    b. Correct.
    c. Incorrect. Many clinicians borrow from the psychodynamic perspective.
    d. Incorrect. This may be true for some clincians but not the majority.

20. a. No. Possibly empathy.
    b. Correct!
    c. No. This is not a technique.
    d. No, this is a Freudian technique.

CHAPTER 6
THE NEUROSCIENCE PERSPECTIVE

LEARNING OBJECTIVES

By the time you have finished studying this chapter, you should be able to do the following:

1. Define and briefly describe the field of behavior genetics, and explain the diathesis-stress model of mental disorder. (131)

2. Briefly explain how family studies, twin studies, adoption studies, and molecular genetics studies are conducted, and list the advantages and shortcomings of each. (132–135)

3. Describe the functions of the cell body, dendrites, axon, axon terminals, myelin sheath, and synapse in connection with the neuron. (136–137)

4. List six neurotransmitters important in the study of abnormal behavior, and describe their major functions as currently understood. (137–138)

5. Name and describe the functions of the four lobes of the cerebral cortex and of the brain structures noted in *italics* in your text. (139–140)

6. Briefly describe the EEG, CT, PET, and MRI as tools for investigating the brain. (141–143)

7. Describe the major functional differences between the right and left hemispheres of the cortex. (139–140)

8. Describe the functions of the somatic and the autonomic divisions of the peripheral nervous system, and further distinguish between the functions of the sympathetic and the parasympathetic divisions of the autonomic system. (144–145)

9. Describe what hormones are, and summarize their role in the functioning of the endocrine system. (146)

10. Evaluate the neuroscience perspective. (146–147)

11. Understand the integration of neuroscience and the psychodynamic perspective. (147–148)

12. Understand the integration of neuroscience and the cognitive-behavioral perspective. (148)

KEY TERMS

The following terms are in bold print in your text and are important to your understanding of the chapter. Look them up in the text and write down their definitions.

autonomic nervous system (144)
central nervous system (135)
cerebral cortex (139)
chromosomes (131)
computerized tomography (CT) (142)
concordant (133)
corpus callosum (139)
diathesis (131)
diathesis-stress model (131)
dizygotic (DZ) twins (133)
down-regulation (137)
endocrine system (146)
event-related potentials (142)
frontal lobe (139)

functional MRI (fMRI) (142)
genes (131)
genetic marker (135)
genotype-environment correlation (131)
hormones (146)
lateralization (143)
magnetic resonance imaging (MRI) (142)
mind-body problem (131)
monozygotic (MZ) twins (132)
nervous system (135)
neurons (136)
neuroscience perspective (131)
neurotransmitter (137)
occipital lobe (140)

parasympathetic division (145)
parietal lobe (140)
peripheral nervous system (144)
phenotype (131)
polygenic (131)
positron emission tomography (PET) (142)
postsynaptic receptors (137)
psychopharmacology (138)

psychosurgery (143)
reuptake (137)
single photon emission computer tomography (142)
somatic nervous system (144)
sympathetic division (144)
synapse (136)
temporal lobe (140)
up-regulation (137)

GUIDED SELF-STUDY

The Neuroscience Perspective

1. Let's start with the basics. Fill in the blanks with the proper terms.

   a. _____ Two factors that interact according to the neuroscience perspective

   b. _____ Formal name of the biological/psychological interaction question

   c. _____ Threadlike structures that contain the recipe for you

   d. _____ The elements of those threadlike structures of inheritance

   e. _____ Event when your physical inheritance was determined

   f. _____ Debate over the extent to which genes control behaviors

   g. _____ Field that studies influence of genetics in behavioral abnormalities

   h. _____ A constitutional predisposition

   i. _____ Idea that psychopathology results from biology *and* environment

2. List three types of clinical genetic studies.

3. How much genetic material do you share with each of the following relatives: parents, siblings, aunts and uncles, and first cousins? Indicate whether that percentage is known with certainty or just on the average, and explain how we know this.

4. Match the terms on the right to the correct phrases. Terms may be used more than once.

   a. _____ Individual units of inheritance information   *chromosomes*

   b. _____ Constitutional predisposition   *co-twin*

   c. _____ Share the same disorder   *concordant*

   d. _____ Another name for a proband case   *diathesis*

   e. _____ A "diagnosed" case   *dizygotes*

   f. _____ Identical twins   *genes*

   g. _____ Fraternal twins   *genotype*

   h. _____ Observable characteristics   *index case*

   i. _____ Twin of an index case   *linkage analysis*

   j. _____ One's biological inheritance   *monozygotes*

   k. _____ String of genes that form a chain   *phenotypes*

   l. _____ Research to find genetic markers

5. How are DZ twins different from MZ twins? List the names of MZ and DZ twins you know.

6. What are the problems with conducting abnormal psychology research with the "genetically ideal" MZ twins?

7. What form of adoption study is the most fruitful in abnormal psychology research and why?

8. Use the following terms to identify the parts of the cell: *cell body, dendrites, axon, axon terminal,* and *myelin sheath.*

   a. _____   Branching fibers from the nucleus that "receive"

   b. _____   Contains the nucleus and provides for the cells function

   c. _____   Insulation on an axon that increases speed of neural transmission

   d. _____   Branched fiber that "sends" the message

   e. _____   Jumping off point for the neural meassage to leave the neuron

9. List six neurotransmitters. Highlight those thought to be particularly related to abnormal behavior.

   a.   d.
   b.   e.
   c.   f.

10. Here are the steps of the electrochemical transmission process that occurs when a message passes through a neuron. Arrange them in the correct sequence. The starting and end points are already marked for you.

   __1__   Neurotransmitter released at the buttonlike ends of axon terminals
   ____   Cell body tallies incoming excitatory and inhibitory messages
   ____   Excitatory messages pass critical all-or-none threshold
   ____   Message moves down axon
   ____   Message moves up the dendrite
   ____   Message arrives at axon terminals
   ____   Neurotransmitter in the synapse
   ____   Neurotransmitter floats into receptors sites
   __9__   Neurotransmitter released at the ends of axon terminals

11. How do psychoactive drugs influence the activity of neurotransmitters?

12. List the five main categories of drugs used to treat abnormal behavior.

13. List the four lobes of the brain. Give one or two functions that each of them serves.

   a.

   b.

   c.

   d.

14. How many lobes does the brain have *altogether*?

15. Identify the major structures of the brain. Use the following terms; they may be used more than once. *Basal ganglia, cerebellum, pons, reticular activating system, hypothalamus, ventricles, corpus callosum, hippocampus, amygdala, thalamus, brainstem, medulla, cerebral cortex*

a. _____ Responsible for posture and balance

b. _____ Regulates heartbeat, breathing, and blood pressure

c. _____ Cavities of cerebrospinal fluid

d. _____ Includes pons, medulla, and reticular system

e. _____ Key structure in memory

f. _____ Midbrain sensory relay system

g. _____ Regulates sleep and arousal

h. _____ Band of nerve fibers connecting the two hemispheres

i. _____ Limbic structure essential for emotional responses

j. _____ upper, outermost part, the wrinkled gray matter

k. _____ Controls hunger, thirst, and sexual desire

l. _____ Regulates body temperature and involved in emotion

m. _____ Connects spinal cord to cerebellum

n. _____ Involved in planned, programmed behaviors

16. Use the following terms to complete the brief overview history of brain mapping: *brain-damaged, brain surgery, expense, invasive, radioactive, sites, timing,* and *x-rays.*

For many years, brain mapping could be done only by inferences drawn from debilitation of

(a)_____-_____ patients and patient reports during (b)_____ _____.

Today there are a variety of techniques. Each has strengths and weaknesses. Some focus on localizing

(c)_____ of activities; others measure (d)_____ of brain activity. Some are more

(e)_____ because using them exposes the brain to some risks, such as injection of (f)_____

materials or exposure to (g)_____. Another issue is the (h)_____ involved in the

procedure.

17. Write the name or abbreviation of the brain research technique in front of its description:

Computerized tomography (CT)
Electroencephalography (EEG)
Event-related potentials (ERPs)
Functional magnetic resonance imaging (fMRI)
Magnetic resonance imaging (MRI)
Positron emission tomography (PET)
Single photon emission computer tomography (SPECT)

a. _____ is based on radio waves in a magnetic field.

b. _____ uses many, many cross-sectional x-rays.

c. _____ uses radioactive tracer substances to form a picture of brain activity.

d. _____ measure brain activity in response to a particular stimulation.

e. _____ measures cerebral cortex electrical patterns.

f. _____ uses radioactive water to monitor blood flow and glucose metabolism.

g. _____ is a very sensitive measure based on magnetic action of blood oxygen.

18. When imaging techniques are used to look at the brain structure of schizophrenics, compared to

nonschizophrenics, the brain ventricles appear to be (a)_____, and the frontal lobes appear to be

(b)_____.

19. Psychosurgery is the most (a)_____ of the biological therapies for abnormal behaviors. Recent

improvements in technologies have led to (b)_____ destruction of brain tissue and therefore

(c)_____ side effects.

20. _____ is the "sidedness" of the brain, the extent to which the different sides of the brain develop and function differently.

21. Write a brief summary of how recent research has redefined the sidedness of the brain.

22. Fill in the correct division of the nervous system to complete the following thoughts.

   Autonomic nervous system   *Parasympathetic nervous system*
   Central nervous system   *Somatic nervous system*
   The entire nervous system   *Sympathetic nervous system*

   a. _____ was formerly called the involuntary nervous system.

   b. _____ senses and acts on the external world.

   c. _____ regulates heartbeat and respiration.

   d. _____ contains the brain and spinal cord.

   e. _____ specializes in "meeting emergencies."

   f. _____ has fibers that emerge from top and bottom of the spinal cord.

   g. _____ is a vast electrochemical conducting network.

   h. _____ mainly stores and transmits information.

   i. _____ is in general control of pupil dilation and bladder contraction.

   j. _____ has nerve fibers that emanate from the middle of the spinal cord.

   k. _____ plays a critical role in the stress response.

   l. _____ decreases heart rate.

23. Fill in the following blanks. These terms may be used more than once: *endocrine, hormones, hypothalamus, pituitary,* and *regulates.*

   The (a)_____ system releases chemical messengers known as (b)_____ into the blood

   stream. The (c)_____ gland is called the "master gland" because it (d)_____ the other glands. It does this by releasing (e)_____ that cause the other glands to release their

(f)_____. The (g)_____ of the brain controls this "master gland."

24. Why are glands being discussed in connection with abnormal behavior?

25. What contributions does your textbook attribute to the neuroscience perspective?

26. What criticisms does your textbook charge to the neuroscience perspective?

27. What is the ethical question that comes with any scientific discovery?

28. What are three ethical questions about the discoveries in the neuroscience perspective?

    a.

    b.

    c.

29. Drugs are the most common of the biological treatments of abnormal behavior. List the five main categories mentioned in the text.

    a.

    b.

    c.

    d.

    e.

30. Does the findings of a genetic predisposition or chemical imbalance necessarily mean that this is the organic causal factor?

HELPFUL HINTS

1. *Note*! In ecological concerns, TV commercials, etc. environment means nature, *But not* in a psychology course!

   NATURE = GENES

   NURTURE = ENVIRONMENT

2. It is important that we understand how the brain works in order to understand abnormal psychology. Some theories on disorders are mostly biologically based—that is, the neuroscience perspective dominates the research. For example, when we read about schizophrenia and its organic factors, understanding the brain and its mechanics is helpful.

3. This chapter may feel like a review of a biology course; however, psychology students must understand the field of psychology as a science.

PRACTICE TEST

Use the following test questions to check your knowledge of the material in this chapter. You may want to write the answers on a separate sheet of paper so you can take the test more than once.

1. Everyone in Wayne's family is very tall, leading everyone to expect that Wayne would also be tall. However, as a child Wayne developed a chronic illness that stunted his growth. The "tall" genes Wayne received from his parents are part of his

   a. phenotype.
   b. genotype.
   c. diathesis.
   d. nurture.

2. Arrange the following genetic research techniques in order of their scientific value, going from least to most useful.

   a. family studies, adoption studies, twin studies
   b. adoption studies, twin studies, family studies
   c. family studies, twin studies, adoption studies
   d. twin studies, family studies, adoption studies

3. The small gap between the axon terminal of one neuron and the dendrite of the next is called the

   a. axon.
   b. synapse.
   c. nucleus.
   d. dendrite reception area.

4. The substance that acts on the opiate receptors in the brain and may be the body's "natural drug" is

   a. enkephalin.
   b. dopamine.
   c. acetylcholine.
   d. norepinephrine.

5. Which of the following stroke locations would produce the most serious language deficits in the average person?

   a. right frontal lobe
   b. left occipital lobe
   c. right parietal
   d. left temporal lobe

6. What information about the brain do event-related potentials (ERPs) provide?

   a. the shape and size of the ventricles
   b. the size of brain structures
   c. changes in brain activity as a result of stimulation
   d. images of areas of the brain that are damaged

7. What has recent research shown us about the left and right hemispheres' functions?

   a. The right hemisphere controls language while the left controls spatial tasks.
   b. Complex language and emotional processes require both sides.
   c. The left hemisphere controls the left side of the body; the right hemisphere controls the right side of the body.
   d. The left hemisphere controls emotions while the right hemisphere controls language.

8. A man with a loaded gun comes toward you and threatens you. Which part of the autonomic nervous system will "kick in?"

   a. parasympathetic division
   b. sympathetic division
   c. somatic division
   d. endocrine division

9. Which statement about the neuroscience perspective is most accurate?

   a. Researchers usually argue that there is one cause for all disorders: biology.
   b. One ethical problem with drug treatment is that drugs rarely reduce important symptoms.
   c. It is no longer possible to consider the neuroscience and psychological perspectives from an either-or point of view.
   d. Few people believe that genetic engineering will present serious ethical dilemmas.

10. According to the _____, certain genes or gene combinations produce a predisposition to a disorder.

    a. neuroscience perspective
    b. diathesis stress model
    c. twin studies
    d. down regulation

11. A growing number of theorists have suggested that integrating neuroscience and this perspective, _____, might improve psychologists' understanding of some psychopathology, such as depression and mania.

    a. cognitive-behavioral
    b. biological
    c. sociocultural
    d. psychodynamic

12. The brain and the spinal cord constitute the

    a. central nervous system.
    b. peripheral nervous system.
    c. autonomic nervous system.
    d. symphathetic nervous system.

13. A technique for studying the brain that measures blood flow and glucose metabolism in the brain is called
    a. single photon emission computer tomography.
    b. electroencephalography.
    c. magnetic resonance imaging.
    d. event- related potentials.

14. The _____ is the forebrain structure that monitors eating, drinking, and sexual behavior.

    a. thalamus
    b. hypothalamus
    c. medulla
    d. cerebullum

15. According to the text, even when identical twins do not grow up in the same household, they are likely to

    a. have little in common.
    b. look different from each other.
    c. have a great deal in common.
    d. have the same pathology.

16. A neurotransmitter associated with schizophrenia is

    a. GABA.
    b. acetylcholine.
    c. norepinephrine.
    d. dopamine.

17. The layer of fat cells that insulates most axons is the

    a. myelin sheath.
    b. cell body.
    c. ion.
    d. channels.

18. The hypothalamus can be described best as a(n)

    a. regulator.
    b. screen.
    c. advisor.
    d. protector.

19. New neuroimaging technologies have led to the advances in _____; early forms of this procedure were known as prefrontal lobotomies.

    a. mind surgery
    b. neurosurgery
    c. psychosurgery
    d. brain surgery

20. Just below the hypothalamus is the _____, called the "master gland" because it regulates hormone secretion by the other glands in the body.

    a. medulla
    b. adrenal gland
    c. pons
    d. pituitary gland

ANSWERS

Guided Self-Study (p. 78)

1. a. physical and psychological factors
    b. mind-body
    c. chromosomes
    d. genes
    e. conception
    f. nature-nurture
    g. behavior genetics
    h. diathesis
    i. diathesis-stress model

2. Family studies, twin studies, adoption studies (132–133)

3. With each parent—50% with absolute certainty
    With siblings—50% on the average
    With aunts and uncles—25% on the average
    With first cousins—12.5% on the average
    Parents are the only ones to whom genetic kinship can be stated with certainty. At each gene site along the chromosomes the offspring got one gene from its mother and one from its father. Kinship between siblings can be only averaged because each offspring receives different genetic code as its 50% share from each parent. In other words, if you could compare your genetic recipe to each of your biological parents, you would find an exact 50% match in each case. If you compared your genetic recipe to each of your siblings, you might find that you had 30% or 80% identical material. On the average you would find 50% similarity with a sibling. (132–135)

4. a. genes
   b. diathesis
   c. concordant
   d. index case
   e. index case
   f. monozygotes

   g. dizygotes
   h. phenotypes
   i. co-twin
   j. genotype
   k. chromosomes
   l. linkage analysis

5. MZ twins were originally one person; DZ twins were always two different people. Dizygotic (DZ) twins came from two entirely independent egg-sperm unions and are no more genetically alike than any of their other siblings (on the average 50%). Monozygotic (MZ) twins were originally one egg-sperm union destined to be only one person; some unpredictable event led to the fertilized egg becoming two separate people who have identical genetic material (100% genetically the same with certainty).

   The point of listing names is to personalize this information to your world. Connecting information to your own experience is a very effective memory aid.

6. MZ twins are rare; even rarer are MZ twins with mental disorder. Also, because MZ twins are so similar physically and are always the same sex, their life experiences may be more similar than DZ twins, who can look quite dissimilar and be of different sexes.

7. The most ideal arrangement of adoption studies is to compare adopted children whose biological mothers had no record of mental health problems to adopted children whose biological mothers had serious mental health problems. This pool of research subjects is more substantial than that of mentally ill MZ twins because mothers who are severely disturbed are likely to have to give their children up for adoption.

8. a. dendrites
   b. cell body
   c. myelin sheath
   d. axon
   e. axon terminal (136)

9. *acetylcholine
   *dopamine
   *norepinephrine
   *serotonin
   enkephalins
   GABA (137–138)

10. 1. Neurotransmitter released at the buttonlike ends of axon terminals
    2. Neurotransmitter in the synapse
    3. Neurotransmitter floats into receptor sites
    4. Message moves up the dendrite
    5. Cell body tallies incoming excitatory and inhibitory messages
    6. Excitatory messages pass critical all-or-none threshold
    7. Message moves down axon
    8. Message arrives at axon terminals
    9. Neurotransmitter released at the ends of axon terminals (136–137)

11. Psychoactive drugs alter neuronal firing patterns by affecting the amount of neurotransmitter or the level of its activity.

12. Antipsychotics, antidepressants, antimanic/mood-stabilizer drugs, antianxiety drugs, sedative-hypnotic drugs (139)

13. a. Temporal lobes—auditory perception (hearing); some vision and memory
    b. Parietal lobes—intrasensory perception; motor (movement); and sensory somatic functions (knowing where in space your own body parts are; you cannot walk if your brain does not know where your foot is and what position it is in at every moment).
    c. Occipital lobes—visual discrimination and visual memory
    d. Frontal lobes—language ability; regulation of fine voluntary movements; ordering of stimuli; sorting of information (139–141)

14. Although we speak of "the four lobes of the brain" in each hemisphere, both hemispheres together total eight lobes. (139–140)

15. a. cerebellum
    b. medulla
    c. ventricles
    d. brainstem
    e. hippocampus
    f. thalamus
    g. reticular activating system
    h. corpus callosum
    i. amygdala
    j. cerebral cortex
    k. hypothalamus
    l. hypothalamus
    m. pons
    n. basal ganglia

16. a. brain-damaged
    b. brain surgery
    c. sites
    d. timing
    e. invasive
    f. radioactive
    g. x-ray
    h. expense

17. a. Magnetic resonance imaging (MRI)
    b. Computerized tomography (CT)
    c. Positron emission tomography (PET)
    d. Event-related potentials (ERPs)
    e. Electroencephalography (EEG)
    f. Single photon emission computer tomography (SPECT)
    g. Functional magnetic resonance imaging (fMRI)

18. a. enlarged
    b. smaller

19. a. controversial
    b. less
    c. fewer

20. Lateralization

21. The simplistic approach of attributing particular global functions to particular hemispheres has been replaced by an emphasis on complex interplay between the two hemispheres—each with its own unique contributions to every sophisticated mental process. Said another way, yes, the two hemispheres do engage in specific individualized behaviors, but the two hemispheres have to interact very closely with each other in order to produce the complex mental processes that were previously attributed to one hemisphere or the other.

22. a. Autonomic nervous system
    b. Somatic nervous system
    c. Autonomic nervous system
    d. Central nervous system
    e. Sympathetic nervous system
    f. Parasympathetic nervous system
    g. The entire nervous system
    h. Central nervous system
    i. Autonomic nervous system
    j. Sympathetic nervous system
    k. Sympathetic nervous system
    l. Parasympathetic nervous system

23. a. endocrine
    b. hormones
    c. pituitary
    d. regulates
    e. hormones
    f. hormones
    g. hypothalamus

24. Dysfunctions in certain glands are associated with some abnormal behaviors.

25. Organic explanations help reduce the stigma of mental illness.

    Organic disorders may be more readily cured by biological treatments than by using more expensive and time-consuming psychological methods.

    The biological perspective has contributed significant information toward the understanding of abnormal behavior .

    Biological researchers have often embraced the diathesis-stress model, which emphasizes that genes and environment interact to shape the individual.

26. a. Advocates of the biological perspective must not assume that the predictable coexistence (correlation) between some biochemical abnormalities and abnormal behavior reflect a causal relationship. Correlations can never prove causality! In a correlational relationship the second factor (abnormal behavior) may be causing the first factor (the biochemical abnormality), or some third factor may be controlling both the first and the second factor.
     b. Not all biological therapies have been successful, and some have been even dangerous.
     c. The biological perspective has raised ethical concerns.

27. How will the scientific knowledge be used?

28. a. Should "bad" genes be repaired?
     b. Should people carrying undesirable genes be allowed to reproduce?
     c. What should be done with sufferers of mental illness who no longer need to be confined thanks to medications but who are not functional enough to establish satisfactory living conditions for themselves?

29. a. antipsychotic drugs
     b. antidepressants
     c. antimanic/mood stabilizers
     d. antianxiety drugs
     e. sedative-hypnotics

30. No. Finding a genetic predisposition or chemical imbalance that accompanies a disorder does not necessarily mean that the organic factor is the only principal cause.

Practice Test (p. 83)

1.   a. Sorry. Remember: "Ph" sounds like "F," and "F" stands for "form." Phenotype is form.
     b. Right!
     c. Close, but no. This term is used in connection with a biological predisposition for disorder.
     d. No. Nurture is environmental influence.

2.   a. No. The last two are out of order.
     b. No. This is going from most useful to least useful.
     c. Yes!
     d. This time the last one is right, and the first two are out of order.

3.   a. No, the axon is a physical structure, not a gap between structures.
     b. Correct!
     c. No. This is the heart of the cell body, where the chromosomes are located.
     d. No such thing. This is just a nonsense phrase.

4.   a. Right!
     b. Sorry, this one is associated with thinking processes.
     c. No. This is associated with muscle movement, among other things.
     d. No. If anything this is just the opposite of an opiate—it fires you up.

5.   a. No. First of all, is language mainly left or right hemisphere?
     b. Sorry. The occipital lobe deals with vision.
     c. Incorrect. Language starts with "L" as in "left."
     d. Correct!

6.   a. No. The key here is event-related. It has something to do with the way the brain responds.
     b. Sorry. Remember it is not structure, it is responding.
     c. Yes!
     d. No, this relates to structure again.

7.   a. No. Actually, it is just the other way around, and even then it is oversimplified.
     b. Right!
     c. No. This is just the reverse of the actual situation.
     d. No, this is an oversimplification, and backward to boot.

8. a. Wrong guess. This is the part that calms you down.
   b. Yes!
   c. No. This isn't a part of the autonomic nervous system; it is the sensory and motor part of the peripheral system.
   d. No such thing. Endocrine *glands* will be involved in you reaction, but they are not a part of the nervous system.

9. a. Not at all. Biology is important, but there are environmental factors as well.
   b. No. In fact they do a better job of symptom control than most other treatments.
   c. Right! It all works together.
   a. No. Actually, this is a very serious concern.

10. a. No, too broad.
    b. Correct!
    c. No, not a perspective.
    d. Not even close.

11. a. Correct!
    b. Sorry, this is just another way of saying neuroscience
    c. Incorrect.
    d. No, this speaks to the importance of the role of early childhood experiences.

12. a. Correct!
    b. No, this is everything outside.
    c. No, this controls the smooth muscles, the glands and internal organs
    d. Sorry, review chart on page.

13. a. Correct.
    b. No, measures brain activity
    c. Wrong, measures magnetic tracks.
    d. No, measures change in brain activity.

14. a. No, the thalamus is not involved in these behaviors.
    b. Correct!
    c. No, the medulla controls breathing.
    d. No, the cerebellum plays a major role in motor behavior.

15. a. No. Twins tend to have a lot in common.
    b. Not true.
    c. Right!
    d. Untrue.

16. a. No.
    b. Not so.
    c. Incorrect.
    d. Right!

17. a. Correct!
    b. No. Review the diagram.
    c. No.
    d. Incorrect.

18. a. Correct!
    b. No.
    c. No, not its role.
    d. Not true.

19. a. No.
    b. Incorrect.
    c. Correct!
    d. No.

20. a. Incorrect.
    b. No.
    c. Wrong. Review pages 139–141.
    d. Correct!

CHAPTER 7
ANXIETY DISORDERS

LEARNING OBJECTIVES

By the time you have finished studying this chapter, you should be able to do the following:

1. List three characteristics of anxiety, and define the concept of anxiety disorder. (151)

2. Define the Freudian concept of "neurosis," and explain why this concept is no longer used as a diagnostic category in *DSM-IV-TR*. (151)

3. Describe two varieties of panic disorder, and explain its relationshp to agoraphobia. (161–163)

4. Describe generalized anxiety disorder, and distinguish it from panic disorder. (153–154)

5. Define phobia, and describe two categories of phobia mentioned in your text. (152–153)

6. Define obsessive-compulsive disorder, distinguish between obsessions and compulsions, and distinguish between two varieties of compulsions. (154–157)

7. Define posttraumatic stress disorder, list the factors associated with its occurrence, and discuss the problems associated with posttraumatic stress disorder as a diagnostic category. (157–161)

8. Explain how the psychodynamic perspective views the causes of anxiety disorders and how such disorders should be treated. (170–171)

9. Explain how the behavioral perspective accounts for and treats anxiety disorders, making specific reference to the two-process model and exposure therapy. (168–170)

10. Explain the role of misperception in the cognitive perspective on anxiety disorders, and describe cognitively based treatment techniques. (163–168)

11. Describe the findings of genetic and biochemical research into anxiety disorders. (171)

12. Describe biological treatments for anxiety disorders, making specific reference to the use of minor tranquilizers and antidepressant drugs. (171–176)

13. Describe the role of neurotransmitters and their relationship to anxiety disorders and treatment. (172–173)

14. Describe the neuroscience perspective and the relationship of biochemistry and medicine. (171–176)

KEY TERMS

The following terms are in bold print in your text and are important to your understanding of the chapter. Look them up in the text and write down their definitions.

acrophobia (152)
agoraphobia (162)
antidepressant drugs (175)
anxiety (151)
anxiety disorders (151)
benzodiazepines (172)
claustrophobia (152)
compulsion (154)
exposure (170)
flooding (170)
generalized anxiety disorder (153)

MAO inhibitors (175)
minor tranquilizers (174)
obsession (154)
obsessive-compulsive disorder (154)
panic attack (151)
panic disorder (162)
phobia (152)
posttraumatic stress disorder (157)
selective serotonin reuptake inhibitors (175)
social phobia (152)
specific phobia (152)

systematic desensitization (169)   withdrawal (174)
tricyclics (175)

IMPORTANT NAMES

Identify the following persons and their major contributions to abnormal psychology as discussed in this chapter.

David Barlow (171)   William Cullin (151)
John Bowlby (170)   Sigmund Freud (151)
David Clark (164)

GUIDED SELF-STUDY

1. What do you personally experience when you are nervous or anxious?

2. List the three basic components of an anxiety response.

   a.

   b.

   c.

3. In what way does the information you gave in question one relate to the three basic components of question two? Did you list elements for each one of the components? If you did not, what did you not include? Give an example of that component.

4. Fill in the blanks with the correct name or term.

   a. _____   Man who coined term "neurosis"

   b. _____   Term for "sane" but very counterproductive behavior

   c. _____   Edition of diagnostic system that eliminated neurosis

   d. _____   Disorder for unidentified "nerve" problem

   e. _____   New criteria for diagnosing what used to be called neurosis

   f. _____   Single largest mental health problem in United States.

5. Although anxiety disorders are not so severe and debilitating as disorders that involve psychosis, there can be some serious consequences. Which of the following are true statements about the complications and the consequences of anxiety disorders?

   _____   Coping is very inefficient; too much energy for too little success

   _____   Largest mental health problem in the United States

   _____   Can lead to more severe disorders, such as depression and alcoholism

   _____   Can lead to physical disorders such as heart disease

Anxiety Disorder Syndromes

6. What are the three basic patterns of behaviors seen in the anxiety disorders?

    a.

    b.

    c.

7. Fill in the blanks with the most specific correct term. Here are your choices (some are used more than once):

    agoraphobia
    claustrophobia   *panic disorder*
    generalized anxiety disorder   *posttraumatic stress disorder*
    normal   *specific phobia*
    obsessive-compulsive disorder   *social phobia*

    a. _____   Fear of purple pencils

    b. _____   A man still re-experiencing horrors of combat ten years after the war

    c. _____   Chronic state of diffuse anxiety

    d. _____   A mechanic who washes his hands five times an hour

    e. _____   A dentist who washes her hands five times an hour

    f. _____   A person suddenly, unaccountably, feels fearful and unreal to herself

    g. _____   Fear of the marketplace

    h. _____   Fear of leaving one's house

    i. _____   A young executive turns down a job that requires public speaking

    j. _____   A cab driver panics when he loses count of the number of buses seen

    k. _____   A student who will take classes only in auditorium-sized classrooms

    l. _____   Going back four times to see if you unplugged the blow dryer

    m. _____   Fear of encountering icy roads during a winter storm

8. How does panic disorder turn into agoraphobia?

9. Where is agoraphobia classified in *DSM-IV-TR*?

    a.

    b.

10. Why would panic attacks be induced in the laboratory?

11. Besides the unpleasant experience of anxiety, what are other possible consequences of having generalized anxiety disorder?

12. What is "secondary anxiety?"

13. Generalized anxiety disorder and panic disorder are currently classified as two separate disorders. Why do some advocate classifying these two disorders as one?

14. List three research findings suggesting that generalized anxiety and panic disorder are indeed separate entities.

    a.

    b.

    c.

15. The two elements to a phobia are intense, persistent (a)_____ fear and (b)_____ of the phobic stimulus.

16. a. A phobia about snakes (*is / is not*) a big problem if you live in New York City.

    b. A phobia about snakes (*is / is not*) a big problem if you live the a tropical jungle.

    c. A phobia about elevators (*is / is not*) a big problem if you live in New York City.

    d. A phobia about elevators (*is / is not*) a big problem if you in a tropical jungle.

17. a. List some common social phobias.

    b. Do you have any of these? Do they interrupt your life?

18. What is the vicious cycle pattern of a social phobia?

19. What possible causes are proposed for social anxiety?

20. An _____ is a thought or an image that keeps intruding on one's thoughts.

21. A _____ is a behavior or mental act that the person is driven to repeat.

22. The purpose of the obsession or compulsion is to reduce or prevent _____.

23. a. _____ The two most common categories of compulsions

    b. _____ Themes commonly seen in obsessions and compulsions

    c. _____ Diagnosis if the person has an obsession

    d. _____ Diagnosis if the person has a compulsion

    e. _____ Type of medications that are used to treat OCD

    f. _____ Another disorder that tends to overlap with OCD

24. List two disorders that use the term *compulsive* but are not obsessive-compulsive disorders.

25. _____ _____ _____ is an anxiety disorder caused by a horrible event that happened to the person, with intense emotional reactions that last at least a month.

26. _____ _____ _____ is the diagnosis if the previous described condition lasts only two to four weeks.

27. _____ _____ is an anxiety disorder that is a reaction to an "ordinary" trauma.

28. What are the symptoms that a person with posttraumatic stress disorder is likely to display?

   a. re- . . .

   b. avoid- . . .

   c. numb- . . .

   d. signs . . .

29. The period after the traumatizing event before the PTSD symptoms start to manifest themselves is called the

   _____ _____.

30. What factors correlate with increased likelihood of developing posttraumatic stress disorder? List four that are features of the trauma, four that are features of the victim, and two that are features of the posttrauma environment.

   Features of the trauma (in any order):

   •

   •

   •

   •

   Features of the victim (in any order):

   •

   •

   •

   •

   Features of the posttrauma environment (in any order):

   •

   •

31. Name the two kinds of coping styles. Which one do you tend to use most in your life? Which one is more effective in averting PTSD?

   a.

   b.

32. Symptoms of PTSD vary widely.

   (a.) What symptoms are more likely seen in people who have witnessed or suffered violence?

   (b.) What symptoms are more likely seen in people who have committed the violence?

Perspectives on the Anxiety Disorders

33. Having already studied the basics of each of the perspectives, you should already be able to roughly identify the explanations of anxiety for each of the perspectives. Label each of the following explanations with the perspective most likely to be associated with that concept.

    a. _____   Unconscious conflict between id impulses and ego actions

    b. _____   Faulty learning

    c. _____   Misperceiving or misinterpretation of internal and external stimuli

    d. _____   Genes and biochemistry

34. Fill in the following blanks with identifying concepts from the psychoanalytic perspective.

    a. Psychodynamic term used for anxiety disorders: _____

    b. Result when ego can't cope with id, demands of superego, and reality: _____

    c. Behavior when defense mechanisms are rigid and/or inappropriate: _____

    d. Result of consistently inadequate ego defense mechanisms: _____

    e. Result when id impulses move too close to conscious mind: _____

    f. Result when anxiety has been displaced onto a logical substitute: _____

    g. Result of reaction formation to deal with fecal interest of anal stage: _____

    h. Theory that nature of disorder determines how anxiety will manifest: _____

    i. Bowlby's more recent psychodynamic explanation of anxiety: _____

35. What three techniques will psychodynamic therapists use?

36. The goal of psychodynamic therapy when treating an anxiety disorder is to help the patient bring

    (a)_____ conflicts to consciousness in order to neutralize them, so that the (b)_____ will

    not have to use all of its energy to cope with the conflict.

37. The key word in behaviorism is *always* (a)_____, which the person then uses to try to

    (b)_____ anxiety.

38. Assign the correct order to the following sequence of two-stage anxiety learning.

    _____ Avoidance response to conditioned stimulus

    _____ Conditioned stimulus elicits fear

    _____ Negative reinforcement of avoidance behavior by anxiety reduction

    _____ Neutral stimulus paired with involuntary fear stimulus

    _____ Neutral stimulus becomes condition stimulus

39. Use terms from the behavioral perspective to identify the concepts in the following phrases:

    a.   Wolpe's two stage method: _____ _____

    b.   Wolpe's method minus relaxation technique: _____

    c.   Behavioral assignments done with real stimuli, not imagined stimuli: _____ _____

    d.   Diagnosis for avoidance-reinforced anxiety behaviors: _____ _____

    e.   Exposure done by imagination rather than in vivo: _____

    f   Confrontation (sudden or gradual) with the feared stimulus: _____

    g.   Exposure that becomes increasingly more anxiety-producing: _____

40. Prioritize the following list as a hierarchy of fears for graded exposure: 1 (least feared) to 7 (most feared)

    _____ Looking at a stuffed snake

    _____ Looking at a live snake

    _____ Seeing color pictures of a snake

    _____ Seeing black and white pictures of a snake

    _____ Seeing a child's simple drawing of a snake

    _____ Touching a live snake

    _____ Touching a stuffed snake

41. Define the type of therapy known as EMDR?

42. List some possible elements of multicomponent behavioral therapies for anxiety disorders.

Cognitive Perspective

43. Label the following concepts from the cognitive perspective.

    a.   Central focus (one word) of the cognitive perspective: _____

    b.   Cognitive explanation of anxiety disorders: _____ _____ _____

    c.   The best predictor of avoidance behavior according to Bandura: _____ _____

    d.   Tendency for anxious people to be very alert to the negative stimuli: _____ _____

    e.   Stimulus that leads to a panic attack: _____

    f.   Exposure to internal anxiety cues that a person interprets as panic: _____ conditioning

44. What are the three elements in cognitive therapy for directly addressing panic disorder?

    a.   Identify . . .

    b.   Suggest . . .

    c.   Help . . .

Neuroscience Perspective

45. Use terms from the biological perspective to identify the following phrases.

   a.   Anxiety disorder most likely to have a genetic basis: _____ _____

   b.   Anxiety disorder having least evidence of heritability: _____ _____ _____

   c.   Term for inherited vulnerability: _____

   d.   Neurotransmitter involved in anxiety: _____

   e.   Class of drugs that lowers gneralized tension: _____

   f.   Class of drugs that is used for panic disorder: _____

   g.   Brain stem area that "mellows out" in middle age: _____ _____

   h.   Theorized process that will not let a memory fade: _____

   i.   Name of effect when drugs multiply each other's effect: _____

   j.   Drugs that are CNS depressants: _____

   k.   Redoubling of symptoms after withdrawal of certain drugs: _____

   l.   Explanation for panic attacks during sleep: _____ _____ _____
        _____

46. List three categories of antidepressants.

   a.

   b.

   c.

47. List some negatives about medications.

   •

   •

   •

48. Identify the role of neurotransmitters with regard to anxiety disorders.

HELPFUL HINTS

1. Everyone experiences anxiety from time to time. The type of anxiety focused on in this chapter is very intense, has become maladaptive, and has both cognitive and affective components. When studying some of these disorders, don't be surprised if you notice you have some of the symptoms. This happens frequently for two reasons. First, everyone does some of these things sometimes. The question is *not* whether you do these things at all; rather, ask yourself how extreme your symptoms are. Do they disrupt your life? Are you dangerous to yourself or others? These are the questions that determine whether professional help should be sought. The second reason students fear they have these disorders is called "medical student syndrome." That is, students tend to become sensitive to the symptoms of whatever disorder they are studying at the time. By the end of the course students may have an issue or two to look at. Interestingly, they do often conclude that some of their friends and family members may meet some of the criteria mentioned in the course. However, occasionally a student realizes that his/her anxiety level is higher than it needs to be and that some professional help could improve the quality of his/her anxious life. If, after taking this class, you decide that perhaps that you really do have a problem and may need help, do seek out a professional opinion.

2. Many of the debates about where specific anxiety disorders should be listed in *DSM-IV-TR* are mentioned in this chapter. To reduce confusion, be sure to learn the established categories before you try to understand the debates on categorization. Always learn the simple basics before you add any complications. Your instructor will definitely expect you to know the existing categories. Check with him/her to see how much information you need to know about the debates. *BUT BE SURE YOU KNOW THE ESTABLISHED SYSTEM FIRST!* Also check with your instructor to see if you must know all the drug names and categories mentioned in this chapter.

PRACTICE TEST

Use the following test questions to check your knowledge of the material in this chapter. You may want to write the answers on a separate sheet of paper so you can take the test more than once.

1. Which statement about anxiety is true?

   a. Anxiety has no functional value.
   b. Most people feel intense anxiety most of the time.
   c. In the right amount, it can promote survival by acting as a powerful motivator.
   d. Anxiety cannot be considered a normal part of human existence.

2. Why has the use of the term *neurosis* been removed from recent editions of the *DSM*?
   a. The term implies a Freudian view of disorder, and non-Freudians objected to its continued use as a diagnostic category.
   b. The term has acquired a social stigma that prevents many people from seeking help.
   c. The *DSM* was designed to be neutral with respect to theories, and the term was judged to be too medically oriented.
   d. The term implies a biological component in anxiety, and there is no evidence to support such a position.

3. Situationally bound and unexpected are two varieties of

   a. phobias.
   b. panic attacks.
   c. posttraumatic reactions.
   d. compulsions.

4. Jean gradually developed her symptoms of worry, restlessness, and insomnia. Betsy suddenly developed her problem when rapid heart beat, sweating, and dizziness came on for no reason. Jean is most likely suffering from _____ while Betsy is most likely suffering from _____.

   a. panic disorder; generalized anxiety disorder
   b. social phobia; panic disorder
   c. generalized anxiety disorder; panic disorder
   d. generalized anxiety disorder; obsessive-compulsive disorder

5. Acrophobia is

   a. fear of open spaces.
   b. fear of water.
   c. fear of enclosed spaces.
   d. fear of heights.

6. Place the following phobias in order of severity, that is, how much they interfere with the living of a normal life, from least severe to most severe.

   a. specific phobia, social phobia, agoraphobia
   b. agoraphobia, social phobia, specific phobia
   c. social phobia, specific phobia, agoraphobia
   d. specific phobia, agoraphobia, social phobia

7. Betsy cannot go to bed at night without repeatedly checking to see if she has turned off the stove and locked the door. Betsy is suffering from
   a. obsessive-compulsive disorder.
   b. social phobia.
   c. generalized anxiety disorder.
   d. panic disorder.

8. The difference between a true compulsion and other so-called compulsive behaviors such as gambling and eating is that in a true compulsion
   a. the behavior is seen as an end in itself.
   b. NOT doing the behavior results in much anxiety and distress.
   c. DOING the behavior results in much anxiety and distress.
   d. there is a physiological addiction involved.

9. From a biochemical point of view, obsessive-compulsive disorder may be actually more closely related to _____ than to the other anxiety disorders.
   a. schizophrenia
   b. substance abuse disorder
   c. posttraumatic stress disorder
   d. depression

10. Survivors of the September 11, 2001, terrorist attack on the World Trade Center are most likely predisposed to which type of anxiety disorder?
   a. phobias
   b. neurosis
   c. post traumatic stress disorder
   d. obsessive compulsive disorder

11. Which of the following is a problem with the classification of posttraumatic stress disorder?
   a. It shares many of the symptoms of both anxiety and dissociative disorders.
   b. Its symptoms mimic those of schizophrenia and conversion disorder.
   c. It is diagnosed by psychoanalytic clinicians only.
   d. It occurs so rarely that diagnosticians cannot recognize it.

12. A Freudian interpretation of obsessive-compulsive disorder places the source of the problem in the _____ stage of development.
   a. oral
   b. anal
   c. phallic
   d. genital

13. Larry's therapist has him lie on a couch and say whatever comes to his mind. The therapist probably has a _____ approach and is using the therapy technique called _____.
   a. psychodynamic; projective personality test
   b. cognitive; decatastrophizing
   c. behavioral; systematic desensitization
   d. psychodynamic; free association

14. Your psychoanalyst notes that recently you have been argumentative and resentful and have in fact begun interacting with him in the same way you describe interacting with your father. The analyst will probably conclude that this is an example of

    a. resistance.
    b. free association.
    c. transference.
    d. reinterpretation.

15. According to Seligman, phobias are more easily developed to certain objects or situations than they are to others. These objects or situations tend to be ones that

    a. have been natural dangers during the course of human evolution.
    b. are encountered most frequently in the life of the individual.
    c. promote the expression of sexual or aggressive tendencies.
    d. involve a lot of effort to manage effectively.

16. Flooding is a form of behavior therapy in which

    a. clients are taught to swim to overcome their fear of water.
    b. clients imagine a feared stimulus in an intense way for a long period of time.
    c. clients are confronted with the hidden significance of their fears until they are recognized on a conscious level.
    d. the therapist exposes him/her self to the feared situation and acts as a model for the client.

17. Research suggests that if Wayne, who suffers from generalized anxiety disorder, listens to tape recordings of homophone words such as moan/mown, pain/pane, and die/dye he will

    a. choose the more threatening of the two possible spellings.
    b. say he did not hear the more threatening-sounding word.
    c. have a panic attack at the sound of these words.
    d. not be able to recall hearing any of the words.

18. The anxiety disorder for which there is the weakest evidence of genetic vulnerability is

    a. panic disorder.
    b. generalized anxiety disorder.
    c. obsessive-compulsive disorder.
    d. posttraumatic stress disorder.

19. Recent research on aging and anxiety disorder shows that as people get older, they tend to experience less anxiety, possibly as a result of the deterioration of an area of the brain called the

    a. locus ceruleus.
    b. hippocampus.
    c. indusium gresium.
    d. hypothalamus.

20. Which of the following is the most valid argument against the use of medication to control anxiety?

    a. Use of medications sets one up for abuse of other drugs.
    b. Medications do not cure anxiety; they just cover symptoms and allow us to avoid the real problem.
    c. Almost all the drugs used to control anxiety have side effects that are just as bad as the anxiety.
    d. Medications often reduces memory to the point where behavioral techniques will not work.

21. Among the minor tranquilizers, or drugs taken to reduce anxiety, the most popular are

    a. SSRIs.
    b. tricyclics.
    c. MAO inhibitors.
    d. bezodiazepenes.

22. Valium, Xanax, Ativan, and Tranxene are used to treat symptoms of anxiety disorders. They are from which classification of drugs?
    a. antidepressants
    b. antipsychotics
    c. benzodiazepines
    d. tricyclics

23. _____ is when a person is confronted with the feared stimulus for a prolonged period of time.
    a. Gradual exposure
    b. Imaginal exposure
    c. Flooding
    d. EMDR

24. For panic disorder, _____ therapy seems to have an 80% cure rate, and the gains are maintained.
    a. psychodynamic
    b. relaxation techniques
    c. flooding
    d. cognitive-behavioral

25. No antianxiety medication is curative. Drugs may suppress symptoms; therefore, it is widely accepted in mental health practice to introduce _____, as well.
    a. psychotherapy
    b. psychodynamic therapy
    c. antidepressants
    d. meditation

26. The following statement is **true** in regard to anxiety disorders.
    a. Panic disorder manifests itself in a very physical form.
    b. Anxiety affects only our cognitions.
    c. People with social phobias are usually most comfortable in front of an audience.
    d. If you avoid a stimulus that triggers a panic attack, you are cured.

ANSWERS

Guided Self-Study (p. 92)

1. Your own experience—some possibilities are sweating palms, tight stomach, general bodily tension, or mental preoccupation with your problem.

2. a. subjective report
   b. behavioral responses
   c. physiological responses (151)

3. Subjective reports of tension and impending danger; Behavioral responses such as talks too much, shaking knees, tremor in voice; Physiological responses such as rapid heart rate, knot in stomach, sweaty palms (158)

4. a. William Cullen (151)
   b. neurosis (151)
   c. *DSM-III* (151)
   d. neurosis (151)
   e. behavioral patterns (151)
   f. anxiety disorders (151)

5. All are true of anxiety disorders. (152)

6. a.   unfocused anxiety
    b.   fear of a particular object or situation
    c.   a disruptive behavior designed to help keep anxiety down (151)

7. a.   specific phobia (152)
    b.   posttraumatic stress disorder (157–158)
    c.   generalized anxiety disorder (153)
    d.   obsessive-compulsive disorder (154)
    e.   normal (151)
    f.   panic disorder (161)
    g.   agoraphobia (162)
    h.   agoraphobia (162)
    i.   social phobia (152)
    j.   obsessive-compulsive disorder (154)
    k.   claustrophobia (152)
    l.   obsessive-compulsive disorder (154)
    m.   normal (151)

8. Panic involves a feeling of being out of control, so panic disorder patients may stay in an environment in which they feel protected and safe—typically the home environment. Eventually, they may be unable to leave home. (162)

9. a.   as an illness itself
    b.   as a complication of panic disorder (161)

10. To assist in treating, using pharmacological agents such as sodium lactate, yohimbine, or caffeine; through breathing procedures such as exercise, hyperventilation, or carbon dioxide inhalation; through confronting a phobic stimulus (162)

11. Development of secondary anxiety; difficulty in memory, concentration, and decision making; many physical complaints (153)

12. Fear of fear itself (153)

13. Some argue that generalized anxiety is the "resting state" of panic disorder. (153)

14. a.   Symptom profiles are different.
    b.   Generalized anxiety disorder seems to be a more gradual process compared to panic disorder.
    c.   Both disorders tend to run in families, but not the same families. (153)

15. a.   unreasonable or irrational
    b.   avoidance (153)

16. a.   is not
    b.   is
    c.   is
    d.   is not (152)

17. a.   Possibilities include speaking before groups, eating in public, using public bathrooms.
    b.   If you said "no," did you ever have to do a music recital as a child? Were you anxious? Do assignments involving oral reports give you a "knot in your stomach?" (152)

18. A person with a social phobia is anxious in social situations and therefore more likely to make a social blunder, which serves only to make the social phobia worse. (152–153)

19. Genetic cause: Shyness runs in families
    High-risk parenting styles:
        Parents who are overprotective yet emotionally unsupportive
        Parents who are overly concerned about dress, grooming, and manners
        Parents who discourage their children from socializing, which prevents them from practicing their social skills (153)

20. obsession (154)

21. compulsion (154)

22. anxiety (154)

23. a. cleaning, checking   d. obsessive-compulsive disorder (154)
    b. embarrassment, violence   e. antidepressants (156)
    c. obsessive-compulsive disorder   f. depression (156)

24. compulsive disorders (meaning excessive, such as can occur with gambling) and obsessive-compulsive personality disorder (156)

25. Posttraumatic stress disorder (PTSD) (157)

26. Acute stress disorder (161)

27. Adjustment disorder (161)

28. a. re-experiencing the trauma (flashbacks or nightmares)
    b. avoidance of circumstances that bring the event to mind
    c. numbness to their present surroundings
    d. signs of increased arousal: difficulty sleeping and irritability (157)

29. incubation period (157)

30. *Features of the trauma*
      Intensity of exposure
      Duration of exposure
      Extent of threat
      Nature of the trauma—natural vs. manmade (157)
    Features of the person
      Pretrauma psychological adjustment
      Family history of psychopathology
      Cognitive and coping styles
      Feelings of guilt (158–159)
    Features of the posttrauma environment
      Availability and quality of social support
      Additional major stressors (157)

31. a. problem focused (more effective in averting PTSD)
    b. emotion focused (157)

32. a. re-experiencing symptoms
    b. denial symptoms (157)

33. a. psychodynamic (170–171)
    b. behavioral (168–170)
    c. cognitive (163–168)
    d. neuroscience (171–176)

34. a. neuroses (170)   f. phobia (170)
    b. anxiety (170)   g. obsessive-compulsive (170)
    c. neurotic (170)   h. defensive style (170)
    d. generalized anxiety disorder (170)   i. anxious attachment (170)
    e. panic attack (161)

35. Free association, dream analysis, resistance, transference (170)

36. a. unconscious
    b. ego (170)

37. a. learning
    b. avoid (168)

38. 4, 3, 5, 1, and 2 (168)

39. a. systematic desensitization (169)
    b. exposure (170)
    c. in vivo (70)
    d. anxiety disorders (168)
    e. flooding (170)
    f. exposure (170)
    g. graded (170)

40. Hierarchies of fear are very subjective because no two people fear the same things or fear them to the same extent. Your arrangement may be slightly different: 4, 6, 3, 2, 1, 7, and 5. (168)

41. EMDR, Eye Movement Desensitization and Reprocessing, is an approach in which clients are asked to move their eyes from side to side while they visualize disturbing events. This process can be seen as a desensitizing process through visualizing, that is, by exposure. (170)

42. exposure
    relaxation training
    anger management
    problem solving, along with cognitive restructuring

43. a. thinking
    b. misperception of threat
    c. efficacy expectations
    d. selective attention
    e. trigger
    f. interoceptive (163–168)

44. a. Identify patients' negative interpretations of body sensations
    b. Suggest alternative, non-catastrophic interpretations
    c. Help patients test the validity of these alternative explanations (165–66)

45. a. panic disorder (171)
    b. generalized anxiety disorder (171)
    c. diathesis (172)
    d. GABA (gamma-aminobutyric acid) (172)
    e. benzodiazepines (174)
    f. antidepressants (175)
    g. locus ceruleus (174)
    h. overconsolidation (174)
    i. synergistic (174)
    j. benzodiazepines (174)
    k. rebound (174)
    l. suffocation false alarm hypothesis (172)

46. MAO inhibitors
    tricyclics
    selective serotonin reuptake inhibitors (SSRIs) (175)

47 Side effects (174)
   None of the medications are curative. (174)
   Medications may reduce symptoms, and thus reduce motivation to work on underlying problems.
   Skills learned while taking medications may be state-dependent learning—that is, not maintained after the medication is withdrawn.

48. GABA is an inhibitory neurotransmitter and plays a role in forms of anxiety that involve the experience of generalized tension. Norepinephrine is implicated in panic disorder, intense alarm reactions, and a variety of anxiety disorders. (172)

Practice Test (p. 99)

1. a. No, in fact, anxiety is probably what has you going over this material right now.
   b. No, again. Some anxious people, however, are surprised to find that this is not the case.
   c. Right!
   d. Sorry, but it is very normal, and it keeps us moving.

2. a. Yes!
   b. No. There may have been some stigma, as with any term implying mental problems, but this is not the reason.
   c. Wrong. Theoretical objections were raised, but not about the medical approach.
   d. False. Its *original* meaning was biological, but that was long ago.

3. a. No. Phobias are categorized as specific and social.
   b. Correct!
   c. Sorry, no such distinction there; all posttraumatic reactions are situation-bound.
   d. No. Compulsions are divided into cleaning and checking types.

4. a. Sorry, you got it backward.
   b. Half right, but there is no mention of a social situation here.
   c. Yes!
   d. Another case of half-right. No obsessive or compulsive symptoms are mentioned.

5. a. Sorry, you have to know some Greek or just plain memorize it. (Hint: the Acropolis is on a hill.)
   b. No. See hint in "a."
   c. Wrong. I bet you'll get it right on your next try.
   d. Correct!

6. a. You got it!
   b. Sorry. Agoraphobia keeps you a prisoner in your own home—that's significant.
   c. No. Social phobias are serious because it is hard to avoid people when engaged in either work or pleasure.
   d. Good start, but the last two are out of order.

7. a. Correct!
   b. No. There's no mention of other people here.
   c. No, this sounds pretty specific to me.
   d. Incorrect. There is no indication of overwhelming panic here, just unwarranted concern.

8. a. No, that is the case with the other behaviors mentioned here.
   b. Right!
   c. No, just the opposite.
   d. Not that we know of, but neither is this the case with gambling and eating.

9. a. No. The disease we're talking about here is more common than schizophrenia.
   b. Actually, no. There doesn't seem to be an addictive process here in the sense of substance abuse.
   c. No. There does not need to be an event-related reaction here.
   d. Right!

10. a. No. Phobias are irrational intense fears.
    b. No. This is not an anxiety disorder.
    c. No. The key characteristics of this disorder are obsessions and compulsions, not necessarily a history of trauma.
    d. Correct!

11. a. Right!
    b. No. Many disorders overlap symptoms with many others, but here there is a better match.
    c. No, if it is in the *DSM,* everybody uses it.
    d. Sorry, it's not that rare at all.

12. a. No, the oral stage shows itself in dependency issues.
    b. Right! These folks are preoccupied with keeping their "stuff" together.
    c. Sorry, but this would be a sexual manifestation.
    d. No. Little is said about crises in the genital stage; if there were one, it would probably revolve around mature relationships.

13. a. No. This is half right, but projective tests are more structured than this.
    b. No both times. Think, who made the couch so famous?
    c. No way. Behaviorists would be bored to death with this approach.
    d. You got it!

14. a. No. The first part of the question resembles resistance, but the second half points to a different answer.
    b. Sorry, free association is a therapy process, not a manifestation of a problem.
    c. Right!
    d. No. The therapist interprets, but there is no Freudian concept of reinterpretation.

15. a. Correct!
    b. Perhaps in the ancient past this was true, but not today in developed countries.
    c. No. Think about it: If our ancestors were phobic about sex, we wouldn't be here.
    d. No. Think in terms of survival value.

16. a. No, this is a clever distractor playing on the flood-water similarity.
    b. Yes!
    c. Sorry. This would be a Freudian approach. Flooding is a behavioral treatment.
    d. This is sometimes done, but it is not flooding. (Hint: A flood is an overwhelming thing.)

17. a. Right!
    b. Sorry, he hears it but interprets it according to his disorder.
    c. Not altogether impossible, I suppose, but in general, no.
    d. This would be amnesia, and the response of people in this test does not go that far.

18. a. No, the genetic evidence here is the strongest.
    b. Correct!
    c. No. Check page 154 in the textbook.
    d. Sorry. Once again, check page 157.

19. a. Correct!
    b. No. Deterioration here would probably cause memory problems.
    c. Sorry. This part of the brain has such a neat name, I couldn't resist, but it is not mentioned in your text.
    d. No. Many emotion-related functions involve the hypothalamus, but this is not the area we are interested in.

20. a. No, this has not been shown to be true.
    b. Right!
    c. No. There are side effects, but in cases of real need, the benefits are worth it.
    d. No, this is just an off-the-wall statement. (Hint: Drugs are often a quick fix that keeps us from doing something more important.)

21. a. No, these are antidepressants.
    b. No, these are antidepressants.
    c. No, these too are antidepressants.
    d. Correct!

22. a. Incorrect
    b. Incorrect.
    c. Correct!
    d. Incorrect.

23. a. Incorrect.
    b. Incorrect.
    c. Correct!
    d. Incorrect.

24. a. Incorrect.
    b. No. This is a technique, but not a therapy.
    c. Incorrect.
    d. Correct!

25. a. Correct!
    b. No, not necessarily this type of therapy.
    c. Incorrect.
    d. No, not necessarily.

26. a. Correct!
    b. No, anxiety has cognitive and biological effects.
    c. No, completely opposite.
    d. No, avoidance does not mean cured.

CHAPTER 8
DISSOCIATIVE AND SOMATOFORM DISORDERS

LEARNING OBJECTIVES

By the time you have finished studying this chapter, you should be able to do the following:

1. Compare and contrast dissociative and somatoform disorders, describing their similarities and differences. (180)

2. Define dissociative amnesia, and describe five patterns of this disorder mentioned in the text. (181–182)

3. Define dissociative fugue, and differentiate it from dissociative amnesia. (182–184)

4. Define dissociative identity disorder, and describe ways in which personalities can manifest themselves. (184–185)

5. Describe the problems with diagnosing dissociative identity disorder and in determining the validity of cases of recovered childhood memories. (187–188)

6. Define depersonalization disorder, and describe the symptoms that accompany it. (188–189)

7. Describe the characteristics of body dysmorphic disorder. (198–199)

8. Describe the characteristics of hypochondriasis. (199–200)

9. Define somatization disorder and pain disorder and distinguish them from hypochondriasis. (200–201)

10. Define conversion disorder, and list the characteristics that distinguish it from a biologically based disability. (201–203)

11. Describe how the psychodynamic perspective would explain and treat each of the disorders in this chapter. (192–193, 204–205)

12. Describe how the behavioral and sociocultural perspectives would account for and treat the disorders in this chapter. (193–195, 205–207)

13. Describe how the cognitive perspective would explain and treat each of the disorders in this chapter. (195–197, 207–208)

14. Describe the neuroscience perspective on, and the treatment of, the disorders in this chapter. (197, 208–209)

KEY TERMS

The following terms are in bold print in your text and are important to your understanding of the chapter. Look them up in the text and write down their definitions.

abreaction (193)

alters (184)

amnesia (181)

body dysmorphic disorder (198)

coconscious (185)

conversion disorder (201)

depersonalization (188)

depersonalization disorder (188)

derealization (189)

dissociative amnesia (181)

dissociative disorders (180)

dissociative fugue (182)

dissociative identity disorder (DID) (184)

episodic memory (182)

explicit memories (182)

host (184)

hypochondriasis (199)

hysteria (180)

iatrogenic (188)

implicit memories (182)

la belle indifférence (202)

malingering (188)

pain disorder (201)
primary gain (201)
procedural memory (182)
secondary gain (201)
semantic memory (182)

somatization disorder (200)
somatoform disorder (197)
source-monitoring deficit theory (196)
state-dependent memory (196)

IMPORTANT NAME

Identify the following person and his major contribution to abnormal psychology as discussed in this chapter.

Pierre Janet (192)

GUIDED SELF-STUDY

1. Dissociative disorders and somatoform disorders are grouped together. Identify the following concepts:

    a. What they were grouped together as and called in early *DSM*s: _____ _____

    b. Old term for a psychogenic disorder that mimics a biogenic disorder: _____

    c. Term for psychogenic disorder that disrupts higher cognitive function: _____ _____

    d. Term for psychogenic disorder that disrupts sensory or motor function: _____ _____

Dissociative Disorders

2. List the four dissociative disorders discussed in your text.

    a.

    b.

    c.

    d.

3. Before treating a client with amnesia a determination must be made as to the cause of the amnesia. Is it organic or psychogenic? Identify each of the following symptoms as organic or psychogenic.

    a. Anterograde (blotting out time after precipitating stress): _____

    b. Only selected material is lost from memory: _____

    c. Victim is not particularly upset about having amnesia: _____

    d. Victim remains oriented in time and place and can learn new information: _____

    e. Lost material is not really lost; can be recalled under the right circumstances: _____

4. Label each of the following patterns of amnesia: *continuous, selective, localized, generalized,* and *systematized.*

    a.. _____   The person forgets his/her entire past life.

    b. _____   The person has spot erasures of memory for a certain period of life.

    c. _____   Forgetting occurs from a specific point onward, including present events.

    d. _____   The person forgets all the events of a certain time period.

    e. _____   Only certain categories of information are forgotten.

5. Draw a line to connect each type of memory with its definition and circle the one that is usually affected by dissociative amnesia.

   a. episodic   how to do skills

   b. semantic   general knowledge

   c. procedural   personal experiences

6. The text suggests three possible explanations for an accused person's claim to have no memory of committing a crime. What are these explanations?

7. Write at least five statements that are descriptive of dissociative fugue.

   -
   -
   -
   -
   -

8. Identify concepts associated with dissociative identity disorder (DID) using the following terms:

   dissociative identity disorder   *coconscious*
   schizophrenia   *internal homicide*
   host   *childhood abuse*
   alters   *iatrogenic*
   alternating personality   *malingering*

   a. Formerly known as multiple personality disorder: _____ _____ _____

   b. Sometimes confused with dissociative identity disorder: _____

   c. Personality corresponding to person before onset of disorder: _____

   d. Later-developing personalities: _____

   e. Two identities take turns controlling behavior, each unknown to other: _____ _____

   f. An alter aware of the host and covertly influencing host's activities: _____

   g. One personality trying to kill another personality: _____ _____

   h. Likely explanation for DID: _____ _____

   i. A dissociative disorder induced by therapy: _____

   j. Conscious faking: _____

9. In the special interest box on "Who Committed the Crime? Subordinate Personalities and the Law" what two legal questions arise?

   a.

   b.

10. Identify the following concepts associated with depersonalization disorder.

    a. _____ _____   Element that is disrupted depersonalization disorder

    b. _____   Feeling of strangeness about the world

    c. _____ _____   Sense of having experienced a novel event previously

    d. _____ _____   Sense of unfamiliarity in a familiar circumstance

11. Answer the following questions about depersonalization disorder.

    a. Is reality contact lost?

    b. Does the person suffer amnesia?

12. Under what circumstances could any person experience depersonalization?

Perspectives on the Dissociative Disorders

13. Identify which perspective would propose each of the following explanations for dissociative disorders.

    a. The _____ perspective sees it as a memory disorder.

    b. The _____ perspective sees it as a serotonin abnormality.

    c. The _____ perspective sees it as a form of learned coping response.

    d. The _____ perspective sees it as a product of social reinforcement.

    e. The _____ perspective sees it as a result of unconscious conflict over basic urges.

    f. The _____ perspective sees it as undiagnosed epilepsy.

    g. The _____ perspective sees it as failure of the hippocampus to integrate memories.

    h. The _____ perspective sees it as extreme and maladaptive defenses.

14. List three stages of treatment for dissociative disorders from the psychodynamic perspective.

Stage 1:

Stage 2:

Stage 3:

15. Identify the major difficulty that can arise from the three-stage psychodynamic therapeutic approach.

    a. _____ is retraumatizing the patient through overwhelming re-exposure to the emotional crisis that initially triggered the dissociation defense mechanism.

    b. _____ _____ is the therapeutic technique to retrieve the memory gradually without emotionally overwhelming the patient.

16. Identify the following perspectives.

    a. The _____ perspective sees dissociation as a straightforward learned avoidance to unbearable stress.

    b. The _____ perspective sees dissociation in the same way as the previous group but then goes on to discuss the "hypnotic role" that is then validated by the "expert" therapist.

17. The two cognitive theories proposed to explain dissociative disorders are each based on memory retrieval failures. Identify each one based on its key concept:

    a. _____-_____ _____ assumes that moods form the context in which memories are filed.

    b. _____ _____ assumes that cues for some memories are personal facts.

18. What is the prognosis for each of these dissociative disorders?

    a. Dissociative amnesia:

    b. Dissociative fugue:

    c. Dissociative identity disorder:

Somatoform Disorders

19. Match the five following somatoform disorders to their definitions: *body dysmorphic disorder*, *pain disorder*, *conversion disorder*, *hypochondriasis*, and *somatization disorder*.

    a. _____ Preoccupation with imagined or exaggerated bodily defects

    b. _____ Fear of particular diseases

    c. _____ Manifested motor or sensory dysfunctions

    d. _____ Many varied, vague, and recurrent physical symptoms

    e. _____ Physical suffering beyond what medical causes would predict

20. Concern about bodily appearance is pervasive in today's society. How do you feel about your appearance? Which of your features do you like least? Do you ever border on body dysmorphic disorder about that feature?

21. Identify the somatoform disorder suggested in the following situations.

    a. A co-worker who is never asked how she is because there is always a long list of physical complaints.

    b. A relative that gives a seemingly unworried, even cheerful detailed account of his/her sensory and/or motor incapacitation.

    c. A neighbor who is anxious about possible symptoms of a serious disease.

22. Why is a glove anesthesia almost certainly a conversion disorder?

23. Fill in the blanks, choosing from the following terms: *episodic memory, semantic memory, explicit memories, procedural memory, implicit memories*

In some cases of amnesia, patients are unable to identify who they are and are unable to recognize family or friends; they may be experiencing (a)_____ loss. Typically, however, their (b)_____, or general knowledge, is spared. They are capable of identifying a picture of a previous president; however, they cannot identify a picture of their spouse. They are able to read, write, add, and subtract; therefore, their (c)_____, or memory for skills, is intact. They have memories that they are aware of, (d)_____, but often the person shows evidence of (e)_____, which are memories that cannot be called into our conscious awareness but still affect our behavior—for example, when Jane Doe dialed a telephone number of the mother she didn't remember she had.

24. In Freudian terms, "gain" is what you hope (unconsciously) to get out of your disorder.

    a. The primary gain in conversion disorder is

    b. The secondary gain in conversion disorder is

Perspectives on the Somatoform Disorders

25. Draw a line to connect the perspective to its explanation for somatoform disorders. *Be sure to check the answer on this question immediately after you attempt it.*

Explanation	Perspective
the sick role	psychodynamic
genetics	behavioral
defense against anxiety	cognitive
misinterpreting bodily sensations	sociocultural
brain dysfunction	biological

26. What kind of therapy will each perspective suggest? Fill in the blanks with the perspectives: *biological, psychodynamic, behavioral, sociocultural,* and *cognitive.*

    a. _____   uses the "talking cure" to uncover the conflict.

    b. _____   focuses on nonreinforcement.

    c. _____   would move society to be more accepting of mental stress so people would not convert it into physical symptoms.

    d. _____   tries to help the individual to stop catastrophizing every physical symptom.

    e. _____   treatments are not well developed, but serotonin reuptake inhibitors have provided some improvement.

27. Specify the type of amnesia that applies to each of the following cases (assume the amnesia applied only to the period or memory loss described).

    a. A man forgets everything that happened during the month while his wife was dying of cancer.

    b. A young man serving in the Marines has no recall of events in his past life while serving in the Persian Gulf war.

    c. A young woman cannot recall anything about the burning building she was trapped in. All she recalls is seeing the fireman bust open the door.

    d. An incest victim remembers her childhood only through the time when she was abused.

    e. A young man forgets all information about his family. Other areas remain intact; however, he is not able to recall any information about his family.

28. The biological perspective has found some interesting information that points to organic factors in somatoform disorder. Name the organic level or structure that belongs with each of the following items.

    a. Correlation between somatization disorder in women and antisocial personality disorder in men:

    b. Level of brain at which sensory suppression occurs:

    c. Brain hemisphere that seems to be significant in these problems:

29. Research indicates that somatization and conversion disorders are seen more in some cultures than others. What does this suggest?

30. Bits and pieces to review: Do you recognize them as they connect to this chapter? The terms may be used more than once.

anterograde	implicit
antisocial personality disorder	Janet's désagrégation
biogenic	lateralization
body dysmorphic disorder	malingering
couvade	neuroscience
déjà vu	paralysis
diversiform somatizer	retrograde amnesia
explicit	semantic
fugue	somatic
hippocampus	source amnesia
hysteria	

    a. _____ Syndrome when husband experiences labor pains

    b. _____ Traveling amnesia

    c. _____ Area within biological perspective

    d. _____ Differences in right and left hemispheres in brain

    e. _____ Having a biological beginning

    f. _____ Motor impairment

    g. _____ Moving forward

    h. _____ Clearly present

    i. _____ Present but not obvious

    j. _____ From Latin word for "flight"

    k. _____ Amnesia for events prior to precipitating event

l. _____   Caused by a wandering uterus

m. _____   Brain structure that plays a key role in memory

n. _____   Name of memory for a person's general information

o. _____   Related to the physical body

p. _____   Deliberately faking

q. _____ _____   One explanation for recovery of false memories

r. _____ _____   Already seen

s. _____ _____   Original conception of mental dissociation

t. _____ _____   Individual has less frequent complaints, but they are more varied

u. _____ _____ _____   Chronic indifference to the rights of others

v. _____ _____ _____   Closely linked to obsessive-compulsive disorder

HELPFUL HINTS

1. Note that the term is "dissociative" not "disassociative." They are the same in meaning, but you do need to know that the name of the disorders that are the result of some mental disassociation is *dissociative*.

2. *Do not confuse dissociative identity disorder (formerly known as multiple personality) with schizophrenia.* Multiple personality is commonly referred to as "split personality," and the term schizophrenia means "split mind." Other than the common connection of a loose usage of the word "split," these two disorders are not related. The person who suffers from schizophrenia has a serious problem testing reality accurately (an extreme example of problems with reality testing would be seeing little green men over in the corner of the room). In multiple personality, the person may have more than one personality, but at any given moment he/she is in touch with reality through the personality that is active.

3. Multiple-personality *is not a personality disorder*. It is a dissociative disorder. A separate chapter is devoted to personality disorders.

4. I have found that people use the word "psychosomatic" disorder when they want to say that the health problem is really in the person's mind. That is incorrect. As you will learn in the next chapter, psychosomatic illnesses have observable physical problems that are caused or aggravated by psychological stress.

5. The term *hypochondriasis* is also often misused. It is often used to describe someone with varied, vague physical complaints. This is actually somatization disorder. The complaints of the hypochondriac are specific and related to his/her fears of a particular disease. If you choose to continue using these terms in the colloquial manner to communicate with others who misuse them in the same way, that is your choice. Just know that on a psychology test you need to know them as they are defined in psychology books.

6. There are numerous references in this chapter to movie characters and real-life people who typify the disorders in this chapter. Check with your instructor to see if testing will cover the specific references to these characters and individuals.

7. Beware of the terms *primary gains* and *secondary gains*. Try to remember that a primary gain is first and foremost the avoidance of burdensome responsibilities! You are able to get out of your responsibilities. What comes next are your secondary gains—attention and sympathy.

PRACTICE TEST

Use the following test questions to check your knowledge of the material in this chapter. You may want to write the answers on a separate sheet of paper so you can take the test more than once.

1. In early editions of the *DSM*, the dissociative and somatoform disorders were grouped under a heading called

    a. hysterical neuroses.
    b. retrenchment disorders.
    c. borderline personality.
    d. cathartic reactions.

2. Bob cannot remember past events. Barbara cannot see with her left eye. Neither have their problems because of neurological damage. Bob probably has a _____ disorder; Barbara probably has a _____.
    a. somatoform; dissociative disorder
    b. dissociative; somatoform disorder
    c. somatoform; somatoform disorder, too
    d. dissociative; dissociative disorder, too

3. _____ amnesia is a rare form of disorder in which a person forgets his/her complete past. Such a person does not know who he/she is or where he/she came from.

    a. localized
    b. generalized
    c. continuous
    d. selective

4. Dissociative fugue is characterized by

    a. memory loss and physical removal to a new location.
    b. a variety of physical symptoms that have no biological basis.
    c. loss of implicit memory without loss of explicit memory.
    d. the appearance of alternative personalities replacing ones lost to amnesia.

5. When fugue victims remember their original identity, they
    a. usually integrate their fugue and pre-fugue experiences in a healthy way.
    b. often develop dissociative identity disorder.
    c. experience depersonalization.
    d. are completely amnesiac for the fugue period.

6. Which of the following is an accurate description of the personalities one often finds in dissociative identity disorder?

    a. When there are only two personalities, both tend to be aggressive.
    b. Personalities will specialize in different areas of life such as job role or family life.
    c. Males with the disorder have male personalities; females with the disorder have female personalities.
    d. Surveys find an average of three alters per patient.

7. Many children are severely abused, yet only a minority develop dissociative identity disorder. One characteristic of those who develop the disorder is
    a. an ability to be hypnotized easily.
    b. experiencing the most severe level of abuse.
    c. lack of a support system.
    d. failure to get help until adulthood.

8. A researcher into dissociative identity disorder suspects that many cases may be iatrogenic. This means she suspects them to be
   a. caused by the therapy process itself.
   b. organically caused.
   c. the result of conscious faking.
   d. the result of childhood abuse.

9. According to current understandings of the phenomenon of "recovered memories" of childhood abuse, which of the following is true?
   a. There is no evidence that recovered memories reflect real experiences.
   b. Most recovered memories of abuse are probably true because care has been taken to provide supporting physical evidence.
   c. There may be some real cases of recalled abuse, but patient suggestibility and carelessness and bias on the part of therapists make the whole issue very cloudy.
   d. Freud's original belief that his patients' dreams and symptoms merely reflected sexual fantasy has finally been supported with modern hypnosis experiments.

10. Research on depersonalization indicates that
    a. it is rarely seen in normal individuals under any circumstances.
    b. when experienced *during* a trauma, it tends to reduce anxiety and depression later.
    c. when experienced *after* a trauma, it tends to reduce the likelihood of posttraumatic stress disorder later.
    d. all of the above

11. Individuals who are chronically preoccupied with their bodily functioning and with fears of developing a disease are suffering from
    a. hypochondriasis.
    b. conversion disorder.
    c. depersonalization disorder.
    d. dissociative disorder.

12. Jack is convinced he has cancer even though many doctors have pronounced him healthy; Jill complains of over a dozen vague pains and problems from dizziness to gastrointestinal symptoms. A good diagnosis for Jack is probably _____; for Jill it is probably _____.
    a. conversion disorder; somatization disorder
    b. somatization disorder; conversion disorder
    c. hypochondriasis; somatization disorder
    d. hypochondriasis; conversion disorder

13. Which of the following is NOT characteristic of a person with pain disorder?
    a. The pain changes for the worse when the person is physically active.
    b. The pain is seen as the problem, not as a symptom of a problem.
    c. The pain is vague and hard to describe.
    d. The person may have had other family members experience chronic pain.

14. Jack, a victim of conversion disorder, appears to be paralyzed from the waist down. He has a handicapped sticker on his car and needs people to open doors for him in his wheelchair. These life-easing consequences of his paralysis are what many psychologists would call
    a. secondary gains.
    b. primary gains.
    c. symptom substitution.
    d. transference neuroses.

15. Which statement about conversion disorder is accurate?

    a. Conversion disorder is so rare, a physician is unlikely to ever encounter one.

    b. The wealthier the community, the higher the likelihood of seeing conversion disorder.

    c. Many cases of conversion disorder are diagnosed as organic, but the reverse is also true.

    d. Conversion symptoms such as glove anesthesia and paralysis are much more common today than in Freud's time.

16. Lena is seeking help for dissociative identity disorder. She most likely will be treated with which type of therapy?

    a. behavioral

    b. drug

    c. cognitive

    d. psychodynamic

17. What seems to be the most effective therapy for somatoform disorders?

    a. psychodynamic treatment

    b. aggressive medical treatment of the reported problems

    c. minimal medical treatment and supportive group therapy

    d. no treatment—somatoform problems usually remit spontaneously after a time.

18. Which psychological perspective assumes that dissociative symptoms are "strategic enactments" for avoiding responsibility for unacceptable behavior and that they are likely to be repeated when they are successful?

    a. sociocultural perspective

    b. cognitive perspective

    c. biological perspective

    d. psychodynamic perspective

19. Behaviorally based treatment for somatoform disorder relies heavily on

    a. hypnosis.

    b. regression therapy.

    c. systematic desensitization.

    d. non-reinforcement of symptoms.

20. There is research that suggests that migraine headaches, marijuana use, and depersonalization disorder may have one thing in common. What is it?

    a. damage to the hypothalamus

    b. history of serious drug abuse

    c. high frequency of psychosis in the immediate family

    d. fluctuations of serotonin levels in the brain

ANSWERS

Guided Self-Study (p. 110)

1. a. hysterical neuroses (201)

    b. hysteria (201)

    c. dissociative disorders (180)

    d. conversion disorder (201)

2. a. dissociative amnesia

    b. dissociative fugue

    c. dissociative identity disorder

    d. depersonalization disorder (188)

3. All these indicators point to a psychogenic amnesia. (181)

4. a. generalized
   b. selective
   c. continuous
   d. localized
   e. systematized (182)

5. a. Episodic memory is memory of personal experiences.
   b. Semantic memory is memory of general knowledge.
   c. Procedural memory is memory of how to do skills. (182)

6. Drug-induced blackouts, faking, and dissociative amnesia because of extreme emotional arousal surrounding the crime (182)

7. Forgets all or most of his/her past
   Takes a sudden, unexpected trip away from home
   Behaviors are purposeful and may even assume a new identity
   Have amnesia for earlier, normal life
   When earlier identity returns (individual "wakes up"), individual has no memory of his/her identity and events during the fugue
   Length and elaborateness of fugues vary considerably
   Person seeks help only after returning to normal identity and is concerned about his/her amnesia during recent unexplained absence (182)

8. a. dissociative identity disorder (184)
   b. schizophrenia (184)
   c. host (184)
   d. alters (184)
   e. alternating personality (184)
   f. coconscious (185)
   g. internal homicide (185)
   h. childhood abuse (186)
   i. iatrogenic (188)
   j. malingering (188)

9. a. Is the whole person guilty if one of his/her personalities commits a crime?
   b. If one personality consents, can another personality within that individual claim to have been victimized (184)

10. a. personal identity (188–189)
    b. derealization (189)
    c. déjà vu (189)
    d. jamais vu (189)

11. a. no (188–189)
    b. no (188–189)

12. Brief experiences in the course of normal life: very tired; meditating; drug induced; as a component of a number of different mental disorders; or after a near-death experience (188)

13. a. cognitive (195)
    b. biological (197)
    c. behavioral (193)
    d. sociocultural (193)
    e. psychodynamic (192)
    f. biological (197)
    g. biological (197)
    h. psychodynamic (192)

14. Stage 1: Establish safe environment to develop trust and reduce stress
    Stage 2: Help client bring troubling repressed memory to consciousness for awareness and grieving
    Stage 3: Help client integrate now-defused material into conscious identity

15. a. Abreaction
    b. Fractionated abreaction

16. a. behavioral (193)
    b. sociocultural (193)

17. a. State-dependent learning
    b. Control elements

18. a. Dissociative amnesia tends to remit without treatment.
    b. Fugue tends to remit without treatment.
    c. Dissociate identity is much more difficult to overcome and may leave the individual vulnerable to relapse in future times of stress.

19. a. body dysmorphic disorder (198)
    b. hypochondriasis (199)
    c. conversion disorder (201)
    d. somatization disorder (200)
    e. pain disorder (201)

20. Your personal response: This becomes a disorder when the concern about the bodily feature interferes with self-esteem and quality of life.

21. a. somatization disorder (200)
    b. conversion disorder (201)
    c. hypochondriasis (199)

22. A short glove pattern on the hand is inconsistent with the neurology of the hand and lower arm. (203)

23. a. episodic memory (182)
    b. semantic memory (182)
    c. procedural memory (182)
    d. explicit memories (182)
    e. implicit memories (182)

24. a. reduction of mental conflict.
    b. being relieved of responsibilities and gaining attention and sympathy. (197)

25. By now I hope you are learning to identify the perspectives.
    Role—Sociological word (205)
    Genetics—Organic word—Must be biological (208)
    Anxiety—Freudian word—Psychodynamic (204)
    Misinterpret—Cognitive word (207)
    Brain—Organic word—Biological again (208)
    There was a trick in this question, *not* to make you feel stupid but to call your attention to a fact if you have not already noticed it. There were two terms that went with "biological," so that left one perspective with no explanation. The point is this: In this chapter, for both dissociative and somatoform disorders, the behavioral perspective shares a view that is very similar to the sociocultural perspective. So, to solve the puzzle in this question you had to use "sick role" twice, once for the sociocultural perspective and again for the behavioral perspective. The reason the two perspectives are so similar here is that the coping response the behaviorists see as being learned (there's that behavioral word!) involves a whole complex pattern that is so elaborate as to overlap with what the sociocultural perspective calls a "social role." Then, to make the behavioral and sociocultural overlap even more dramatic, the sociocultural perspective says that society "reinforces" the individual in the role. To separate these two, see what the focus of the theory is. Is the focus the *learning* that the person does? Then you are dealing with the behavioral perspective. Or, is the focus learning what *society* (as a whole) is reinforcing? That is the sociocultural perspective.

26. a. Psychodynamic (204)
    b. Behavioral (205)
    c. Sociocultural (205)
    d. Cognitive (207)
    e. Biological (208)

27. a. localized amnesia (181)
    b. generalized amnesia (181)
    c. selective amnesia (181)
    d. continous amnesia (181)
    e. systematized amnesia (182)

28. a. genes (208)
    b. cerebral cortex (209)
    c. right (209)

29. A sociocultural perspective! Cultures that have value systems that say physical illness is acceptable but a show of emotional distress is not acceptable can expect to see psychological problems expressed in physical symptoms. (205)

30. a. couvade (201)
    b. fugue (182)
    c. neuroscience (208)
    d. lateralization (209)
    e. biogenic
    f. paralysis
    g. anterograde (181)
    h. explicit (182)
    i. implicit (182)
    j. fugue (182)
    k. retrograde amnesia (181)

    l. hysteria (201)
    m. hippocampus (197)
    n. semantic (182)
    o. somatic (197)
    p. malingering (188)
    q. source amnesia (182)
    r. déjà vu (189)
    s. Janet's désagrégation (192)
    t. diversiform somatizer
    u. antisocial personality disorder (208)
    v. body dysmorphic disorder (198)

Practice Test (p. 117)

1. a. Correct!
   b. Sorry—no such thing. (Hint: Early editions of the *DSM* we heavily influenced by Freud.)
   c. No. That's an unstable personality in another chapter.
   d. That's in the ballpark—it's a Freudian term, but *catharsis* means emotional release.

2. a. Sorry, just the other way around.
   b. Right!
   c. No. These are two different symptom patterns.
   d. No. They do not have the same problem.

3. a. No. This is the one where only a circumscribed period of time is lost.
   b. Yes!
   c. No. This is one where no new memories will stick (it goes on continuously).
   d. Sorry. This is the one with spot erasures.

4. a. You got it!
   b. No. Remember, "fugue" means to flee.
   c. Remember what the word "fugue" means; if any memory is lost, it is explicit.
   d. No. In fugue, the personality doesn't change.

5. a. Unfortunately, no. It is more complicated than that.
   b. *Fortunately*, no. It is not *that* complicated.
   c. No consistent evidence of this.
   d. Right!

6. a. No. There is no such predictable pattern.
   b. Correct!
   c. Sorry. This can happen, but there is no pattern to it.
   d. Actually, the number is thirteen.

7. a. Right!
   b. No. This was checked on, but it turns out not to be significant.
   c. Sorry, this does not seems to be a factor either.
   d. No. Again, this is not mentioned as an issue.

8. a. Right!
   b. No; "-genic" refers to causes, but organicity is not the cause here.
   c. Sorry. The term for that is *malingering*.
   d. Incorrect. (Hint: It happened while "I-at" the therapist's office.)

9. a. No. Too sweeping a statement. Unfortunately, childhood abuse is a real phenomenon.
   b. Sorry. Physical evidence is hard to come by and is often not available.
   c. Correct!
   d. Incorrect. The point with this issue is the notorious unreliability of hypnosis for proving *anything*.

10. a. Not true. Many people encounter this experience occasionally.
    b. Right!
    c. Just the reverse—depersonalization later may get in the way of resolving the issue.
    d. Incorrect. There is only one right answer here.

11. a. Yes!
    b. No. Fear of disease is the crucial element here. Conversion disorder patients just show a disability.
    c. False. This has to do with feelings of unreality.
    d. Sorry. We are discussing a somatoform disorder here.

12. a. Sorry. Half right, but neither of the problems here qualifies as a conversion disorder.
    b. No. Not even half right this time.
    c. Correct!
    d. Half right, but there are no conversion disorder symptoms here.

13. a. Correct! It doesn't change with the situation, as real pain would tend to do.
    b. This is a true statement, not an exception as was asked for.
    c. This is also true of pain disorder.
    d. Sorry, this is also a characteristic of pain disorder patients.

14. a. Right—fringe benefits!
    b. No. Primary gain is anxiety reduction.
    c. Incorrect. This is where one symptom is replaced by another.
    d. Sorry. This has to do with bringing relationship issues into therapy.

15. a. Incorrect. The physician may encounter them but not recognize them for what they are.
    b. Sorry. Just the opposite.
    c. Right!
    d. Incorrect. Just the opposite is true.

16. a. No. Behaviorists are somewhat at a loss with these problems; more mental than they like to deal with.
    b. Incorrect. Little has been accomplished with drug treatments here.
    c. Cognitive people deal with these problems as memory losses, but the complex mental dynamics are the bread and butter of another group.
    d. You got it!

17. a. Not particularly effective, but psychodynamic types are not alone in that situation.
    b. No. This just results in unnecessary medical interventions and complications.
    c. Right!
    d. Sorry, this is not the case; they usually linger indefinitely.

18. a. Correct!
    b. No. The focus here is external, not thought processes.
    c. Sorry. Nothing in the question hints at a biological issue.
    d. Incorrect. Psychodynamic types would be much more subtle and "unconscious" in their analysis.

19. a. No, this would be more of interest to the psychodynamic people.
    b. Sorry. This sort of thing would get at the inner turmoil psychodynamic types focus on.
    c. Incorrect. This is a behavioral treatment, but it is used for phobias.
    d. Correct!

20. a. No, that structure of the brain is not mentioned in this connection.
    b. Incorrect. There is no evidence of this.
    c. Once again, there is no evidence supporting this.
    d. Correct!

CHAPTER 9
PSYCHOLOGICAL STRESS AND PHYSICAL DISORDERS

LEARNING OBJECTIVES

By the time you have finished studying this chapter, you should be able to do the following:

1. Define the relationship between psychology and health, and summarize your text's position on the mind-body problem. (211–214)

2. Define stress, and explain how stimulus specificity and individual response specificity interact to determine a person's reaction to stress. (214)

3. Summarize the impact of stress on body regulatory processes, behavior, the functioning of the immune system, and the susceptibility to illness. (214–215)

4. Describe the relationship between coronary heart disease and sudden cardiac death (SCD) and stress, making reference to the impact of social status, gender, and personality characteristics. (215–216, 221)

5. Describe essential hypertension, and discuss its possible stress-related causes. (216, 224)

6. Summarize research on psychological factors affecting patients' susceptibility to and survival of diseases such as cancer and AIDS. (225–230)

7. Define migraine headache and discuss current thinking on the biogenic vs. psychogenic nature of this disorder. (230–231)

8. Define obesity, and discuss the biological and psychological factors assumed to be responsible for the problem. (231–232)

9. Describe the physiological and psychological factors associated with sleep disorders such as insomnia and circadian rhythm disorder. (233)

10. Describe how gender, ethnicity, and socioeconomic status relate to the risk for stress-related disorders. (235–236)

11. Discuss how behavioral psychologists explain and treat stress-related disorders through the mechanisms of learning. (236–237)

12. Summarize the cognitive perspective's view of stress-related disorders. (238–239)

13. Describe the psychodynamic perspective's concept of "organ neurosis" as an explanation for stress-related disorders, and discuss the usefulness of catharsis in treatment. (239–241)

14. Describe the interpersonal perspective and the effects of social change on the family as they relate to stress-related disorders. (241–242)

15. Describe the sociocultural perspective and the role of ethnicity and socioeconomic status as it relates to stress-related disorders. (242)

16. Summarize the neuroscience perspective on stress-related disorders. (242–243)

KEY TERMS

The following terms are in bold print in your text and are important to your understanding of the chapter. Look them up in the text and write down their definitions.

acquired immune deficiency syndrome (AIDS) (228)
biofeedback training (237)

circadian rhythm disorders (234)
coronary heart disease (220)

essential hypertension (224)
feedback (215)
general adaption syndrome (214)
health psychology (212)
human immunodeficiency virus (HIV) (228)
hypertension (224)
immune system (217)
individual response specificity (214)
insomnia (233)
migraine headache (230)

mind-body problem (212)
muscle-contraction headaches (230)
negative feedback (220)
obesity (231)
psychoneuroimmunology (PNI) (218)
psychophysiological disorders (212)
relaxation training (237)
stimulus specificity (214)
stress (214)
Type A (223)

IMPORTANT NAMES

Identify the following persons and their major contributions to abnormal psychology as discussed in this chapter.

Walter B. Cannon (214)
Sheldon Cohen (211)
René Descartes (213)
Meyer Friedman (223)

Janice Kiecolt-Glaser (218)
R.H. Rosenhan (223)
Gary Schwartz (220)
Herbert Weiner (220)

GUIDED SELF-STUDY

1. Fill in the following blanks.

   a. Organic diseases that were long acknowledged to have emotional factors: _____

   b. Another term for those same disorders with emotional components: _____

   c. New science that sees body and mind as one concept: _____

   d. Another term for that unified mind-body science: _____ medicine

   e. The concept that means all-in-one-piece; mind and body as one: _____

   f. Descartes' concept of mind and body as separate entities: _____

2. Which of the following definitions of stress is the correct one?

   a. environmental demands

   b. autonomic nervous system activation

   c. interaction between the stimulus and the person's appraisal of the stimulus

3. How do you personally know when you are stressed? What are your physiological signs of stress?

4. Are you aware of someone else's physical stress reactions—maybe a family member, friend, roommate, or coworker? Are her/his stress reactions similar to yours, or quite different from yours?

5. Identify the following stages of Hans Selye's general adaptation syndrome.

   a. _____ A state of rapid general arousal when the body's defense are mobilized

   b. _____ The state of optimal biological adaptation to environmental demands

   c. _____ Stage when body loses its ability to cope with the prolonged demands

6. Define the following concepts about stress reactions.

   a. _____ _____ Different kinds of stress produce different physiological responses

   b. _____ _____ _____ Individuals have their own unique response patterns

   c. _____ _____ Physical trait that may reflect an innate hypersensitivity to stress

   d. With the first two factors in mind, explain how an actual stress reaction is determined.

7. The study of stimulus specificity has revealed more subtleties about this determinant of stress. The stress reaction will vary, depending on

   a. whether the stimulus is ongoing or _____, and

   b. whether the stimulus is _____-term or _____ -term. These factors combine to produce

   c. elaborate patterns of physiological responses, including _____ expressions, _____-wave changes, and _____ secretions.

8. Identify the theorist whose name is associated with each of the following statement.

   Gary Schwartz   *Holmes and Rahe*   *Herbert Weiner*
   Hans Selye   *W. B. Cannon*   *Janice Kiecolt-Glaser*

   a. _____ Described massive activation of the entire sympathetic division

   b. _____ Described the general adaptation syndrome

   c. _____ Devised the disregulation model of stress disorders

   d. _____ Devised the oscillation model of stress disorders

   e. _____ Studied living bereavement in connection with Alzheimer's disease

   f. _____ Studied the correlation between major life crises and illness

9. Mark which of the following could lead to a stress response in a person.

   a. _____ Getting fired

   b. _____ Losing one's car keys

   c. _____ Finding no milk to pour on the bowl of cereal

   d. _____ Finding a five-dollar bill

   e. _____ Getting a significant pay raise

   f. _____ Winning the lottery

10. Identify the term for the following cardiac malfunctions that are influenced by stress.

    a. Blockage in the arteries of the heart: _____ _____

    b. Rapid, irregular contractions: _____ _____

    c. Reduced blood flow during acute stress: _____ _____ _____ _____

11. Identify which part of the nervous system is associated with each of the following concepts

    a. _____ Once thought to be beyond voluntary conscious control

    b. _____ Controls the smooth muscles, glands, and internal organs

    c. _____ Regulates heartbeat, respiration, blood pressure, bladder contraction, perspiration, salivation, adrenaline secretion, and gastric acid production

    d. _____ Allows body to cope with ebb and flow of environmental demands

    e. _____ Has sympathetic and parasympathetic divisions

    f. _____ Contributes to the fight-or-flight response

12. Match these terms to their definitions: *antibodies, immune, lymphocytes, mitogens, psychoneuroimmunology,* and *stressor.*

    a. _____ White blood cells that defend the body

    b. _____ System that defends body against invaders

    c. _____ Any life event that requires an adaptive response

    d. _____ Compounds that mimic actions of foreign substances in the body

    e. _____ Study of stress, illness, and the immune system

    f. _____ Proteins produced by lymphocytes to attack foreign substances

13. Choose the correct definition of the term *negative feedback* in Schwartz's disregulation model.

    a. Personal criticism as a destructive environmental stimulus

    b. Unpleasant physiological arousal

    c. A self-regulating process in a bodily system

    d. Misinformation from a malfunctioning organ

14. Another effect of stress is a change toward more high-risk behaviors. List some high-risk behaviors that tend to increase when people are under stress.

Now list a beneficial effect of stress on health.

Psychological Factors and Physical Disorders

15. Identify the term for the following concepts related to coronary heart disease.

    a. Formation of fatty deposits on the inside walls of the arteries: _____

    b. Blood clot: _____

    c. Reduced and inadequate blood flow: _____

    d. Heart attack: _____ _____

    e. Chest pain from transient reductions of oxygen to heart: _____ _____

    f. Bodily event that goes unnoticed to the individual: _____

16. List traditional risk factors for coronary heart disease.

17. List new risk factors that have been shown to contribute to coronary heart disease.

18. Identify the following concepts in regard to hypertension.

    a. _____ is the organ most likely to be the identifiable organic cause of hypertension.

    b. _____ hypertension is hypertension for which there seems to be no organic cause.

19. List controllable factors that contribute to hypertension.

20. Which of the following two facts is particularly dangerous in the case of hypertension?

    a. Hypertension produces no immediate discomfort for many of its victims.

    b. Individuals experiencing long-term exposure to stress habituate to it, so that they no longer even notice stress operating on them.

21. The psychological component for cancer is seen in improved survival rates for cancer victims who are in support groups. List benefits that support groups can provide. Which one is considered to be the most important?

22. What experimental condition made rats less able to fight cancer?

23. What psychological interventions are being used to deal with the AIDS epidemic?

24. What are the two types of headaches?

25. Fill in the following blanks to complete the five characteristics that differentiate migraine headaches from other kinds of headaches: *affective, aura, cognitive intolerance, intense, localized,* and *physical.*

    a. _____ on one side of the head

    b. More _____ than other headaches

    c. Sometimes preceded by an _____

    d. Often accompanied by _____ problems (nausea, vomiting), _____ problems (confusion), and _____ problems (depression, irritability)

    e. May involve _____ to light and/or sounds

26. The long dominant theory on the cause of migraine headaches was a pattern of stress-induced blood vessel

    (a)_____ and (b)_____ in the brain. More recent research has led to a newer theory about

    (c)_____ disorder involving the neurotransmitter (d)_____.

27. "Obesity is a socially defined condition." What does that mean?

28. Identify the following concepts in connection with disorders in eating.

    a. _____ _____ is failure to eat to the point of extreme malnutrition.

    b. _____ is a chronic pattern of binge eating.

    c. _____ is the typical chronic dieter's reaction to food or food cues.

29. What are the three different patterns of insomnia?

    a.

    b.

    c.

30. When studying sleep, researchers operationally define sleep as when a subject

    a. no longer responds to his name whispered at 60 db.

    b. begins to have rapid eye movements.

    c. relaxes the major muscle groups of the body.

    d. shows an EEG brain pattern labeled as indicating sleep.

31. Choose the correct terms for the following blanks (not all are used): *anterograde state, sleep-state misperception, hypoglycemic, anticipatory anxiety*, and *hypervigilance*.

    a. _____ Person can't sleep because he/she is worried that he/she will be unable to fall asleep

    b. _____ An individual's extreme underestimation of amount of sleep actually occurring

    c. _____ Remaining to some degree alert instead of relaxing into sleep

32. List at least four factors that cause or worsen insomnia.

    •   •

    •   •

33. Lagniappe—a little something extra: Fill in the term for each of the following concepts. These are concepts on which you may be directly tested or indirectly tested because they are assumed to be in your general knowledge base.

    a. _____ Cells that are sensitive to arterial pressure

    b. _____ Most common and most dangerous stress-related disorder

    c. _____ Virus that destroys immune cells

    d. _____ Sleeping pills

    e. _____ Involved with regulating the biological clock

    f. _____ Accounts for almost 25% of deaths in the United States

    g. _____ Progressive breakdown of mental functioning

    h. _____ Nightmares that result from having used sleeping medications

    i. _____ Term for chronically high blood pressure

    j. _____ Word meaning full-up or satisfied

    k. _____ Speed at which the body converts food into energy

    l. _____ Rapid, irregular heart contractions

    m. _____ Number one cause of death in the Western world

    n. _____ Rhythmic back-and-forth cycles

34. What is the stress-inducing factor in the Stroop color-word test?

    a. Monotony of reading color names repeatedly

    b. Reading color names printed in a color inconsistent with the color named in the word itself

    c. Having to report ink color of words that are themselves names of other colors

    d. Pressure to produce in having to name as many colors as possible in thirty seconds

35. Circle those who are at higher risk for the following stress-related disorders.

    a. Coronary heart disease: *Africans / Caucasians*; also, *men / women*

    b. Hypertension: *Africans / Caucasians*

    c. Cancer: *Africans / Caucasians*

    d. Migraine headache: *men / women*

    e. Obesity: *Africans* / Caucasians

    f. Insomnia: *men / women;* also, *younger / older*

36. Why are anorexia nervosa, bulimia, nightmares, night terrors, and sleepwalking not discussed in detail in this chapter? Where will they be discussed?

The Behavioral Perspective

37. a. What's *always* the right word for the behavioral perspective?

    b. Right after that right word, what two mechanisms (or processes) for behaviorism should pop into the forefront of your memory?

    c. This means that behaviorists will attempt to explain psychophysiological disorders in terms of

    _____.

38. For many decades behavioral theorists believed that the stress responses from the autonomic nervous system were learned and controlled through (a)_____ conditioning only. Then, in the 1960s, research demonstrated that people could learn to control autonomic processes by (b)_____ conditioning as well. This discovery gave birth to a behavioral therapy technique known as (c)_____ training for dealing with stress.

39. Biofeedback is learning to listen to your body. How can you actually learn to "listen" to your body?

40. What other two behavioral techniques are used to teach people to cope with stress?

41. List some bits of news that would cause you to have physical reactions. Also, consider exactly what physical reactions you experience.

The Cognitive Perspective

42. Predictability and _____ are the two cognitive variables that researchers have found that make dramatic differences in stress reactions.

43. According to this research, which of the following students is going to have the lowest catecholamine level?

   a. The very bright student who knows the material thoroughly but experiences very high test anxiety

   b. The student who feels that he/she hasn't a clue what will be on the test, doesn't understand the material very well, and feels that at best he/she will make a low C in the class

   c. The student who says, "I will schedule two hours of study time to this class every Thursday because the instructor always schedules tests on Fridays"

   d. The student who says, "This class is not worth the trouble. I am wasting my time and effort with it"

44. Assign the correct numerical order to the following stages of Lazarus's interactive dynamic model of stress.

   _____ Coping

   _____ Environmental event

   _____ Health outcomes

   _____ Outcomes of coping

   _____ Primary appraisal

   _____ Secondary appraisal

45. a. What is the name given to the training sessions that cognitive therapists use to help people learn to cope?

   b. What specific training is likely to be offered in these sessions?

The Psychodynamic Perspective

46. The underlying problem from the psychodynamic perspective is always (a)_____ conflict.

   Psychodynamic theorists refer to stress-related physical disorders as organ (b)_____.

   Psychodynamic treatment tries to uncover the repressed material and emotionally get it out in the open,

   using a process called (c)_____. PNI research has verified that writing out one's stressful events

   does something to relieve stress, as indicated by increased activity in the person's (d)_____ system.

The Interpersonal Perspective

47. The interpersonal perspective would see modern industrialized (a)_____ as contributing to stress.

   One effect industrialization has had is the disruption of (b)_____ and families. This disruption leads

   to the (c)_____ systems perspective whose focus is family. Research leaves no doubt that

   interpersonal relationships are a major factor in stressful circumstances: People who do not have social

   support networks are (d) *more / less* at risk for illness than people who do have a social support network.

The Sociocultural Perspective

48. In addition to the break up of the family, other changes in our society appear to be affecting susceptibility of certain groups to particular illness. Another sociocultural point focuses on the fact that socially and economically (a)_____ people are more at risk for stress-related illnesses. There is an irony: As women get equal opportunity for employment, they are also getting a more equal opportunity for (b)_____. In fact, (c)_____ are twice as likely as European Americans to develop hypertension.

The Neuroscience Perspective

49. The neuroscience perspective emphasizes the role of (a)_____ and, increasingly, the (b)_____ in stress and illness.

50. Review the model linking stress (figure 9.2, p. 243) to the reactivation of disease-causing agents. Is it easier to have a flare-up of an old disorder or develop a new disease?

HELPFUL HINTS

1. I hope this hint will sound very familiar to you. It was in the previous chapter. I repeat it here because it is fundamental to this chapter. People use the word "psychosomatic" to say that someone's health problem is really only in the person's mind. That is incorrect. As you learned in the last chapter, that would be either psychogenic pain disorder or a somatoform disorder. Psychosomatic illnesses are observable physical problems that are caused or aggravated by mental issues. The term *hypochondriasis* is often misused as well. It is often used to describe someone with varied, vague physical complaints. This is actually somatization disorder. According to the psychological definition, the hypochondriac fears particular diseases. If you choose to continue using these terms in the colloquial manner to communicate with others who misuse them in the same way, that is your choice. Just know that on a psychology test, you are going to need to know them as they are defined in psychology books.

2. Remember that respondent conditioning is always based on (involuntary) reflex responses. Yes, you are a puppet on a string in respondent conditioning. Operant conditioning is behavior change because of consequences the response brought. In operant conditioning *you* are deciding which consequence you will take by the behavior you choose; that means you are pulling *your own* strings to bring the consequences you want. If, at this point, you are swearing off being a puppet on a string (respondent conditioning), and you are becoming a devotee to pulling your own strings (operant conditioning), reread "operant versus respondent conditioning" in the chapter on behaviorism. *You need both kinds of conditioning to survive.* Being on a string that alerts you to danger is not bad!

3. Since you are taking this course, you are a college student; so by definition this chapter on *stress* is for you! Learn it not only for the test, but also for managing your own quality of life. Look into your time and stress-management skills and your study skills. I have seen very few students (including myself) who do not benefit from a class self-help book on these issues.

4. Check to see how much of the physiology for the disorders you need to know. For instance, under obesity, do you need to know the physical health risks for obesity? Also, do you need to know the specifics of those models on page 233?

PRACTICE TEST

Use the following test questions to check your knowledge of the material in this chapter. You may want to write the answers on a separate sheet of paper so you can take the test more than once.

1. In discussing the mind-body problem, your text takes the position that
   a. mind and body are just two aspects of one unified person.
   b. mind dominates the body and controls it.
   c. mind and body are essentially unrelated.
   d. physical disorders give rise to mental illness.

2. "Stress" has been defined in three ways. Which of the following accurately lists those definitions?
   a. Attitude, personality style, physiological reaction
   b. Stimulus, response, interaction between stimulus and appraisal
   c. Behavior pattern; physiological reaction, disorder
   d. Minor events, major events, appraisal

3. The part of the nervous system most responsible for the stress response is the
   a. spinal cord.
   b. autonomic nervous system's sympathetic division.
   c. autonomic nervous system's parasympathetic division.
   d. endocrine system.

4. According to your text, research has shown that the continual stress of daily hassles
   a. has less effect on physical illness than do major life traumas.
   b. influence men more than women because of hormonal differences.
   c. is related to poor mood, not poor health.
   d. is a better predictor of declining physical and psychological health than are major life events.

5. Shift workers often experience trouble with sleeping and may have other problems as well. According to Weiner, this is because
   a. they are angry about their shift schedules and need catharsis to relieve their stress.
   b. they have paired waking and sleeping with many different times of day in a respondent conditioning situation.
   c. they have disrupted their natural rhythms or oscillations of sleep and waking.
   d. they have accepted social expectations about sleeplessness in shift workers.

6. According to recent research into Type A personalities, the characteristic that produces the highest risk for cardiovascular disease is
   a. hostility.
   b. procrastination.
   c. time urgency.
   d. competitiveness.

7. The clinical term for high blood pressure with no identifiable organic cause is
   a. psychogenic hypertension.
   b. pathological hypertension.
   c. hypertension.
   d. essential hypertension.

8. Which of the following is most closely related to essential hypertension?

   a. dramatic expressions of emotion
   b. depression
   c. defensiveness
   d. moderate anxiety

9. Animal studies on the relationship between cancer and stress suggest that

   a. stress has no direct effect on the cancer, but animals with cancer cannot deal as effectively with stress.
   b. when the immune system is destroyed by stress, cancer progresses to AIDS.
   c. stress makes it more difficult for the body to reject cancer cells.
   d. at least in rodents, cancer and stress do not affect one another at all.

10. The most productive application of behavior therapy in the fight against AIDS is in

   a. training people to consciously control their immune systems.
   b. reducing the likelihood of high-risk behavior.
   c. changing homosexuals into heterosexuals.
   d. reducing the public's fear of the human immunodeficiency virus (HIV).

11. The most current idea on the cause of migraine headaches is that

   a. it is a stress reaction in the muscles of the neck and head.
   b. it is associated with constriction and dilation of blood vessels in the head.
   c. it is induced primarily by hormonal changes after menopause.
   d. it is associated with abnormal levels of serotonin in the brain.

12. Consider this statement: There were fewer "fat" people in the United States one hundred years ago. If this is true, the most likely explanation is that

   a. diets were more effective before the development of commercially processed food.
   b. people in the nineteenth century were more exercise conscious than people are today.
   c. technology has enabled us to be more precise about weight surveys than was possible one hundred years ago.
   d. one hundred years ago, one had to weigh a lot more before people thought of a person as being fat.

13. Tim, who is quite overweight and constantly dieting, is working away at his boring job sorting birdseed. Unbeknownst to him, a coworker playing a practical joke changes the clock from 3 P.M. to 5 P.M. Tim looks up and thinks it is two hours later than it really is. According to research, his most likely response will be

   a. Ooh—suppertime; lets eat!
   b. Wow—time sure flies when you're having fun!
   c. Hey—I didn't get nearly as much done today as I thought!
   d. Gee—so late and I'm not even hungry yet!

14. One problem with insomniacs is "anticipatory anxiety." This means that

   a. worrying about insomnia ahead of time makes it worse.
   b. sleep loss results in higher anxiety levels later in the day.
   c. worrying about nightmares is likely to bring them on.
   d. sleeping medications tend to raise anxiety levels with continued use.

15. Which of the following is a recently introduced non-benzodiazepine sleeping aid that has few side effects?

   a. Restoril
   b. Dalmane
   c. Ambien
   d. Halcion

16. The discovery that heart rate and blood pressure could be modified through operant conditioning suggested that

    a. operant conditioning and respondent conditioning were really the same process.
    b. to some degree the functions of the autonomic nervous system could be changed voluntarily.
    c. respondent conditioning was not responsible for autonomic responses.
    d. respondent conditioning was also responsible for voluntary behavior.

17. When men being tested for HIV were instructed to exercise regularly, the ones who later turned out to be HIV positive were

    a. nearly indistinguishable in their immune functioning from the men who were HIV negative.
    b. more likely to reject the HIV and return to normal health.
    c. less likely to benefit from the exercise.
    d. more likely to develop AIDS because of the added stress of exercise.

18. Two cognitive variables that seem to be very important in how one handles a stressful situation are the perception of one's ability to _____ the situation.

    a. suppress and forget
    b. predict and control
    c. describe and understand
    d. endure and ignore

19. Your text reports that catharsis is useful in managing the potentially harmful effects of stress. Catharsis means

    a. replacing destructive feelings with socially acceptable ones.
    b. the suppression of damaging emotions.
    c. analyzing the symbolic content of fears and dreams.
    d. getting negative feelings out of your system by expressing them.

20. According to the text, which of the following is evidence supporting a genetic connection in stress-related disorders?

    a. People with hypertensive parents are more likely to experience hypertension themselves.
    b. There is an identifiable gene associated with the development of breast cancer.
    c. MZ twins and DZ twins are equally likely to develop asthma.
    d. Insomnia can be induced in all members of any given family.

ANSWERS

Guided Self-Study (p. 126)

1. a. psychophysiological (212)
    b. psychosomatic (212)
    c. health (212)
    d. behavioral (212)
    e. holistic (212)
    f. dualism (213)

2. All these are definitions of stress discussed in your text. This was a trick question to call your attention to the fact that there are different ways to define stress. (214)

3. Your personal observations

4. Your personal observations

5. a. alarm and mobilization
    b. resistance
    c. exhaustion and disintegration (214)

6. a. stimulus specificity (214)
    b. individual's response specificity (214)
    c. hemispheric asymmetry (215)
    d. It is an extremely complex process whereby the two factors operate simultaneously. The degree of reaction to a stimulus is determined by the person's individual response specificity. (215)

7. a. anticipated
    b. short or long
    c. facial, brain, hormone (214)

8. a. W. B. Cannon (214)
    b. Hans Selye (214)
    c. Gary Schwartz (214)
    d. Herbert Weiner (214)
    e. Janice Kiecolt-Glaser (218)
    f. Holmes and Rahe (216)

9. All these are stressors because both positive and negative changes require adaptation (adjustment) from the person. (214)

10. a. coronary occlusion
    b. electrical accident
    c. constriction of coronary vessels (216)

11. Every answer is *autonomic nervous system* (*ANS*)! The first answer is found on page 216, and all others are found on page 217. The point of this question is to emphasize the importance of the autonomic nervous system in this chapter.

12. a. lymphocytes (217)
    b. immune (217)
    c. stressor (214)
    d. mitogens (218)
    e. psychoneuroimmunology (218)
    f. antibodies (217)

13. "c" is correct (220)

14. High-risk behaviors can be summarized as behaviors that harm the body instead of being health producing. (In other words, they do more harm than good.) For instance, overeating, undereating, failure to maintain a proper diet, sleep loss, drug use, smoking, and failing to take needed prescribed medications. (220–221) The beneficial effect of stress is that people under stress are more likely to seek medical attention for health problems that they might ignore if they were not as stressed. (221)

15. a. atherosclerosis (221)
    b. thrombus (221)
    c. ischemia (221)
    d. myocardial infarction (221)
    e. angina pectoris (221)
    f. silent (221)

16. Family history of the disease, increasing age, males more than females, high blood cholesterol, high blood pressure, smoking, obesity, physical inactivity, and diabetes mellitus (221)

17. Stress and personality traits (221); social environment/status (222); high levels of anger, hostility, and aggression based on distrust and cynical attitudes toward other people (221)

18. a. Kidney (224)
    b. Essential (224)

19. Long-term exposure to stressful occupation, smoking, obesity, high salt intake (224)

20. b. Lack of awareness of the condition (224)

21. Education, stress management, coping skills, learning to control pain through self-hypnosis, learning improved communication and assertiveness skills. Most important is social support, particularly from other cancer victims who can lend understanding that even family members cannot provide. (225–226)

22. helplessness (226)

23. Teaching people how to avoid high-risk behaviors, assertiveness training to help them demand safety for themselves, problem solving to reduce circumstances that make high-risk behaviors more likely to occur, and reinforcing people for protecting themselves. The research on effectiveness of after-infection psychological treatments is still unclear. (228)

24. Migraine and tension headaches (also called muscle-contraction headaches) (230)

25. a. Localized
    b. intense
    c. aura
    d. physical, cognitive, affective
    e. intolerance (230)

26. a. constriction (230)
    b. dilation (230)
    c. neurological (230)
    d. serotonin (230)

27. All people must have some fat to carry out the required chemical processes of the body, but how much is the right amount to have "in storage" in the body is defined by the culture. (231)

28. a. Anorexia nervosa (232)
    b. Bulimia (232)
    c. Overresponsiveness (231)

29. a. Taking a long time to fall asleep
    b. Awakening too early in the morning
    c. Going to sleep easily but waking up repeatedly during the night
    To summarize for easy recall—awake too long, too early, or too often (233)

30. "d" (233–235)

31. a. anticipatory anxiety (233)
    b. sleep-state misperception (233)
    c. hypervigilance (233)

32. Drugs, alcohol, caffeine, nicotine, stress, anxiety, physical illness, psychological disturbance, inactivity, poor sleep environment, and poor sleep habits are all listed in the text. (233)

33. a. baroreceptors (215)
    b. hypertension (219)
    c. HIV (228)
    d. hypnotics (233)
    e. circadian rhythm (234)
    f. cancer (225)
    g. dementia (2)
    h. REM rebound (233)
    i. hypertension (224)
    j. satiated (231)
    k. metabolic rate (231)
    l. fibrillations (221)
    m. heart disease (221)
    n. oscillations (221)

34. "a" (214)

35. a. Africans, men (235)
    b. Africans (235)
    c. Africans (235)
    d. women (235)
    e. Africans (235)
    f. women; older (235)

36. All these disorders are most likely to appear in childhood or adolescence, so they are discussed in detail in Chapter 15, which is about childhood and adolescence: anorexia nervosa (231) and bulimia (231); nightmares, night terrors, and sleepwalking. (233)

37. a. Learning!
    b. Respondent and operant conditioning! (236)
    c. learning, specifically respondent and operant conditioning (237)

38. a. respondent (same as classical)
    b. operant
    c. biofeedback (237)

39. In the biofeedback training a machine monitors the body function of interest (temperature, blood pressure, etc.) and indicates how it is changing. You then note what you were feeling or doing when the change occurred and use that knowledge to more consciously produce the desired bodily response. (237)

40. Progressive relaxation and physical exercise (237)

41. Your own experience. Some possibilities that may cause a "sick feeling" are news of disasters or personal tragedies, certainly, but on a less disastrous level, overdrawing your checking account; being forced to deal with someone you distinctly dislike (parent, in-law, ex-roommate, or ex-boyfriend/girlfriend/spouse); and that always-dreaded word "test."

    Here are possibilities for physical sensations: hit in the stomach; stomach goes into a knot; stomach seems to jump or to flip over; a sinking feeling in your stomach and/or heart; sense of heart stopping and then racing; pain in the head; tight jaw from teeth clenching; full body tension; or numbness in the sense of existing but not feeling.

42. control (238)

43. "b" is correct because this student has little sense of predictability or control, copes very poorly, and has subjective self-judgments of minimal ability to cope. (238)

44. 1. Environmental event
    2. Primary Appraisal
    3. Coping
    4. Outcomes of coping
    5. Secondary appraisal
    6. Health outcomes

45. a. Stress management programs
    b. Goal setting, coping skills (for instance, time management), assertiveness training, muscle relaxation techniques, self control (238) (see Hint 4)

46. a. unconscious (239)
    b. neurosis (239)
    c. catharsis (240)
    d. immune (239)

47. a. society (241)
    b. marriage (241)
    c. family (241)
    d. more

48. a. disadvantaged (242)
    b. ulcers (242)
    c. African Americans

49. a. genetic (242)
    b. interactive (242)

50. Flare-up of an old disorder (learn the term *reactivation of latent pathogens*) (243)

1. a. Right!
    b. No. Hint: The text does not adopt a dualistic position.
    c. Not true. Remember the last time you had a fever or a little too much to drink?
    d. Sorry. This is true, but it is only half the story.

2. a. Incorrect. These are things that can influence stress, but they do not define stress.
    b. Correct!
    c. No. These are all concepts related to stress, but they are not definitions of stress.
    d. Sorry. These things influence the stress response, but they do not define it.

3. a. No. This is a part of the central nervous system connecting the brain to the body.
    b. Yes!
    c. Incorrect. Hint: When you are under stress, you want a lot of sympathy.
    d. Wrong. The endocrine system is the glandular system; it is not part of the nervous system.

4. a. Incorrect. If that were true, as long as you avoided major trauma, you would have it made.
    b. Sorry, no evidence of this.
    c. No, because mood and health are related to each other.
    d. Right!

5. a. No, it doesn't have much to do with attitude toward the schedule.
    b. No. This is not impossible, I suppose, but it is not Weiner's position.
    c. Correct!
    d. This sounds sociocultural, but there is no evidence for this.

6. a. Correct!
    b. No, this is unrelated.
    c. Sorry. This is a good Type A characteristic, but all by itself it does not seem to be a factor.
    d. Incorrect. Hint: A fighting attitude does more harm than a merely competitive attitude.

7. a. No. A good guess but not the right term.
    b. Sorry. It is pathological, but the technical term is different.
    c. No. This is just plain high blood pressure, without an adjective relating to cause.
    d. Right!

8. a. No, if anything, this would tend to relieve high blood pressure.
    b. No. There is no mention of this.
    c. Correct!
    d. Sorry, if this were true, we would all have high blood pressure.

9. a. Sorry. The process is stated backward here.
    b. Not true. Cancer and AIDS are unrelated problems.
    c. Right!
    d. Incorrect, there is a relationship.

10. a. No. This may not be impossible, but it is not where the success is right now.
    b. Correct!
    c. Incorrect. This would be unethical and besides, AIDS is not just a homosexual problem.
    d. Sorry. This would actually be a bad idea if fear of the virus motivates careful behavior.

11. a. No, this never was a hypothesis regarding migraines.
    b. Incorrect. This *was* the thought recently, but it has since been changed.
    c. Wrong. Many people besides post-menopausal women get migraines.
    d. Yes!

12. a. No. In fact, fewer people were dieting a hundred years ago and foods were probably fattier.
    b. Incorrect. There was probably more physical labor, but they also knew less about nutrition.
    c. No. Scales aren't that much better now, and there were probably fewer surveys of any kind.
    d. Right! Remember the thing about social definitions.

13. a. You got it! External eating cues have a big impact.
    b. Unlikely, considering his job.
    c. No. We don't know how much he planned to get done, but we do know about his weight problem.
    d. Very unlikely. Tim is probably ready to eat anytime.

14. a. Right!
    b. No evidence of this, but it may make the person more tired.
    c. No. Insomnia is not necessarily connected to nightmares.
    d. No. Sleep medications can cause a variety of problems, but the key word here is "anticipatory."

15. a. No. This is one is hard to figure out from context; you just have to know it.
    b. No. Try again. Hint: "Bien" is Spanish for "good." So taking this one gives good results.
    c. Right!
    d. Sorry. This one does have side effects.

16. a. Not that far, but it got people thinking about the things these processes could do.
    b. Yes!
    c. No. This is carrying things too far. Respondent conditioning is definitely involved.
    d. Sorry. Just because operant spills over into the respondent domain does not mean that the reverse is also true.

17. a. Correct!
    b. Too optimistic, the idea is on the right track.
    c. Sorry, just the other way around, at least with respect to their infection.
    d. No. Just the reverse—the exercise helped them.

18. a. Actually, this just tends to make matters worse.
    b. You got it!
    c. This could be useful, but another one is better.
    d. No. This does not solve the problem and does not reduce its effects.

19. a. Sorry. This would be the defense of sublimation.
    b. No, just the opposite.
    c. Sorry. This is useful for a psychodynamic type, but it is not catharsis.
    d. Correct!

20. a. Right!
    b. Taken by itself, this statement is unrelated to the issue of stress.
    c. Not true.
    d. No. Even if this were true, it would not prove a genetic link—it could all be related to the environment that was imposed.

CHAPTER 10
MOOD DISORDERS

LEARNING OBJECTIVES

By the time you have finished studying this chapter, you should be able to do the following:

1. List and describe nine characteristics of a major depressive episode. (246–247)

2. List and describe eight characteristics of a manic episode. (247–248)

3. Describe the patterns of mood episodes that are characteristic of major depressive disorder and bipolar disorder. (248–252)

4. Summarize the population data that differentiate major depression from bipolar disorder. (249)

5. Define dysthymia and cyclothymia, and distinguish them from major depressive disorder and bipolar disorder. (252–253)

6. Distinguish between neurotic versus psychotic disorders, endogenous versus reactive disorders, the effects of early versus late onset, and describe the phenomenon of comorbidity. (253–257)

7. Summarize the population data concerning suicide. (257–263)

8. List some common myths about suicide and the major behavioral, environmental, and cognitive predictors of suicide, and evaluate the effectiveness of suicide prevention. (257–263)

9. Explain the "reactivated loss" and "anger in" hypotheses held by the psychodynamic perspective, and describe psychodynamic attempts to treat mood disorder. (269)

10. Explain how behavioral and interpersonal perspectives account for mood disorders and suicide in terms of learning processes and extinction, and describe behavioral treatments for mood disorder. (263–264)

11. Explain how cognitive theorists account for mood disorders and suicide in terms of destructive thinking, learned helplessness, and poor self–schemas, and describe cognitive treatments for mood disorder. (264–269)

12. Summarize sociocultural factors that may affect mood disorders and suicide, and describe what the sociocultural perspective would recommend to solve these problems. (272)

13. Summarize recent biological research on mood disorder and the neuroscience perspective making reference to genetic studies, neurophysiological studies, neuroimaging work, and biochemical research. (273–279)

14. Discuss biological treatments for mood disorder, including drug treatments and electroconvulsive shock treatments. (279–284)

KEY TERMS

The following terms are in bold print in your text and are important to your understanding of the chapter. Look them up in the text and write down their definitions.

agitated depression (247)
anhedonia (247)
antidepressant medication (279)
antimanic medication (280)
attachment theory (270)
bipolar disorder (251)
catecholamine hypothesis (278)
comorbidity (257)

continuity hypothesis (255)
cyclothymic disorder (253)
delusions (253)
depression (246)
dexamethasone suppression test (DST) (277)
dysthymic disorder (252)
electroconvulsive therapy (ECT) (282)
endogenous (255)

hallucinations (253)
helplessness-hopelessness syndrome (246)
hypomanic episode (248)
interpersonal psychotherapy (IPT) (271)
learned helplessness (265)
lithium (280)
major depressive disorder (248)
major depressive episode (246)
mania (246)
manic episode (247)

MAO inhibitors (249)
mixed episode (248)
mood disorders (246)
premorbid adjustment (249)
reactive (255)
retarded depression (247)
seasonal affective disorder (SAD) (275)
selective serotonin reuptake inhibitors (SSRI) (279)
social-skills training (264)
tricyclics (279)

IMPORTANT NAMES

Identify the following persons and their major contributions to abnormal psychology as discussed in this chapter.

Karl Abraham (269)
Aaron Beck (266)
Emile Durkheim (272)

Emil Kraepelin (269)
Abraham Lincoln (246)
Martin Seligman (264)

GUIDED SELF-STUDY

Use the following terms to complete the blanks in Questions 1–5.

affective   Hippocrates   temporary
Aretaeus   manic   duration
episodic   mild

1. Variations in mood are quite normal when they are _____ and _____.

2. When mood variations become so extreme and prolonged that the victim's life is disrupted, that is a mood

    disorder, or an _____ disorder.

3. (a)_____ described depression and mania in the fourth century B.C.

    (b)_____ observed that sometimes manic and depressive behaviors occurred in the same person.

4. A distinctive characteristic of mood disorders is their _____ quality.

5. Whether the episode is (a)_____ or depressive, its severity and its (b)_____ will determine
    which mood disorder diagnosis is applied.

6. List nine characteristic features of a major depressive episode. Try to list these from memory to see which
    you already know. If you just copy them straight from the book first without trying to recall them or make
    them up yourself, you will not have "exercised" your neurons. Remember *No pain, no gain* (or no brain)!

    a.   f.

    b.   g.

    c.   h.

    d.   i.

    e.

7. What is the helplessness-hopelessness syndrome?

8. Now list eight characteristics of a manic episode. (How many can you do from memory?)

   a.   e.

   b.   f.

   c.   g.

   d.   h.

9. How can you tell whether a person is manic or just very happy, self-confident, and energetic?

10. Mark each of the following time factors as indicating a *manic* episode or a *depressive* episode.

    a. _____ Ends abruptly over a few days

    b. _____ More gradual onset over weeks

    c. _____ Shorter in duration, lasting only several days to several months

    d. _____ Starts rather suddenly over a few days

    e. _____ Subsides slowly over weeks or months

Mood Disorder Syndromes

Use these terms to complete Questions 11 and 12.

bipolar I	chronic	dysthymia
bipolar II	cyclothymia	major depression
bipolar disorder	depressive	manic

11. There are typically two patterns (syndromes) in which people experience mood disorders. There are people

    who have one or more (a)_____ episodes, and there are those who have some combination of

    (b)_____ episodes and (c)_____ episodes. If one has only depressive episodes, one is

    diagnosed as having (d)_____ _____ disorder. If one has the combination of episodes, the

    diagnosis is (e)_____ _____. Then this category is broken down into two types.

    (f)_____ disorders are disorders consisting of at least one manic or mixed episode and usually (but

    not always) depressive episodes as well. (g)_____ disorders are disorders showing depression and

    only hypomanic symptoms—but not full-blown manic symptoms.

12. If one experiences one of the two patterns of mood disorders described in question 11 but to a lesser degree,

    not disabling enough to merit a diagnosis of major depression or bipolar disorder; the disorders are called

    (a)_____ and (b)_____, respectively. Although these disorders are milder, they are

    particularly troublesome because they are (c)_____.

13. (a) _____ percent of the population will experience major depression at some time in their lives.

(b) Explain the textbook's quote that some experts believe we are in an "age of depression."

14. What segments of the population are more likely to have depression?

15. If you have a major depressive episode, what are the chances that you will have another one?

16. How can one depressive episode contribute to the likelihood of another one occurring?

17. Give the appropriate diagnosis for each of the following mood patterns. Remember, in bipolar disorder, there is Type I, which can be mixed or rapid cycling, and then there is Type II.

   a. _____ Manic—normal—depressive—normal—manic—normal—depressive

   b. _____ Both manic and depressive symptoms at once

   c. _____ One manic episode

   d. _____ Manic—normal—manic—normal—manic—normal

   e. _____ Depressive—hypomanic

   f. _____ Depressive—normal—depressive—normal—depressive—normal

18. Write the correct disorder (either *major depression* or *bipolar disorder*) before each of the following descriptions that differentiate the two disorders.

   a. _____ is the much less common of the two disorders.

   b. _____ occurs in the two sexes equally.

   c. _____ is not avoided by having close emotional relationships.

   d. _____ typically shows a normal premorbid personality.

   e. _____ involves depression which seems to be a pervasive slowing down.

   f. _____ has episodes that tend to be briefer and more frequent.

   g. _____ is very likely to run in the family.

19. Draw lines to connect the terms that go together with regard to the dimensions of mood disorders.

   endogenous   psychotic
   neurotic   early
   late   reactive

20. The psychotic-neurotic dimension is used to indicate severity of impairment, which refers to the person's

   ability to do (a)_____ testing. Psychosis can involve distortions in perceptions that are so drastic

   that the person can actually experience a false sensory experience called a (b)_____. If the person

   holds false beliefs, he/she is said to have (c)_____.

21. a. Draw a box around the following depressions which *may* reach psychotic proportions.

    b. Circle those that *never* reach psychotic proportions.

    c. Put a star next to those that are *always* at a psychotic level.

    dysthymia   *major depression*
    bipolar disorder   *cyclothymia*

22. Use these terms to complete the following blanks.

    bodily movements   *loss*   *sleep*
    cognitive   *melancholic*   *vegetative*
    emotional   *people*   *weight*
    exit   *precipitating*

    Originally, the reactive-endogenous dimension indicated whether the depression was preceded by a

    (a)_____ event, which often is about uncontrollable (b)_____, particularly of

    (c)_____. These are referred to as (d)_____ events. However, such a determination was

    often not so easy to make. Currently, the term *reactive* is assigned to people whose impairment is mainly

    characterized by (e)_____ and (f)_____ dysfunction. The term *endogenous* is assigned to

    those people who have primarily (g)_____ symptoms, which are physical symptoms such as

    (h)_____ disturbance, _____ loss, and slowed _____. *DSM-IV-TR* lists these as

    (i)_____ features.

23. Circle the best place to be on each of the three dimensions to produce the best prognosis.

    neurotic   .   .   .   psychotic

    endogenous   .   .   .   reactive

    early onset   .   .   .   late onset

24. Complete the following blanks using these terms: *anxiety, comorbidity, depression, intraepisode,* and *lifetime.*

    (a)_____ means two pathological events happening together in the same individual. When this

    happens at the very same time, the events are said to have (b)_____ comorbidity. If a person's

    whole life is considered, then the term is (c)_____ comorbidity. Two disorders that have a high rate

    of lifetime comorbidity and even intraepisode comorbidity are (d)_____ and _____.

Suicide

25. Why are accurate statistics on suicide really unknown?

26. a. Who commits more suicide, *married* or *single* people?

    b. Who commits more suicide, *men* or *women*?

    c. Who attempts more suicide, *men* or *women*?

    d. What is one reason for the statistics of "b" and "c?"

    e. Does the likelihood of suicide increase or decrease with age, or is it uncorrelated?

27. Teenage suicide has risen alarmingly in recent years (200% since 1960). Use the following words to fill in the blanks explaining possible reasons for this trend: *drug, parenting, resources, stresses, depression, sexual abuse,* and *communication.*

Teenagers approaching adulthood face many of the same (a)_____ that adults face but do not yet

have the adult (b)_____ to cope with them. Increasing rates of (c)_____ among the young

plus high levels of (d)_____ use leave them even less able to cope. In such cases, one might expect

the family to take up the burden and provide love and assistance, but all too often families of teenage suicide

victims are characterized by generally poor (e)_____ as indicated by high levels of conflict and

inadequate (f)_____ skills and high rates of childhood (g)_____ _____.

28. Here are some myths about suicide. Write the truth below the myth.

    a. People who threaten won't actually do it.

    b. People who attempt suicide are not serious or they would not have failed.

    c. Don't talk about suicide; you might give somebody ideas.

29. What are some behaviors that should make you think that someone is suicidal?

-
-
-
-
-
-
-

30. What percent of those who attempt suicide are sure they really do want to die?

31. Explain why others may attempt suicide.

Perspectives on the Mood Disorders

32. The (a)_____ perspective was the first to challenge Kraepelin's biogenic theory of mood disorder.

    An early explanation was offered by (b)_____, one of Freud's students. His approach assumes that

    when a love object is lost, anger about the loss can be turned (c)_____, especially if one has

    (d)_____, or mixed, feelings about that person.

33. Modern psychodynamic theorists have expanded on Abraham's original ideas. Draw a line from the psychodynamic assumption about depression on the left to the correct explanatory concept on the right.

    a. Early loss or threat of loss   Divorce, loss of job

    b. Loss is reactivated   You must help me cope with life

    c. Helplessness-hopelessness   There must be something wrong with me

    d. Ambivalence toward love object   Mother dies of cancer

    e. Low self-esteem   Feelings not clear or well understood

    f. Depression is functional   I can't deal with this—it's too big

34. Review! Review! Review the psychodynamic approach to therapy presented in Chapter 6! If the terms *free association*, *dream analysis*, and *analysis of transference and resistance* don't ring bells for you, you need to go back and look them up again, because they will appear repeatedly in future chapters. Also, if your professor has a fondness for cumulative finals, you will need to know it for sure!

    Right now, however, let's focus on a more recent psychodynamic development, IPT, which stands for

    (a)_____ _____. This treatment by Klerman is based on the work of (b)_____

    _____ _____. It is a brief form of treatment in which core problems are identified and dealt

    with. Four common core problems mentioned in your text are (c)_____ (d)_____ disputes,

    (e)_____ transition, and lack of (f)_____ Does it work? It can be useful in preventing

    (g)_____ in patients who are discontinuing drug therapy, and it may be superior to either cognitive

    or behavioral treatment for patients who are (h)_____ depressed.

35. What does the behavioral perspective on mood disorders assume is the primary causal process behind these problems?

36. Review of a basic learning process—when behavior is no longer reinforced, it diminishes or stops. This process is called

    a. punishment.

    b. negative reinforcement.

    c. extinction.

    d. discrimination.

37. How does the loss of a loved one or a job result in depression from the lack-of-reinforcement point of view?

38. What does the text mean when it refers to "aversive social behavior" in depressives?

39. How does social skills training fit into a behavioral treatment program for depressives? What can it accomplish?

40. Purely behavioral therapies for mood disorder have not been shown to be faster, cheaper, or more effective than some other approaches, particularly drug treatments and (a)_____ therapy. As a result, behavioral treatments that did not include a (b)_____ component have largely fallen by the wayside. Therefore, it is to the (c)_____ perspective that we turn next.

41. One cognitive approach to depression is helplessness-hopelessness theory. The original research on learned helplessness was done by (a)_____ using (b)_____ as subjects. When exposed to shock the animals could neither avoid nor escape from, they eventually became passive sufferers. Later, when they *could* escape from the shock, they (c)_____ _____. When people are exposed to uncontrollable events, it was assumed that they would act in a similar way, producing the characteristic passivity found in cases of (d)_____

42. The key difference between extinction theory on the behavioral side and helplessness theory on the cognitive side is

    a. extinction refers to the death of a loved one, but helplessness refers to no-win conflicts.
    b. extinction refers to real, objective events, but helplessness refers to expectations about events.
    c. extinction occurs only in adults, but helplessness has its roots in childhood.
    d. no difference at all; these are just two different terms for the same process.

43. Although helplessness explained the passivity of depression, it did not explain the sadness, guilt, and suicidal tendencies. According to Abramson and colleagues, hopelessness is also involved, meaning that not only are things bad, but they will (a)_____ be bad and there is (b)_____ I can do about it. In turn, hopelessness comes from certain kinds of explanations or (a)_____ people make about events.

44. Considering research on attributions and inferences that people make regarding stressful events, which of the following people is the most likely to be depressed? A person who thinks:

    a. This is strange—a freak accident.
    b. It's my fault—I always make mistakes.
    c. Why are you always picking on me? I deserve better.
    d. This is a chain of uncommonly bad luck for me.

45. Imagine a student who has just failed her first math test. Draw a line from each attribution on the left to its example on the right.

a. permanent   "I guess college just isn't for me."

b. temporary   "I just had a bad day—tomorrow will be better."

c. internal   "I was prepared, but the test questions were horrible!"

d. external   "Oh, well, I guess calculus just isn't my strong point."

e. generalized   "I've never been good in school; why should it change now?"

f. specific   "Stupid, stupid—what do you expect from a dummy like me?"

46. Of the six attributions listed in the preceding question, which three are a recipe for depression?

47. Another cognitive approach to depression suggests that depressed people have negative (a)_____

_____, which means they tend to see themselves as "losers." In fact, some researchers believe there

are two types of "loser" mentalities that contribute to depression. One has to do with the issue of

(b)_____, and the other has to do with self- (c)_____. An interesting finding is that the

negative outlook of depressives may be more (d)_____ than the cheerier outlook of the rest of us.

Remember Freud's defense mechanisms? It almost seems that depressives have lost the ability to kid

themselves about life, and that a little bit of self-deception may actually be (e)_____

48. According to (a)_____, the modification of negative schemas will give the best inoculation against

depression. Also, patients are taught to revise their (b)_____ style.

49. Use these terms about the sociocultural perspective to fill in the blanks.

earlier	society	stressor
more	economic	teens
restrictions	stability	

The sociocultural perspective ALWAYS relates issues to factors in (a)_____. There is no doubt:

Suicide rates are directly affected by socio- (b)_____ conditions. Research also indicates that

depression is happening (c)_____ frequently and at an (d)_____ age in the United States.

Social change is proposed to be the cause, because this trend toward depression is not seen in traditional,

tight-knit, nonindustrialized communities with stable social structures. Not all sociocultural theories are

based on the benefits of (e)_____ in cultures. The text gives a partially sociological explanation for

why women are more at risk for depression after they enter their (f)_____. However, in this theory, a

stable social structure is a (g)_____. According to this theory, in adolescence young women begin

to confront the (h)_____ of a sex-biased society.

50. In genetic research, we already know that the weakest evidence is derived from (a)_____ studies, and

the best evidence comes from (b)_____ studies, with the evidence from (c)_____ studies

falling somewhere in the middle. Fortunately, in the case of genetic studies on mood disorders the three

types of studies all point in the same direction: There (d) *is / is not* a genetic component in these problems.

With regard to major depression versus bipolar disorder, the evidence of inheritance is strongest for

(e)_____.

51. In connection with neurophysiological research on mood disorder, write the term on the right in front of its
    definition on the left.

a.	_____	Used to treat SAD	*time giver*
b.	_____	Eye movements occur soon after sleep onset	*SAD*
c.	_____	Zeitgeber	*REM*
d.	_____	Used to treat depression	*sleep deprivation*
e.	_____	Rapid eye movements	*light therapy*
f.	_____	Seasonal affective disorder	*short REM latency*

52. Hormone imbalances have been implicated mood disorder. Variations in one hormone, cortisol, are the basis

of the DST, or (a)_____ _____ _____. Depressed patients who fail to suppress

production of cortisol when given a dose of dexamethasone are categorized as having (b) *endogenous /*

reactive depression. Cortisol nonsuppressors also are more likely to be (c) *neurotic / psychotic.* In addition,

cortisol nonsuppressors tend not to respond as well to (d) *drugs / psychotherapy* and are (e) *more / less*

likely to relapse if they continue as nonsuppressors after treatment. It is (f) *likely / unlikely* that cortisol

nonsuppression is a primary cause of mood disorder, since this phenomenon also is seen in other disorders

as well.

53. The catecholamine hypothesis involves the question of whether neurotransmitter imbalance has a role to play
    in mood disorder. Determine whether the following statements are *true* or *false*.

    a. _____ Norepinephrine is assumed to be involved in mood disorders.

    b. _____ High norepinephrine levels are associated with mania, low levels with depression.

    c. _____ Tricyclics work by blocking norepinephrine reception at the postsynaptic neuron.

    d. _____ Low serotonin levels tend to be associated with mood disorder.

    e. _____ L-tryptophan increases levels of serotonin in the brain.

    f. _____ L-tryptophan tends to induce mood disorder because of its effect on serotonin.

    g. _____ Suicide attempters and suicide victims have abnormally low levels of serotonin.

    h. _____ Norepinephrine belongs to a class of molecules called catecholamines.

54. Draw a line from the biological treatment for mood disorders on the left to the statement related to it on the right.

a. MAO inhibitors   Nine or ten treatments over a period of weeks

b. tricyclics   Many side effects but best for "atypical depression"

c. SSRIs   Tends to reduce side effect of memory loss

d. electroconvulsive therapy   Easy to overdose and takes several weeks to work

e. right hemisphere shock Treatment of choice for bipolar disorder

f. lithium   Most popular prescription drug

g. Prozac   Prevent reuptake of serotonin at presynaptic neuron

HELPFUL HINTS

1. Major depression is also called unipolar disorder. Bipolar disorder is also commonly called manic-depression. Getting this terminology locked into your thinking is *very important* so you can follow lectures regardless of which terminology your teacher and fellow students use. To put this info into organized form: "Uni" means one. (A unicycle has one wheel.) Unipolar means one-ended; therefore, unipolar disorder means depression only, also called major depression. "Bi" means two. (A bicycle has two wheels.) Bipolar means two-ended; therefore, bipolar disorder means (usually) mania and depression, or manic-depression. It may also help to recall that polar means opposite—therefore, vascillation between depression and mania.

2. Beware! Even though learned helplessness says "learned," its focus is on expectation, which is a cognitive term.

PRACTICE TEST

Use the following test questions to check your knowledge of the material in this chapter. You may want to write the answers on a separate sheet of paper so you can take the test more than once.

1. A major depressive episode is often characterized by "anhedonia." This means that the individual
   a. suffers from loss of appetite.
   b. gets no pleasure from life.
   c. feels worthless and guilty.
   d. cannot think clearly.

2. Andy is depressed, yet he seems full of restless energy. He constantly paces through his apartment, wringing his hands and moaning about his sorrows. Andy is experiencing _____ depression.
   a. retarded
   b. anhedonic
   c. cyclothymic
   d. agitated

3. In contrast to a depressive episode, a manic episode will typically
   a. create greater personal discomfort.
   b. last longer.
   c. begin more suddenly.
   d. have less effect on mood state.

4. José has his ups and downs. He has been "down in the dumps" so badly in recent weeks that he has been unable to do his job. But today he arrived at the office at 4 A.M. telling jokes to the night watchman and planning to cure all the office problems by noon. It sounds like José has

    a. agitated depression.
    b. mixed depression.
    c. bipolar disorder.
    d. unipolar disorder.

5. The major difference between bipolar I disorder and bipolar II disorder is that

    a. bipolar I disorder does not have the depressive component.
    b. bipolar I disorder is found only in women.
    c. bipolar II disorder has less severe manic components.
    d. bipolar II disorder is generally endogenous.

6. Which of the following is true of bipolar disorder?

    a. It is more common than major depression.
    b. It is more common among the lower socioeconomic groups.
    c. It is more likely to run in families than major depression.
    d. Its victims tend to have a history of low self-esteem and dependency.

7. Cyclothymic disorder is to _____ as dysthymic disorder is to _____.

    a. bipolar disorder; major depression
    b. depressive episode; manic episode
    c. major depression; hypomanic episode
    d. bipolar I disorder; bipolar II disorder

8. The continuity hypothesis argues that

    a. people with mood disorders continue to have problems throughout their lifetimes.
    b. hallucinations and other psychotic conditions occur only in those with bipolar disorder.
    c. normal, sad moods and psychotic depression are different points on a single continuum.
    d. once people reach a level of psychotic depression, they are likely to have bipolar disorder as well.

9. Decreased energy, worry, low self-esteem, dependency, and crying are all symptoms found in

    a. depression alone.
    b. bipolar disorder alone.
    c. anxiety alone.
    d. both anxiety and depression.

10. Which of the following represents the "modal suicide committer?"

    a. Nancy, an African-American nineteen-year-old depressed mother of two
    b. Greg, a twenty-three-year-old single, unemployed Asian-American man
    c. Brenda, a thirty-five-year-old Caucasian-American housewife
    d. Jack, a fifty-year-old Caucasian-American depressed because he has cancer

11. A small city wants to develop a suicide prevention program. Based on research evidence, what advice would you give the mayor?

    a. A school-based program will have only minimal effects on adolescent boys most at risk for suicide.
    b. A telephone hotline will reduce by 60% the number of male suicides committed.
    c. School-based programs will be much more effective with the boys than the girls.
    d. Suicide hotlines are much more effective than school-based programs.

12. A contemporary psychodynamic theorist would be most likely to make which of the following claims about depression and suicide?

   a. "Depression is really a problem in thinking; the depressive attributes failure to himself or herself despite obvious evidence to the contrary."
   b. "Depression has its roots in a very early loss or threat of a loss."
   c. "Depressives take the anger they feel toward themselves and project it onto other people in their families."
   d. "Depressives have a grandiose sense of themselves and unconsciously want to have everyone be under their control."

13. Behaviorists speak of extinction as being a cause of depression. This means that
   a. a loss results in disappearance of behaviors reinforced by the lost object.
   b. thinking about the death of a loved one created a loss of meaning of life.
   c. the loss of a love object lowers one's self-esteem.
   d. loss results in intense anger, which is then turned inward against the self.

14. Throughout her childhood, Gretchen had been exposed to uncontrollable or unescapable stressors owing to her dysfunctional family situation. Eventually she adopted a depressed "What's the point?" attitude toward life and now rarely even attempts to cope. A cognitive theorist would say that Gretchen suffers from

   a. extinction of reinforcement.
   b. learned helplessness.
   c. cognitive restructuring.
   d. SAD.

15. Research on attributional style shows that depressives

   a. see their problems as temporary but nevertheless unbearable.
   b. blame negative events on the world, not on themselves.
   c. generalize their problems over all areas of life rather than limiting them.
   d. tend to feel they have more control over situations than they actually do.

16. Which of the following is true regarding the effectiveness of cognitive therapy for mood disorders?

   a. It can be just as effective as drug treatments.
   b. A combination of cognitive-behavioral treatment and drugs may be better than either one alone.
   c. The behavioral side of cognitive-behavioral treatment may be as effective all by itself as the combination of the two.
   d. All of the above

17. From the sociocultural perspective, the most promising means of preventing depression and suicide are likely to be

   a. telephone hotlines.
   b. school mental health programs.
   c. reducing problems such as teen pregnancy and substance abuse.
   d. making antidepressants more widely available in the community.

18. Linkage analysis provides support for which of the following statements about depression?
   a. Depression is definitely linked to a defect on chromosome 11.
   b. Depression is definitely NOT linked to a defect on chromosome 11.
   c. Depression MAY be linked to a defect on chromosome 11, but it may be related to a number of other genetic factors as well.
   d. None of the above

19. According to the text, hormonal imbalances appear to be particularly characteristic of _____ depressions.
    a. endogenous
    b. reactive
    c. dysthymic
    d. neurotic

20. Frank suffers from endogenous depression; Irving suffers from bipolar. Of the following choices, which drugs would be most effective for each man?
    a. lithium for Frank; tricyclics for Irving
    b. tricyclics for Frank; lithium for Irving
    c. dexamethasone for Frank; lithium for Irving
    d. serotonin for Frank; norepinephrine for Irving

21. _____ as many single people as married people kill themselves.
    a. Three times
    b. Twice
    c. Seventy-five percent
    d. Twenty-five percent

22. Three times as many women attempt suicide, but four times as many men as women succeed in killing themselves. Why?
    a. Women do not have access to the same methods as men.
    b. Men use lethal methods.
    c. Men are more committed to killing themselves than women.
    d. Women's attempts are usually interrupted.

23. Teenage girls are especially at risk of suicide attempts, in fact in the year 2000, suicide
    a. became the third leading cause of death among 15–24 year-olds.
    b. became the first leading cause of death among 15–24 year-olds.
    c. among girls significantly decreased.
    d. among boys and girls were the same.

24. The most common form of therapy for depressed patients is
    a. psychodynamic therapy.
    b. cognitive-behavioral therapy.
    c. antidepressant medications.
    d. antimanic medications.

25. While there are many competing drugs in the antidepressant market, the antimanic medication is dominated by one medication, _____.
    a. MAO inhibitors
    b. Prozac
    c. SSRIs
    d. lithium

ANSWERS

Guided Self-Study (p. 144)

1. mild and temporary

2. affective

3. a. Hippocrates
    b. Aretaeus

4. episodic

5. a. manic
    b. duration

6. a. depressed mood
    b. loss of pleasure or interest in usual activities
    c. disturbance of appetite
    d. sleep disturbance
    e. psychomotor retardation or agitation
    f. loss of energy
    g. feelings of worthlessness and guilt
    h. difficulties in thinking
    i. recurrent thoughts of death or suicide (246–247)

7. The helplessness-hopelessness syndrome is that pattern of thinking that deeply depressed people experience. They feel utter despair and believe they are going to feel that way forever; they are convinced that nothing will be able to lessen the mental anguish that they are experiencing. (246)

8. a. elevated or irritable mood
    b. inflated self-esteem
    c. sleeplessness
    d. talkativeness
    e. flight of ideas
    f. distractibility
    g. hyperactivity
    h. reckless behavior (247–248)

9. A person with mania becomes extremely hyperactive over a short time, maybe even a few days. The behavior has a driven quality to it. If he/she is spending money, the spending is likely to be with no regard for his/her actual financial condition. If the individual is driving a vehicle, the speed may be as fast as the vehicle will go with no concern to the dangers involved. Irritability in the individual is triggered very easily by anyone who interferes.

10. a. manic
     b. depressive
     c. manic
     d. manic
     e. depressive (246, 247)

11. a. depressive
     b. depressive
     c. manic
     d. major depressive
     e. bipolar disorder
     f. bipolar I
     g. bipolar II (251)

12. a. dysthymia
     b. cyclothymia
     c. chronic (252)

13. a. Seventeen
     b. The prevalence of major depression is rising with each successive generation since World War II (249).

14. Divorced or maritally separated; women (one and a half to three times higher than men); the young (women, fifteen to nineteen years; men twenty-five to twenty-nine years) (249)

15. 80%, or eight chances out of ten (249)

16. Recurrent episodes have a tendency to set up conditions for further episodes because the results of a major depressive episode are stressful in themselves: Lowered self-confidence; family and marital relationships are disrupted; progress in school or at work is interrupted; even the immune system is weakened, leaving the person more susceptible to illness. (249)

17. a. bipolar I
    b. bipolar I (mixed episode)
    c. bipolar I (Yes, one manic episode makes a bipolar disorder diagnosis.)
    d. bipolar I
    e. bipolar II (252)
    f. major depressive disorder (248)

18. All these descriptions fit bipolar disorder. (251)

19. endogenous—reactive (255)
    nonpsychotic—psychotic (253)
    late—early (256)

20. a. reality
    b. hallucination
    c. delusions

21. a. 2 boxes, major depression and bipolar disorder
    b. 2 circles, dysthymia and cyclothymia
    c. No stars; no depressive disorders are *defined* as psychotic. (253)

22. a. precipitating   f. cognitive
    b. loss   g. vegetative
    c. people   h. sleep, weight, bodily movements
    d. exit   i. melancholic (255)
    e. emotional

23. neurotic, reactive, and late onset (253–255)

24. a. Comorbidity
    b. intraepisode
    c. lifetime
    d. anxiety, depression

25. Suicides are many times disguised as accidental deaths. (257)

26. a. single
    b. men
    c. women
    d. men use lethal methods (257)
    e. increases (257)

27. a. stresses   e. parenting
    b. resources   f. communication
    c. depression   g. sexual abuse (259)
    d. drug

28. a. People who threaten suicide are at higher risk of doing it. (25–259)
    b. People who attempt suicide are at higher risk of doing it again and succeeding.
    c. Encouraging a person to talk about his feelings is therapeutic.

29. Comments about the futility of life in general or of his/her life in particular
    Becoming withdrawn
    Seeming to make preparations for a long trip
    Giving away treasured possessions
    Suddenly becoming tranquil after signs of depression
    High level of stress in the person's life
    Recent "exit" events in the person's life
    A perspective of hopelessness

30. Only 3–5% (258)

31. Thirty percent are ambivalent about dying. They are the "to be or not to be" group—people who aren't sure they want to die but don't want to live the way they have been doing. Sixty-five percent are trying to say they are in emotional pain that seems unbearable to them. (252)

32. a. psychodynamic
    b. Karl Abraham
    c. inward
    d. ambivalent

33. a. Mother dies
    b. Divorce, loss of job
    c. I can't deal with this
    d. Feelings not clear
    e. There must be something wrong with me
    f. You must help me cope with life (269)

34. a. interpersonal psychotherapy
    b. Harry Stack Sullivan
    c. grief
    d. interpersonal
    e. role
    f. social skills
    g. relapse
    h. severely (269)

35. LEARNING! (263)

36. extinction (263)

37. Our favorite people or valued activities serve as powerful reinforcers for the behaviors that are associated with these people or activities. When the reinforcers are removed, the behaviors go into extinction. Since loved ones and jobs account for a significant part of our daily lives, loss of these reinforcers can be significant, and the person ends up doing very little—depression. (264)

38. Depressed people often act in ways that drive other people away from them—they complain, make demands, and generally go around with a black cloud over their heads. The result is social isolation, which tends to make the depression even worse. (263)

39. Social skills training is on the one hand a means for reducing the aversive social behavior mentioned in the previous question. This allows the person to find others reinforcing and to be reinforcing to them in return. In the long run, this could enable the person to replace significant reinforcers that were lost when the depression began. (264)

40. a. cognitive
    b. cognitive
    c. cognitive (264)

41. a. Seligman
    b. dogs
    c. remained passive
    d. depression (264)

42. "b" is correct (264)

43. a. always
    b. nothing
    c. attributions (264–66)

44. "b" is correct. This statement suggests the idea that the individual sees the problem as internal to an widespread within the individual and permanent in duration. (266)

45. a. "I have never been any good . . ."
    b. "I just had a bad day . . ."
    c. "Stupid, stupid . . ."
    d. "I was prepared, but . . ."
    e. "I guess college just . . ."
    f. "Oh well, I guess calculus . . ." (267)

46. Permanent, internal, and generalized attributions for negative events set one up for depression. (267)

47. a. self-schemas
    b. dependency
    c. criticism
    d. realistic
    e. beneficial (267)

48. a. Beck
    b. attributional (266)

49. a. society
    b. economic
    c. more
    d. earlier
    e. stability
    f. teens
    g. stressor
    h. restrictions (272–273)

50. a. family
    b. adoption
    c. twin
    d. is
    e. bipolar disorder (273)

51. a. light therapy
    b. short REM latency
    c. time giver
    d. sleep deprivation
    e. REM
    f. SAD (275)

52. a. dexamethasone suppression test
    b. endogenous
    c. psychotic
    d. psychotherapy
    e. more
    f. unlikely (277–278)

53. a. True
    b. True
    c. False; they work by blocking the reuptake of norepinephrine at the presynaptic neuron.
    d. True
    e. True
    f. False; it relieves mood disorder because it increases serotonin levels.
    g. True
    h. True (278)

54. a. Many side effects, but . . .
    b. Easy to overdose and . . .
    c. Prevent reuptake of serotonin . . .
    d. Nine or ten treatments . . .
    e. Tends to reduce side effect . . .
    f. Treatment of choice . . .
    g. Most popular prescription drug (279–282)

Practice Test (p. 153)

1. a. No. Think of it this way—a hedonist is a pleasure seeker.
   b. Right!
   c. Sorry. Hedonism has to do with pleasure seeking.
   d. Incorrect. This is an important vocabulary word for the chapter; see the comments above.

2. a. No. Retardation refers to slowing down. Does Andy seem slow to you?
   b. No. Again, hedonism is pleasure seeking. The question does not mention that.
   c. Incorrect. This is a mild form of bipolar disorder.
   d. Right!

3. a. No, actually manic people often feel quite good—too good, in fact.
   b. Sorry, most of the time it lasts a shorter time.
   c. Yes!
   d. No, not less effect, just a different effect.

4. a. No. Ups and downs are the giveaway here.
   b. "Mixed" implies contrasting symptoms occurring simultaneously. That is not the case here.
   c. Correct!
   d. No, that would just be depression.

5. a. Incorrect. Both I and II generally involve depression; it's the other half that's important.
   b. No. Any time you see an absolute qualifier like "only," be suspicious. This is psychology, and the absolutes are few and far between!
   c. Right!
   d. No, there is no evidence on this.

6. a. No, it is less common—only about a fourth or a third as common.
   b. Just the opposite. More common among higher socioeconomic groups.
   c. Correct!
   d. No. This is true of unipolar disorder.

7. a. Yes!
   b. No. Don't confuse episodes with disorders. Episodes are the bricks from which disorders are built.
   c. No. Cyclothymic means cycling, or back-and-forth. So it cannot refer to depression alone.
   d. Incorrect. Cyclothymic is bipolar, but dysthymic is not.

8. a. Good guess, but no. The continuity here has to do with type of problem, not time span.
   b. No. This statement has nothing to do with continuity. Continuity means connectedness.
   c. Right! It is a matter of degree, not of kind.
   d. Sorry. Continuity implies a connectedness between extremes, and that is not the issue here.

9. a. Incorrect. Beware of absolute assertions.
   b. No. Many problems share some of the same symptoms.
   c. Hint: This question is getting at the concept of comorbidity.
   d. You got it!

10. a. No. Who is more likely to succeed at suicide, men or women?
    b. No. Who is more likely to commit suicide, Asians or Caucasians?
    c. Sorry. This is the modal suicide *attempter*.
    d. Correct!

11. a. Correct, unfortunately.
    b. Wrong. To the extent hotlines work, they work better with females.
    c. Incorrect, and again they tend to work better with females.
    d. No. Actually, neither one of these approaches works very well.

12. a. Sorry. This is a cognitive point of view—notice the focus on thinking?
    b. Right!
    c. No. To the extent that anger is involved, psychodynamic theorists would say it is just the other way around.
    d. Incorrect. This is not a psychodynamic viewpoint.

13. a. You got it!
    b. This is not behavioral—it is more philosophical/cognitive.
    c. No. Remember, behaviorists generally focus on external events, not internal experience.

14. a. No, extinction is a behavioral concept, and the question asks for a cognitive response.
    b. Right!
    c. Incorrect. This is a cognitive *treatment* process, not a disorder process.
    d. Sorry. This is a season-related form of depression unrelated to rewards and punishments.

15. a. Incorrect. It they thought it was temporary, they would not be so depressed.
    b. Wrong. If the problems were external, they could move away or change something and thus relieve the depression.
    c. Correct!
    d. No. They feel they have less control.

16. a. Yes.
    b. Yes again.
    c. Another true one.
    d. Obviously the right answer!

17. a. No. Remember, the sociocultural perspective believes social ills *cause* the problems, so . . .
    b. Incorrect. Once you identify what you think is the problem, what do you change?
    c. Right!
    d. Sorry. They would see this as just covering up the symptoms.

18. a. No. This is what they originally thought, until there were some replication problems.
    b. No. That is too much on the other side.
    c. Right!
    d. Sorry. You have to throw one of these in occasionally.

19. a. Correct!
    b. No. It turns out that the old meaning of endogenous may have some validity here.
    c. Incorrect. Wrong set of categories.
    d. Wrong. These would be the least severe depressions. In general, the more severe a problem is, the more likely a biological connection will be found.

20. a. Sorry. You got it backward.
    b. Right!
    c. Half right; dexamethasone is not a drug for treating mood disorders—it is part of the DST.
       No. These are neurotransmitters believed to be involved in mood disorders, but they are not medications for it.

21 a. No.
    b. Correct!
    c. No, too high.
    e. No.

22 a. No, women could have access to the same methods.
    b. Correct!
    c. Incorrect, men may not be more committed, just more successful owing to the method used.
    d. No.

23. a. Correct.
    b. Incorrect.
    c. Incorrect.
    d. No.

24. a. No.
    b. No, may be used in conjunction.
    c. Correct.
    d. No, not usually used with depression.

25. a. No, this is an antidepressant.
    b. No, this is an antidepressant.
    c. No, this is a class of antidepressants.
    d. Correct.

CHAPTER 11
PERSONALITY DISORDERS

LEARNING OBJECTIVES

By the time you have finished studying this chapter, you should be able to do the following:

1. Define a personality disorder according to *DSM-IV-TR* criteria, and discuss the reliability of this diagnostic category. (287)

2. List and describe the essential characteristics of the three odd/eccentric personality disorders (paranoid, schizotypal, and schizoid). (287-290)

3. List and describe the essential characteristics of the three dramatic/emotional personality disorders (borderline, histrionic, and narcissistic) discussed in the chapter. (290–298)

4. List and describe the essential characteristics of the three anxious/fearful personality disorders (avoidant, dependent, and obsessive-compulsive). (298–301)

5. Distinguish between paranoid personality disorder, delusional disorder, and paranoid schizophrenia, and distinguish between obsessive-compulsive personality disorder and obsessive-compulsive disorder. (287, 301)

6. Summarize the population statistics regarding personality disorders, and give four examples of impulse-control disorders. (300)

7. Discuss the psychodynamic perspective on the development of personality disorders, and summarize the psychodynamic approach to the treatment of these problems. (303–305)

8. Discuss personality disorders and their treatment from the behavioral and cognitive perspectives. (305-308)

9. Explain the sociocultural perspective's view of personality disorder, including reference to political issues that complicate attempts to define and diagnose these disorders. (308)

10. Explain the neuroscience perspective and summarize genetic and biochemical research into the causes and treatment of personality disorders. (308)

11. Explain the dispute over the gender and cultural bias within personality disorders. (302–303)

KEY TERMS

The following terms are in bold print in your text and are important to your understanding of the chapter. Look them up in the text and write down their definitions.

antisocial behavior (291)
antisocial personality disorder (APD) (290)
avoidant personality disorder (298)
borderline personality disorder (293)
dependent personality disorder (299)
dialectical behavior therapy (306)
histrionic personality disorder (296)
impulse-control disorder (300)

narcissistic personality disorder (297)
obsessive-compulsive personality disorder (301)
paranoid personality disorder (287)
passive avoidance learning (292)
personality disorder (287)
schizoid personality disorder (289)
schizotypal personality disorder (288)

IMPORTANT NAMES

Identify the following persons and their major contribution to abnormal psychology as discussed in this chapter.

Hervey Cleckley (290–291)   Marsha Linehan (306)

GUIDED SELF-STUDY

1. Personality disorders contain key qualities that separate them from other forms of disorder. Here are the qualities; write them into the *DSM-IV-TR*'s definition of personality disorder.

adolescence	enduring	pervasive
deviates	impairment	stable
distress	inflexible	

"An (a)_____ pattern of inner experience and behavior that (b)_____ markedly from the

expectations of the individual's culture, is (c)_____ and (d)_____, has an onset in

(e)_____ or early adulthood, is (f)_____ over time, and leads to (g)_____ or

(h)_____."

In other words, unlike other problems, which can be fairly specific in their effects and which can occur at a variety of times during life, personality disorders are long-term trends in problem behavior covering wide areas of functioning. They are essentially *ways of living that cause problems* for the person or those around him/her.

2.   By the way, on which axis of the *DSM-IV-TR* are personality disorders located?

3. Complete the following statements about the reliability of the personality disorder diagnostic category using these terms:

atypical	personality disorder	reliable
coverage	reliability	

As a diagnostic category, personality disorders has not been very (a)_____. Diagnosticians fairly

well agree on the presence or absence of a (b)_____ _____, but they often disagree as to

which disorder is being manifested in a particular patient. The problem is to make the categories distinct

enough among themselves to ensure high (c)_____ but not so limiting as to reduce

(d)_____ and cause too many people to be put in the "mixed" or (e)_____ categories.

4. The other problem with the personality disorder diagnosis is the assumption that stable personality traits exist. Which perspective objects to this assumption?

5. Draw a line from each personality disorder to the phrase that most closely defines the disorder. Use each disorder and each phrase only once.

paranoid	Withdraws fearing rejection
schizotypal	"Odd"
schizoid	Bogged down in details
borderline	Puts decision making on someone else
histrionic	A "flake" (unstable)
narcissistic	Suspicious
avoidant	Doesn't find social contact worthwhile
dependent	"Ego" maniac (as term is popularly used)
obsessive-compulsive	Overly dramatic

6. Choose among the following to find one or more "good jobs" for the personality disorders listed below. Consider the needs of the job and the characteristics of each of the disorders.

accountant   *comedian*   *private detective*
bookkeeping   *forest ranger in a remote area*   *proofreader*
cartoonist   *long-haul truck driver*   *night watchman*

   a. Obsessive-compulsive:

   b. Paranoid:

   c. Schizotypal:

   d. Schizoid:

7. Place a check mark in front of the three personality disorders that the *DSM-IV-TR* categorizes as odd/eccentric personality disorders. Then, after each of the disorders you checked, tell how the oddness shows itself in the person.

   _____ Paranoid   _____ Borderline

   _____ Schizotypal   _____ Histrionic

   _____ Schizoid   _____ Narcissistic

   _____ Avoidant   _____ Obsessive-compulsive

   _____ Dependent

8. Place a check mark next to three personality disorders that the *DSM-IV-TR* categorizes as dramatic/emotional personality disorders. Then, after each of the disorders you checked, explain how this emotional state or display is manifested.

   _____ Paranoid   _____ Borderline

   _____ Schizotypal   _____ Histrionic

   _____ Schizoid   _____ Narcissistic

   _____ Avoidant   _____ Obsessive-compulsive

   _____ Dependent

9. Check the three personality disorders that *DSM-IV-TR* categorizes as anxious/fearful personality disorders. Then, after each of the disorders you checked, describe how this worry and fearfulness shows itself.

_____ Paranoid		_____ Borderline
_____ Schizotypal		_____ Histrionic
_____ Schizoid		_____ Narcissistic
_____ Avoidant		_____ Obsessive-compulsive
_____ Dependent		

10. List four factors that contribute to the instability of the borderline personality.

    a.

    b.

    c.

    d.

11. Some personality disorders have names that are similar to those of other psychiatric problems. It is important not to confuse the personality disorders with these other diagnoses. After each of the following personality disorders, list the other disorder or disorders from which it must be differentiated.

    a. Paranoid personality disorder:

    b. Schizotypal personality disorder:

    c. Schizoid personality disorder:

    d. Obsessive-compulsive personality disorder:

12. So, how are the paranoid, schizotypal, and schizoid personality disorders different from the other disorders you wrote in?

13. And, how is obsessive-compulsive personality disorder different from the other disorder you wrote in?

14. Some more distinctions: Both the avoidant personality and the schizoid personality have few interpersonal relationships, but for entirely different reasons. For the schizoid, it is simply a lack of (a)_____, but for the avoidant personality it is fear of (b)_____. Also, it is possible that the borderline personality disorder may sometimes overlap and be confused with (c)_____ or dissociative (d)_____

    _____.

15. In connection with narcissistic personality disorder, an interesting set of opposite explanations comes from the social learning and psychodynamic camps. The (a)_____ theorists see narcissism as an effort to make up for inadequate parental affection and approval, whereas the (b)_____ people see it coming directly from too much approval.

16. The text points out that personality disorders are quite rare in the general population but are quite common among people being treated for psychological problems. How is this to be explained? Choose the best answer.

    a. Treatment for other psychological problems can often cause a personality disorder.

    b. People who seek treatment for other problems often have a personality disorder lurking in the background as well.

    c. Insurance companies will pay more for the treatment of a personality disorder than for many other problems.

    d. A *DSM-IV-TR* diagnosis requires an entry for each axis, and Axis II is where personality disorders fit.

17. The correct answer to the previous question addresses a concept we encountered in the chapter on diagnosis and assessment. It is the issue of _____.

18. For each of the personality disorders listed below, tell if it is most commonly found in males, in females, or if it is distributed equally between the genders.

    a. _____ Paranoid

    b. _____ Schizotypal

    c. _____ Schizoid

    d. _____ Avoidant

    e. _____ Dependent

    f. _____ Borderline

    g. _____ Histrionic

    h. _____ Narcissistic

    i. _____ Obsessive-compulsive

19. Another set of disorders in this chapter is characterized by the tendency to act impulsively in a way that is harmful to the self or to others. What is the collective name of these disorders?

20. Draw a line from the disorder on the left to its description on the right.

    a. intermittent explosive disorder   Fire setting for pleasure or tension relief
    b. kleptomania   Compulsive tendency to bet and wager
    c. pyromania   Destructive outbursts
    d. trichotillomania   Stealing things you don't need
    e. pathological gambling   Hair pulling

21. There is some evidence linking trichotillomania with which other disorder?

Perspectives on the Personality Disorders

22. What do psychodynamic theorists call personality disorders?

23. In the character disorders, the ego is not working well because of problems in the pre- (a)_____

    relationship between the child and the (b)_____, what Mahler calls the process of (c)_____

    -_____. The result, psychodynamic theorists believe, is a weakened (d)_____, unable to cope

    well with life.

24. In regard to ego functioning, how do psychodynamic theorists rank *character disorders* with *neuroses* and *psychoses*? Write each disorder in the appropriate space.

    Best-functioning: _____ * _____ * _____ :Worst-functioning

25. Psychodynamic theory says that different personality disorders result from different kinds of ego problems. Match each personality disorder with its ego problem.

    a. _____ Ego is unstable, person "falls apart" in times of stress

    b. _____ Ego forgoes own thinking skills in favor of thinking skills of others

    c. _____ Ego shifts all mental energy into planning

    d. _____ Ego directs all mental energy into scanning the environment

    e. _____ Ego may be defending against a profound sense of inferiority

26. People with character disorders are usually not distressed by their own personality quirks; and if they are distressed, they are likely to perceive the problem as (a)_____ to them. Therefore, they are likely to come to therapy only when (b)_____, and then they are often uncooperative. From this, one might conclude that the prognosis for character disorders is rather (c)_____.

27. In treating personality disorders, psychodynamic therapists take a more (a)_____, parent-like role than psychoanalytic therapists do with other clients. These therapists are trying to provide an opportunity for the patient to rework the disrupted (b)_____-child relationship that is assumed to underlie (c)_____ _____, as the psychoanalysts call these disorders.

28. Use these terms for the behavioral perspective on personality disorders: *learning, traits, personality, trends.* Some behaviorists object to the concept of personality because these behaviorists are unwilling to talk in terms of fixed (a)_____. Some behaviorists see the individual as (b)_____ classes (types) of behaviors that lead to (c)_____ in behavior equivalent to the concept of (d)_____.

29. Check three of the following to identify the learning situations that behaviorists believe can lead to personality disorders.

    invalidating syndrome   *endogenous assertiveness*
    anomie   *premorbidity*
    prognosis   *direct reinforcement*
    parasympathetic retraining   *disregulation syndrome*
    modeling   *fugue*
    biofeedback training   *schema alignment*

Use the following terms for Questions 30 and 31. One of them is used twice.

    adult   *dependent*   *learning*
    calming   *histrionic*   *modeling*
    child   *invalidating*   *obsessive-compulsive*

30. The (a)_____ syndrome is the behavioral pattern in which the parents dismiss a child's emotional

distress unless the distress comes from a problem of (b)_____-sized proportions. As a result, the

child does not get practice in self- (c)_____ and emotional problem-solving on small,

(d)_____-sized problems. For example, when a child is learning to cope with the pain of a tiny hurt

(often not visible to the parent's eye), that child is making beginning steps toward (e)_____ to deal

with the (f)_____-sized pain of personal rejection or losing a job.

31. In (a)_____, the child copies the behavior that he/she sees in others. While the child may copy

problem behavior from others, direct reinforcement or punishment may also play a role. For example, if a

child is consistently punished for any sign of assertiveness, the result may be (b)_____ personality

disorder. If temper tantrums are reinforced by the parent giving the child what he/she wants, the result may

be (c)_____ personality disorder. Finally, (d)_____ personality disorder may result from

excessive reinforcement of neatness, rule-following, and other "goody-goody" behavior.

32. Cognitive psychologists talk in terms of (a)_____, which are the organizational structures that

individuals use to efficiently conceptualize and store information in one's (b)_____. Instead of

remembering every fast food restaurant as a separate place, most people have a schema for a fast food

restaurant. If a place proposed for lunch is known to be a fast food restaurant, everyone knows what to expect

without further description.

33. Check the following concepts which are probably in most people's schemas for fast food restaurants.

servers in formal attire   *drive-through service*
valet parking   *filet mignon on the menu*
self-serve areas   *economical prices*
menu over central counter   *necessity to make reservations*
cloth table napkins   *topless waitresses*
limited menu

Use the following words to fill in the blanks for Questions 34 and 35.

camouflage   *modifying*   *schemas*
compelled   *reinterpreted*   *situation*
faulty   *rigid*   *unlikely*

34. Cognitive theorists see personality disorders as the result of (a)_____ schemas. Many of us may hold beliefs that are counterproductive; however, these become a major problem deserving of a diagnosis only if we feel strongly (b)_____ to exercise the ideas and beliefs across all circumstances without any consideration for the particulars of any given (c)_____. In other words. our thinking and behavior become very (d)_____.

35. The ambitious goal of cognitive therapists is to change faulty (a)_____. A more realistic and practical alternative to complete change, which is very (b)_____ to occur, is to help the person try to limit the use of his/her faulty schemas or to put them to as good use as can be worked into the person's life. For example, the process of (c)_____ a schema means to limit it to some appropriate area of life. A schema can also be (d)_____ by finding activities in which the schema is more useful and productive. The cognitive therapists may also teach socially acceptable ways to deal with situations in which the schema might otherwise cause problems; this is called schematic (e)_____.

36. The next perspective takes a different point of view from the others discussed thus far. A major assumption here is that the problem is actually located in society at large and that personality disorders are simply ways that individuals react to or cope with social injustice. This understanding of personality disorders comes from the (a)_____ perspective. In view of this, these people would recommend changing the (b)_____ in order to remove the causes of the disorder

37. We have already seen that some personality disorders are more common in one gender than in another. Assuming that some of the disorders common to women are not so much the result of personal failings but the consequence of social inequity and labeling, how would one explain dependent personality disorder?

38. How would one explain histrionic personality disorder from this point of view?

39. Two other proposed personality disorders have been discussed for a number of years. Name them in the space before their definitions.

    a. _____ A tendency to inflict harm or abuse on others

    b. _____ A tendency toward chronic pessimism and self-destruction

40. These proposed disorders were opposed and never made it into the *DSM*. Why would a labeled disorder reflecting an uncontrollable tendency to harm others for personal power or gratification not be a good idea?

41. Why would a labeled disorder reflecting an uncontrollable tendency toward pessimism and self-destructive behavior not be a good idea?

42. In view of all this, it seems to be the case that when sensitive areas of people's lives are affected by professional psychological concerns the outcome is as much involved with _____ as it is with science.

43. Biological research has dramatically demonstrated that there is a (a)_____ component to personality. In fact, some twin studies indicate that as much as (b)_____% of personality may be the direct result of genetic influence.

44. Since many of the disorders on Axis I of the *DSM-IV* also appear to have genetic components, there is an argument that the personality disorders on Axis (a)_____ may be long-standing, or

(b) "_____" versions of Axis I problems. It has been proposed that avoidant personality disorder is just a variation on (c)_____ _____, that schizotypal personality disorder is a variation of

(d)_____ (which in fact it was once considered to be), and that borderline personality disorder is a form of (e)_____ _____. The fact that some personality disorders respond to the same

(f)_____ as their counterparts in Axis I also makes some theorists doubt the appropriateness of the personality disorder diagnoses.

HELPFUL HINT

Note that just because someone engages in some of the behaviors described in this chapter some of the time does not mean that the person has a disorder (in fact, just about all of us have engaged in most of the "abnormal" behaviors described in this text at some time or other). Pervasiveness, inflexibility, maladaption, and long duration are the key issues in defining these disorders. In other words, how much does the behavior get in the way of living a happy and productive life?

PRACTICE TEST

Use the following test questions to check your knowledge of the material in this chapter. You may want to write the answers on a separate sheet of paper so you can take the test more than once.

1. Another way of stating the *DSM-IV-TR* definition of personality disorder is
   a. a lifestyle that creates difficulties for the person or others.
   b. a limited behavioral quirk that irritates those around the patient.
   c. a lack of emotional responding that takes that joy out of life.
   d. a retreat from anxiety to the point that reality contact is lost.

2. Which of the following statements about personality disorders is FALSE?
   a. The problem behaviors are rarely evident before adulthood.
   b. Contact with reality is usually maintained.
   c. The disorders may cause more pain to people who deal with such patients than to the patients themselves.
   d. The trait is so much a part of the person that the person does not see it as a disorder.

3. Which of the following is an argument that *behaviorists* would use against the personality disorder diagnoses?

    a. These diagnoses deprive people of their unique individuality by forcing them into pigeonholes.
    b. There is too much overlap between characteristics in these diagnoses, and this results in low reliability.
    c. These diagnoses assume stable personality traits to be the major determinants of behavior while ignoring situational variables.
    d. These diagnoses are often sexist and tend to blame the victim for the problem.

4. Which of the following personality disorders is included under the heading of odd/eccentric disorders?

    a. histrionic
    b. obsessive-compulsive
    c. schizoid
    d. dependent

5. Alfred believes that his coworkers are always talking about him, his neighbors are plotting to have him evicted, and women intentionally avoid him. Yet he is able to perform his job adequately. Alfred is probably suffering from which of the following personality disorders?

    a. schizoid
    b. histrionic
    c. paranoid
    d. borderline

6. The defining characteristic of schizotypal personality disorder is _____; the defining characteristic of schizoid personality disorder is _____.

    a. suspiciousness; dependence on others
    b. odd thinking; shallow emotions
    c. preference to be alone: odd thinking
    d. odd thinking; preference to be alone

7. All of the following are included in the dramatic/emotional group of personality disorders EXCEPT

    a. narcissistic personality disorder.
    b. borderline personality disorder.
    c. schizotypal personality disorder.
    d. histrionic personality disorder.

8. Which perspective has traditionally had the most interest in the borderline personality disorder?

    a. behavioral
    b. sociocultural
    c. psychodynamic
    d. cognitive

9. The histrionic personality and the narcissistic personality are similar in that they both

    a. demand a great deal from others but give little in return.
    b. involve bizarre idiosyncrasies.
    c. are characterized principally by extreme emotional fluctuations.
    d. involve avoidance of social contact.

10. A man is socially withdrawn. He is extremely sensitive to disapproval; in fact, he expects people will dislike him. He also exhibits low self-esteem and an extreme fear of rejection. This man would most likely be diagnosed as suffering from which personality disorder?

    a. narcissistic
    b. avoidant
    c. schizoid
    d. schizotypal

11. Fear of making decisions, self-doubt based on a fear of being abandoned, and worrying that no one cares are key features of the _____ personality disorder.

    a. antisocial
    b. obsessive-compulsive
    c. histrionic
    d. dependent

12. People with obsessive-compulsive personality disorder tend to be

    a. suspicious of others' motives.
    b. filled with both anger and grief.
    c. unconventional and impulsive.
    d. perfectionists.

13. The chief difference between the obsessive-compulsive personality disorder in this chapter and the obsessive-compulsive disorder (OCD) in an earlier chapter is that the personality disorder

    a. is more pervasive in life.
    b. is more likely to involve simply checking and cleaning.
    c. is less common than OCD.
    d. is more severe in its symptoms than OCD.

14. Karen and her husband are seeing a counselor for marital problems. According to your text, which of the following personality disorders is most likely to be diagnosed in Karen while in the process of marital counseling?

    a. dependent personality disorder
    b. avoidant personality disorder
    c. schizoid personality disorder
    d. narcissistic personality disorder

15. Wally likes fire. Sometimes he sets fires just for the excitement of seeing it burn and watching the fire department respond. He knows his behavior is a problem, but he just can't seem to help himself. *DSM-IV-TR* would diagnose Wally with

    a. kleptomania.
    b. pyromania.
    c. trichotillomania.
    d. nothing; this is a crime, not a disorder.

16. The psychoanalytic community has been most involved in the study of two personality disorders. They are

    a. schizoid and schizotypal.
    b. borderline and dependent.
    c. narcissistic and borderline.
    d. histrionic and obsessive-compulsive.

17. Marian's husband has brought her into therapy because she is incapable of making decisions, and, therefore, all decisions and responsibilities are shifted to him. Which perspective would be most likely to view her dependent behavior as resulting from a childhood in which assertiveness was repeatedly punished?

    a. psychodynamic
    b. biological
    c. sociocultural
    d. behavioral

18. From the cognitive point of view, the distinction that separates the schemas of personality disordered patients from those of average people is that with the personality disorder, schemas are

    a. dysfuntional.
    b. unhelpful.
    c. not related to reality.
    d. too rigidly applied.

19. What has the *DSM-IV-TR* done to reduce the likelihood of gender or cultural bias in the application of personality disorder diagnoses?

    a. It warns diagnosticians to be aware that gender or cultural information can unintentionally bias a diagnosis.
    b. It has removed all diagnostic categories that are likely to result in gender or cultural bias.
    c. It has removed all references to gender and culture in the assessment and diagnosis process.
    d. It has done nothing about this issue, on the grounds that scientific rigor will result in sufficient fairness for all.

20. What do certain researchers mean when they propose that personality disorders are just "characterological" versions of other disorders such as phobias or schizophrenia?

    a. Axis II disorders are just more pervasive versions of Axis I disorders.
    b. Personality disorders are the cause of the other disorders mentioned.
    c. Axis I disorders are just more pervasive versions of Axis II disorders.
    d. The other disorders mentioned are the cause of personality disorders.

21. Which personality disorder is characterized by a lack of regard for society's moral and legal standards?

    a. antisocial
    b. borderline
    c. narcissistic
    d. schizotypal

22. It is difficult to treat people with schizoid and schizotypal personality disorder because

    a. they are emotionally unstable.
    b. they tend to misrepresent themselves in therapy.
    c. they are cognitively and emotionally restricted.
    d. their treatment is usually mandated.

23. A key characteristic of narcissistic personality disorder is

    a. mania.
    b. grandiosity.
    c. splitting.
    d. lack of remorse.

24. Serial killers may likely be diagnosed with which personality disorder?

    a. narcissistic personality disorder
    b. schizoid personality disorder
    c. antisocial personality disorder
    d. schizotypal

25. Which of the following statements is TRUE?

    a. Men account for three-quarters of the persons diagnosed with borderline personality disorder.
    b. Women outnumber men three to one in the diagnosis of antisocial personality disorder.
    c. One group at risk for personality disorders is people in psychological treatment.
    d. Men outnumber women three to one in the diagnosis of histrionic personality disorder.

ANSWERS

1. a. enduring
   b. deviates
   c. pervasive
   d. inflexible
   e. adolescence
   f. stable
   g. distress
   h. impairment (287)

2. Axis II

3. a. reliable
   b. personality disorder
   c. reliability
   d. coverage
   e. atypical (287)

4. behaviorists (287)

5. paranoid—suspicious (287)
   schizotypal—"odd" (288)
   schizoid—doesn't find social contact worthwhile (289)
   borderline—a "flake" (unstable) (293)
   histrionic—overly dramatic (296)
   narcissistic—"ego" maniac (297)
   avoidant—withdraws fearing rejection (298)
   dependent—puts decision making on someone else (299)
   obsessive-compulsive—bogged down in details (301)

6. a. Obsessive-compulsive (attention to detail)—accountant, proofreader (301)
   b. Paranoid (hypervigilant)—private detective, night watchman (287)
   c. Schizotypal (unusual perspective and behaviors)—cartoonist, comedian (the ones who see the world from unusual perspectives are some of my favorites) (288)
   d. Schizoid (very content alone)—forest ranger in a remote area, long-haul truck driver (289)

   Be sure to read the Helpful Hint on this issue.

7. Paranoid—is overly suspicious and mistrustful and alienates people. (287)
   Schizotypal—does and says bizarre and outlandish things; seems "off the wall." (288)
   Schizoid—is a loner; has little human warmth and finds people uninteresting. (289)

8. Borderline—is so emotionally unpredictable that friendships are unstable. (293)
   Histrionic—emotionally overboard and overreactive on everything. (296)
   Narcissistic—self-absorption does not leave room for others as equals. (297)

9. Avoidant—too apprehensive about rejection to risk a friendship. (298)
   Dependent—afraid of facing life and lives with a clinging dependency. (299)
   Obsessive-compulsive—constant concern over order and control; can't loosen up. (301)

10. a. Difficulties in establishing a secure self-identity
    b. Distrust
    c. Impulsive and self-destructive behaviors
    d. Difficulty controlling anger and other emotions (293)

11. a. Delusional disorder and paranoid schizophrenia (287)
    b. Schizophrenia (287)
    c. Schizophrenia (289)
    d. Obsessive-compulsive (anxiety) disorder (301)

12. In the case of the paranoid, schizotypal, and schizoid personality disorders, the names reflect a similarity to the symptoms of schizophrenia or delusional disorder, but to a less severe degree. (287)

13. In the case of obsessive-compulsive personality disorder and obsessive-compulsive disorder, the names are similar because of superficially similar behaviors, but the personality disorder is more pervasive; that is, it more significantly affects the person's life. (301)

14. a. interest or capacity (289)
    b. rejection
    c. depression
    d. identity disorder

15. a. psychodynamic
    b. social learning (297)

16. "b" is correct (301)

17. comorbidity (301)

18. a. male
    b. male
    c. male
    d. equal
    e. female
    f. female
    g. female
    h. male
    i. male

19. impulse control disorders (300)

20. a. destructive outbursts
    b. stealing things you don't need
    c. fire setting for pleasure or tension relief
    d. hair pulling
    e. compulsive tendency to bet or wager (300)

21. obsessive-compulsive disorder (301)

22. character disorders (303)

23. a. Oedipal
    b. mother
    c. separation-individuation
    d. ego (304)

24. Best functioning: neuroses * character disorders * psychoses :Worst functioning (304)

25. a. borderline personality disorder
    b. dependent personality disorder
    c. obsessive-compulsive personality disorder
    d. paranoid personality disorder (287)
    e. narcissistic personality disorder (297)

26. a. external
    b. forced to come by others
    c. poor (303)

27. a. directive
    b. parent
    c. character disorders (303)

28. a. traits
    b. learning
    c. trends
    d. personality (305)

29. invalidating syndrome, modeling, direct reinforcement (305)

30. a. invalidating
    b. adult
    c. calming
    d. child
    e. learning
    f. adult (305)

31. a. modeling
    b. dependent
    c. histrionic
    d. obsessive-compulsive (305)

32. a. schemas
    b. memory (306)

33. self-serve areas
    menu over central counter
    limited menu
    drive-through service
    economical prices (306)

34. a. faulty
    b. compelled
    c. situation
    d. rigid (306)

35. a. schemas
    b. unlikely
    c. modifying
    d. reinterpreted
    e. camouflage (305)

36. a. sociocultural
    b. culture or society (308)

37. Society has traditionally placed women in a subservient role, which left them little choice but to be dependent. It would be unfair to then label this dependency as a personal problem. (302)

38. People who have little direct personal control over their lives sometimes gain that control indirectly through emotional manipulation. Once again, such behavior in someone who has been deprived of other methods of control cannot be fairly labeled as a personality problem. (302)

39. a. sadistic personality disorder
    b. self-defeating personality disorder (303)

40. Some argue that such a label would tend to excuse abusers from taking responsibility for their actions. (303)

41. Some argue that such a label would place responsibility for abuse on the person receiving the abuse rather than on the person committing it (he/she was "asking for it"). (303)

42. politics (303)

43. a. genetic   fifty (308)

44. a. II
     b. characterological
     c. social phobia
     d. schizophrenia
     e. mood disorder
     f. drugs (308)

Practice Test (p. 171)

1. a. Correct!
    b. No. Personality disorders are not limited; they are pervasive.
    c. For a schizoid personality, yes, but overall, personality disorders can be quite emotional.
    d. No. That would be psychosis, and personality disorders are not psychoses.

2. a. Right! Actually, the problem is *defined* as being present early in life.
    b. This is true.
    c. This is true, also.
    d. Once again, a true statement.

3. a. This is an argument that some make, but it is not a behavioristic complaint.
    b. This is an argument that is made, but just about everybody says it, not just behaviorists.
    c. Correct!
    d. Again, an argument some make, but more likely to be feminists, not behaviorists.

4. a. No, this one is dramatic/emotional.
    b. No, this one is anxious/fearful.
    c. Yes!
    d. No, this is another anxious/fearful disorder.

5. a. Sorry. A schizoid wouldn't pay that much attention to the people around him.
    b. No. The histrionic personality uses self-centered emotional display, not fear of others.
    c. Right!
    d. Incorrect. The focus here is quite stable—suspicion. Borderlines aren't that consistent.

6. a. No. Suspiciousness = paranoid; dependence = dependent.
    b. Half right, but depression is a mood disorder.
    c. Sorry. Right responses, but in the wrong order.
    d. You got it!

7. a. No, this is in fact a dramatic/emotional disorder.
    b. Sorry, this is in the dramatic/emotional group as well.
    c. Right! This one is in the odd/eccentric group.
    d. Incorrect. This is also a dramatic/emotional disorder.

8. a. No. Hint: The group we're interested in got the *DSM* to include the disorder.
    b. No. Another hint: Who deals most with emotional issues in life and relationships?
    c. Yes!
    d. Sorry. I guess this is one you either know or you don't.

9. a. You got it!
    b. No, that is the schizotypal personality.
    c. Sorry. This is more true of the borderline personality disorder.
    d. No. In fact, histrionic and narcissistic personalities need other people to play off of.

10. a. Wrong. The narcissistic type has too much self-presentation, not too little.
    b. Right!
    c. Close, but no cigar. Schizoids avoid others, but because of lack of interest.
    d. No. Schizotypal personalities are characterized by bizarre behavior.

11. a. No. The antisocial personality is not characterized by self-doubt.
    b. No. This one is characterized by perfectionism.
    c. Incorrect. This one is characterized by emotional overreactions.
    d. Right!

12. a. No, this is the paranoid personality.
    b. Sorry, this is the borderline personality, if anything.
    c. Just the opposite—they tend to stay in their ruts at all costs.
    d. Correct!

13. a. Yes! You remembered the definition of a personality disorder!
    b. No, just the opposite.
    c. Again, just the opposite.
    d. Once more, the characteristics are reversed.

14. a. Correct! This agrees with statistics reported in the text.
    b. Less likely. In fact, with avoidant personality disorder, Karen might not be married at all.
    c. Sorry. Once again, with schizoid disorder, Karen probably would not have a husband.
    d. Not impossible, but the question asks what is most likely, and that is dependency.

15. a. No, this is purposeless shoplifting.
    b. You got it!
    c. No, this is hair pulling.
    d. No, the behavior isn't the issue with the *DSM*, it's the motive behind it.

16. a. No. This is a little difficult because the answer involves more than one page in the text.
    b. Half right, but dependent isn't it.
    c. Yes!
    d. Sorry, I guess this is another one you either know or you don't.

17. a. No. The key word here is "punished." That's a learning process, isn't it? Hmmm.
    b. Wrong. These people would be looking at organic issues, not environmental ones.
    c. Closer, but no. Remember the focus is on Marian's personal life history.
    d. Right!

18. a. No, we all have dysfunctional schemas at times.
    b. Sorry. Unhelpful is just another way of saying dysfunctional.
    c. Once again, unrealistic schemas aren't that rare. I've got some, and so do you.
    d. Correct!

19. a. Yes!
    b. No. That would be extreme and destructive to the whole mental health profession.
    c. No. This would be silly, because gender and race are legitimate factors in determining behavior.
    d. It's a nice thought, but in reality even scientists aren't as unbiased as we would like.

20. a. Correct!
    b. Sorry. You have to know the axes of the *DSM* and the meaning of "characterological."
    c. Just the other way around.
    d. No. In many cases, personality disorders precede the other problems.

21. a. Correct!
    b. No, a key characteristic for this one is splitting.
    c. No, a key characteristic for this one is gradiosity.
    d. No, a key characteristic for this one is odd or eccentric apperance or behavior.

22. a. No, they are not usually "unstable."
    b. No, not correct.
    c. Correct!
    d. No, this is necessarily so.

23.   a.   No, this characteristic may be seen in bipolar.
        b.   Correct!
        c.   No, this is usually seen in borderline personality disorder.
        d.   No, this is usually seen in antisocial personality disorder.

24.   a.   No, review personality disorders.
        b.   No.
        c.   Correct!
        d.   No, incorrect.

25.   a.   No. Actually, women account for three-quarters of those diagnosed.
        b.   No. Men outnumber women three to one.
        c.   Correct!
        d.   Incorrect. More women than men are diagnosed with histrionic personality disorder.

CHAPTER 12
SUBSTANCE-USE DISORDERS

LEARNING OBJECTIVES

By the time you have finished studying this chapter, you should be able to do the following:

1. Define psychoactive drugs, and list seven criteria used by *DSM-IV-TR* to diagnose substance dependence and four criteria used to diagnose substance abuse. (313–314)

2. Describe the effects of various amounts of alcohol on the individual, and summarize the personal and social costs of alcohol dependence. (315–318)

3. Describe the development of alcohol dependence, and summarize data on alcohol dependence and abuse according to gender, race, ethnicity, religion, and age. (318–321)

4. Summarize efforts to treat alcohol dependence, making reference to multimodel treatments, support groups, inpatient and outpatient services, and relapse prevention. (322–326)

5. Describe the physical and psychological effects of nicotine, summarize the major theories of nicotine dependence, and describe legal, social, and treatment-based approaches to reducing nicotine dependence. (326–329)

6. Describe the effects of depressant drugs, and distinguish among opiates, barbiturates, tranquilizers, and nonbarbiturate sedatives. (329–332)

7. Describe the effects of stimulant drugs, and distinguish among amphetamines and the various forms of cocaine. (333–335)

8. Describe the effects of hallucinogenic drugs, and summarize current information on the effects and possible risks associated with the use of marijuana and hashish. (335–340)

9. Summarize the psychodynamic view of substance dependence, and relate it to the issue of why certain high-risk groups are likely to use drugs. (340–341)

10. Describe tension-reduction and positive reinforcement explanations of substance dependence proposed by the behavioral perspective, and trace the evolution of behavioral treatment programs for substance dependence. (341–342)

11. Explain the use of couple and family therapies in treating substance dependence from the family systems perspective. (342–343)

12. Summarize the role of expectancies in the cognitive view of substance dependence, and describe three factors thought to be important in cognitive-behavioral attempts to prevent relapse after treatment. (343–345)

13. Summarize data suggesting genetic and biochemical predispositions for substance dependence, making reference to Type 1 and Type 2 alcoholism, endorphins, and dopamine, and describe the use of drugs in the treatment of substance dependence. (345–349)

14. Summarize the social-environmental causes of substance dependence as seen from the sociocultural perspective, and define and give examples of harm reduction. (349–352)

KEY TERMS

The following terms are in bold print in your text and are important to your understanding of the chapter. Look them up in the text and write down their definitions.

addiction (313)   amphetamines (333)

barbiturates (332)
blood alcohol level (315)
cocaine (334)
crack cocaine (334)
depressant (330)
detoxification (322)
endorphins (347)
hallucinogens (335)
hashish (336)
heroin (331)
LSD (lysergic acid diethylamide) (335)
marijuana (336)
matching (325)
MDMA ("Ecstasy") (336)
methadone (331)

morphine (330)
motivational interviewing (324)
opiates (330)
opium (330)
PCP (phencyclidine) (336)
psychoactive drug (312)
relapse prevention (325)
stimulants (333)
substance abuse (314)
substance dependence (314)
synergistic effect (332)
tolerance (314)
tranquilizers (332)
withdrawal (314)

IMPORTANT NAMES

Identify the following persons and their major contributions to abnormal psychology as discussed in this chapter.

Albert Hoffman (335)   Stanley Schachter (328)

GUIDED SELF-STUDY

The Nature of Substance Dependence and Abuse

1. Psychoactive substances are those that alter one's _____ state.

2. In the past, definitions of drug dependence were divided into two categories: (a)_____ and

    (b)_____. They are no longer separate. In *DSM-IV-TR*, they now form one category called

    psychoactive (c)_____ _____.

3. Fill in the seven *DSM-IV-TR* criteria for substance dependence. Here are the missing terms:

    abandonment   *preoccupation*   *withdrawal*
    control   *tolerance*
    drug-related   *unintentional*

    a. _____ with the drug

    b. _____ overuse

    c. _____ is developed

    d. _____ symptoms when use of the substance is decreased or stopped

    e. Persistent desire or efforts to _____ drug use

    f. _____ of social, occupational, or recreational activities

    g. Continued use despite _____ problems

4. How many of these criteria must be met to allow the diagnosis of psychoactive substance dependence?

5. If an individual does not meet the criteria to be diagnosed with substance dependence, yet "obviously" has a

drug-related problem, the diagnosis can be substance (a)_____. The text lists four criteria in

connection with this: failure to take care of major role (b)_____; creates physically (c)_____

situations; drug-related (d)_____ problems; drug-related social or (e)_____ problems.

Alcohol Dependence

6. Alcohol is a depressant; that means it (a)_____ brain activity, starting at the (b)_____ centers first and then moving downward.

   (c) If it is a depressant, why do some people feel more "up" at a party after a drink?

7.   a. At what blood alcohol level will mood and social behavior be affected?

    b. What is the blood alcohol level at which a person is presently considered to be "intoxicated" in most states? (Some states now have even lower limits.)

8. About how much alcohol would it take to raise your blood alcohol to 0.10%? (Look up your statistic in Table 12.1.)

9. To determine the answer to the previous question you had to look on the chart, which considers your body

(a)_____ and your (b)_____. Your weight determines how much (c)_____ your

body has in which to distribute the alcohol. Your sex must be considered because females have less

(d)_____ per pound of body weight in which to dilute the alcohol.

10. What does Table 12.2 (page 316) indicate could be the outcome for the "winner" in an alcohol chug-a-lug (drinking) contest, if his/her blood alcohol level gets to 0.35 or 0.40%?

11. Beyond the chemical depression of cortical tissues, what else influences how the person will behave when consuming alcohol?

12. Do you know the dimensions of the alcohol problems in the United States? First, give your best estimate on each of the following statistics. Then look up the correct statistic to see how close your estimate was.

      Your guess   Correct data

  a.   _____   _____   Total cost of alcohol-related auto accidents

  b.   _____   _____   1998 alcohol-related problems cost the Amercan economy

13. Rank the three major areas of economic loss caused by alcohol: (a = most costly to c = least costly)

  _____   Motor vehicle accidents

  _____   Health problems

  _____   Decreased work productivity

14. What are some of the physiological effects of the habitual overuse of alcohol?

15. Babies born to mothers who drank during pregnancy may have a disorder called (a)_____

    _____ _____. Characteristics of this disorder are (b)_____ retardation,

    (c)_____ development, and bodily (d)_____

16. While individuals may follow different paths toward the development of an alcohol dependency, what did Jellinek's famous study on the development of alcoholism indicate was the typical time span from the beginning of heavy drinking to complete defeat?

17. There are people who have serious problems with alcohol, yet they do not drink every day. This pattern of

    drinking is called (a)_____ drinking. Individuals can stay sober for periods of time, then some event

    will trigger an alcoholic binge or (b)_____.

18. What other behavioral disorder seems to follow the same sequence found in alcoholics?

19. There are predictable differences in behaviors between male and female alcoholics.

    a. Women usually begin drinking _____ in their lives.
    b. Women are more likely to cite a _____ event as the start of their drinking problems.
    c. Women are more likely to be associated with a problem-drinking _____ or lover.
    d. Socially, women are more likely to drink _____ or with someone _____ to them.
    e. Women are more likely to have a _____ pattern, combining other drugs with alcohol.

20. In each of the following categories, circle the factor that produces the *highest* risk for alcohol use.

    a. Education level: *low / moderate / high*
    b. Economic level: *low / moderate / high*
    c. Ethnic group: *Latino / Native American / Irish*
    d. Gender: *men / women*

21. Besides religious and cultural affiliations, what is the major predictor of alcohol consumption among adolescents?

22. Here are the terms for the multimodal treatment approach:

    detoxification   *nausea*   *variety*
    fluids   *relaxation*   *withdrawal*
    marital   *support*

    Multimodal treatment uses a (a)_____ of therapeutic approaches. First, (b)_____ helps the

    individual withdraw from physical dependency on alcohol. Medication is used as needed to ease the

    symptoms of (c)_____. There is also an emphasis on returning the person to physical

    health—vitamins and plenty of (d)_____. Once "detox" is complete, treatment begins to address

    the many problem areas in the alcoholic's life: occupational therapy, family and (e)_____ therapy, and (f)_____ techniques that directly address bodily stress. Involvement in a peer (g)_____ network such as Alcoholics Anonymous gives the individual opportunities to develop relationships based on reality instead of denial. In addition, Antabuse may help the person's will power against impulsive drinking because (h)_____ occurs if alcohol is consumed within two days after taking Antabuse.

Nicotine Dependence

23. Here are the terms for reviewing nicotine dependence:

addiction	*death*	*paradoxical*
aggressive	*elevate*	*reinforcement*
C	*heart*	*secondhand*
calming	*increasing*	*stimulant*
cancer	*mild*	*stress*
chewing	*mouth*	*withdrawal*

Nicotine has a seemingly contradictory effect on the body, called an (a)_____ effect. Not only does nicotine elevate blood pressure and heart rate, which is the effect of a (b)_____ drug, but at the same time it has a (c)_____ effect. This effect is not just in the minds of smokers; rats became less (d)_____ when injected with nicotine. However, Schachter found that nicotine does not seem to (e)_____ the mood of a smoker; but once a nicotine level in the blood is established, a drop in that nicotine level does lead to symptoms of (f)_____. This research finding contradicts the hypothesis that nicotine dependence is perpetuated by a continuing positive (g)_____ effect for the smoker. Circumstances such as increased vitamin (h)_____ intake or exposure to (i)_____, both of which lower blood nicotine levels, lead to increased smoking. This blood-nicotine-level research indicates at least some degree of (j)_____. However, smokers do not develop tolerance, in which an evers (k)_____ level of nicotine is required to maintain the same level of effect. Withdrawal symptoms are said to be (l)_____ compared to the physical withdrawal of alcohol. The distinct drawback associated with nicotine use is the possibility of eventual (m)_____. Cigarette smoking is associated with higher death rates from (n)_____, (o)_____ disease, and other illnesses. Recent evidence has also revealed that inhaling (p)_____ smoke (from someone else's cigarette) is harmful to one's health. Smokeless tobacco, such as snuff and (q)_____ tobacco, is associated with cancer of the throat and (r)_____.

24. Use these terms in the following blanks.

coping   *motivation*   *support*
extrinsic   *number*
intrinsic   *efficacy*

Here are six factors that affect the likelihood of success in being able to stop smoking: The individual's

(a)_____ level; whether the motivation is (b)_____ (doing it for yourself) or

(c)_____ (doing it to please someone else); the self-(d)_____ level that the person

experiences; that is, does the person believe he/she can successfully stop smoking; how many alternative

(e)_____ mechanisms the person has as resources; (f)_____ by compliments and

encouragement from others; (g)_____ of smokers in one's social environment.

Other Psychoactive Drugs

25. Here are the categories of drugs discussed in this chapter under "Other Psychoactive Drugs." Match each one to its effects: *depressants, hallucinogens, marijuana/hashish,* and *stimulants*

   a. _____ "Downers"—decrease brain activity

   b. _____ "Uppers"—increase brain activity

   c. _____ Cause distortions in sensory processes

   d. _____ Euphoria, passivity, intensified sensory perceptions

26. List three physiological effects common to all depressant drugs.

   a. _____ develops.

   b. _____ symptoms occur.

   c. _____ functions in vital organs, such as respiration; death can result.

27. The _____ effect in depressant drugs is the cumulative potentiating effect (combined multiplied effect) seen as drugs interact with each other in the body:

   1 drug + 1 drug = more than the 2 drugs just added together

   For example, alcohol to help you swallow your barbiturate sleeping med could give you four times the effect of either the alcohol or barbiturate alone; you could end up permanently "asleep."

28. When using tranquilizers and nonbarbiturate sedatives, about how long will it be before the individual develops tolerance and the dosage needs to be increased to obtain the same effect?

   a. two days

   b. two weeks

   c. two months

   d. two years

29. Assign the probable order (1–7) to the following sequence for drug-induced insomnia.

_____ Habitual use of sleeping aid

_____ Higher dose of medication required to achieve sleep

_____ Person takes sleeping aid to avoid bad dreams

_____ Person tries to stop the medication

_____ Problem with disrupted, fitful sleep

_____ REM rebound occurs filled with unpleasant dreams and nightmares

_____ Use of sleeping aid medication begins

30. Identify to which category of drugs (*depressant, stimulant,* or *hallucinogen*) each of the following substances belongs.

Amphetamines: Tranquilizers:
Alcohol: Caffeine:
Opiates: Cocaine:
LSD: Barbiturates:

31. List the source of each of the following drugs.

Opiates: Marijuana:
Nicotine: Hashish:
Caffeine: MDMA
Cocaine:

32. Which drug is

a. America's most common form of drug dependence?

b. America's most widely used psychoactive drug?

c. America's most popular illicit drug?

d. America's most widely used illegal narcotic?

e. America's "club drug" known as "Ecstasy."

33. Amphetamine abuse creates symptoms that resemble those of another serious mental disturbance. What is it?

34. Circle the active ingredient in marijuana and hashish.

CHT   DLS   HCT   LSD   SLD   TCH   THC

35. The two consistent physiological effects caused by marijuana and hashish use are (a)_____ heart rate and (b)_____ of the whites of the eyes.

36. What are four controversial effects from long-term use of marijuana?

a. Reduction of _____ in males, but not necessarily a change in sex drive

b. Possible suppression of the _____ system, but no clear clinical effect

c. Carcinogenic effect of marijuana smoke on the _____

d. Changes in _____, but evidence is incomplete

Substance Dependence: Theory and Therapy

37. What does the word "homeostasis" mean in the sense that psychodynamic theorists use it in connection with drug abuse?

38. This use of drugs to maintain homeostasis is sometimes referred to as

    a. self-regulation.

    b. transference neurosis.

    c. self-medication.

    d. self-instructional training.

39. Behaviorists originally explained alcohol abuse as a learned method of anxiety relief. This is explained in the

    (a)_____ _____ model. More recently, behaviorists have shifted from a focus on avoidance,

    or (b)_____ reinforcement, toward the (c)_____ reinforcing qualities produced with the

    release of certain brain chemicals, such as (d)_____ and norepinephrine, along with the body's

    natural painkillers, the (e)_____.

40. Here are the terms for the behavioral perspective on alcoholism:

aversion	*problem-solving*	*social*
elicit	*respondently*	*stress*
nausea	*shock*	*suppress*

    Behavior therapies initially centered on (a)_____ therapy, which involves the individual being

    (b)_____ conditioned by pairing an aversive stimulus such as (c)_____ or electric

    (d)_____ with alcohol. Current behavioral treatment programs go beyond aversion therapy. Even

    though aversion therapy works to (e)_____ drinking, it does not deal with all the stimuli that

    strongly (f)_____ drinking behaviors. Behavioral programs for alcoholism now teach

    (g)_____ skills and (h)_____-_____ skills to help cope with the difficulties of life.

    Relaxation techniques are taught to directly address bodily (i)_____ reactions. Alcoholics are taught

    to recognize cues and situations that lead to drinking and to practice dealing with these situations without

    drinking.

41. Answer *true* or *false* to the following statements on the interpersonal perspective on substance dependence.

    _____ a. Behavioral couple therapy reduces relationship problems where alcohol is involved.

    _____ b. Approximately 75% of wife-beaters meet the criteria for alcohol dependence.

    _____ c. Gains from couple therapy seem more permanent than gains from other treatments.

    _____ d. About 60 to 80% of drug-dependent people live with or are in close touch with their parents.

    _____ e. "Multi-system" treatment involves not just the family but all groups and institutions in contact with a drug-dependent person.

42. What are the positive expectancies that the cognitive perspective sees as incentives for drinking alcohol?

43. What are the long-term problems with this positive-expectancy theory of drinking?

44. Here are the terms for cognitive treatment methods: *defeatist, planned, recovery, relapse, restructuring, thinking,* and *total*.

Therapy from the cognitive view is always based on changing thinking habits. In addition to this cognitive

(a)_____, the cognitive therapists address (b)_____ prevention in an aggressive manner.

They teach how to deal with inevitable slip-ups in the (c)_____ process and even practice

(d)_____ relapses. The goal of this approach is still focused on the (e)_____ process. They

do not want a little slip-up to cause (f)_____ thinking and lead the person to have a

(g)_____ relapse.

45. Categorize each of the following as one of three the possible factors that could lead to drug relapse: *intrapersonal, environmental,* or *physiological*.

a. Angry at spouse:

b. Withdrawal cravings from your last binge:

c. Fourth of July beer and bratwurst celebration:

d. Feelings of inadequacy:

e. Having "just one" beer in your system:

f. A lot of physical tension:

g. Spouse out of town:

46. Here are the terms for the neuroscience perspective for alcoholism:

adolescence	genetic	quiet
adulthood	low	sexes
autonomic	nine	son
driving	ninety	stressor
father	personality	two

Biological research has demonstrated that a susceptibility to alcoholism has a(n) (a)_____ component. The actual physiological component may be in the (b)_____ nervous system. This evidence also suggests that there are (c)_____ different patterns for this inheritance of a predisposition to alcohol dependence. Type 1 generally begins in (d)_____ and affects both (e)_____ following diathesis-stress predictors; that is, the person is likely to succumb to alcoholism after exposure to a major (f)_____. Type 1 seems to be more common in (g)_____-income level groups and among rather (h)_____-living people. Type 2 generally begins in (i)_____, and it follows a sex-linked pattern that goes from (j)_____ to (k)_____. The sons that inherit this pattern are at (l)_____% risk. In other words, if the father fits this pattern, the son has (m)_____ out of ten chances to also be alcohol dependent if he drinks. There is a(n) (n)_____ pattern also associated with Type 2 alcohol dependence involving traits such as impulsiveness, aggression, risk-taking, brawling, reckless (o)_____, and other criminal behavior.

47. Two theories of brain chemistry are proposed to try to explain drug dependence.

   a. Opiates decrease the production of _____, the body's natural pain-killer.

   b. This results in a body more sensitive to discomfort when opiate use is stopped, thus explaining the occurrence of _____ symptoms.

   c. Most drugs of abuse increase production of _____, which appears to be highly reinforcing.

48. The _____ perspective suggests that socioeconomic factors are a significant force in determining alcoholism problems, because different rates of alcoholism are seen in different social groups.

49. An approach to substance dependence emphasized by the sociocultural perspective is harm reduction. This approach is based on the idea that if society is unwilling to establish policies that are effective in eliminating actual drug (a)_____, we can at least engage in actions that minimize the (b)_____ that drug dependency does to society. A prime example of such an attempt is (c)_____-exchange programs, designed to reduce the spread of the (d)_____ virus among drug users.

50. Contaminated needles spread about (a)_____ of all new AIDS cases nationwide. Drug use accounts for (b)_____ of new cases of HIV among women, and more than (c)_____ of those among children, who as noted, contract it from their mothers' womb.

HELPFUL HINTS

1. Death is definitely one possible outcome of alcohol withdrawal if medical support therapies are not available. As noted in the text, death is also an outcome for habitual overuse of alcohol and drug dependence. Perhaps no one has ever died from nicotine withdrawal, but the person in withdrawal is sometimes irritable enough to provoke death threats from friends and coworkers.

2. The explanation of Schachter's findings in behavioral terms is that smoking is maintained by a negative reinforcer. The smoker smokes to escape or to avoid the unpleasant feeling of low blood nicotine level.

PRACTICE TEST

Use the following test questions to check your knowledge of the material in this chapter. You may want to write the answers on a separate sheet of paper so you can take the test more than once.

1. Which of the following is true concerning substance use, abuse, and dependence?
    a. *DSM-IV-TR* now distinguishes between physical addiction and psychological dependence.
    b. The nature of the drug, for the most part, determines the diagnostic category of the patient.
    c. There are several drugs for which ANY use is automatically considered abuse.
    d. Substance use *becomes* abuse or dependence only when the pattern of use causes problems for the person.

2. Recurrent failure to fulfill major obligations, drug-related legal problems, recurrent drug use in dangerous situations, and continued use despite negative social effects of drug use are signs of
    a. substance abuse.
    b. addiction.
    c. substance dependence.
    d. compulsion.

3. Brenda and Bob go out for drinks. They both weigh about 140 pounds. Each has six drinks in one hour on an empty stomach. It can be expected that
    a. Brenda and Bob will be equally intoxicated.
    b. Bob will be more intoxicated than Brenda.
    c. neither Brenda nor Bob will be intoxicated.
    d. Bob will be less intoxicated than Brenda.

4. In developing alcohol dependence, which of the following applies more to females?
    a. Begins drinking earlier, solitary drinker, drinks longer before treatment
    b. Starts drinking later, solitary drinker, shorter drinking time before treatment
    c. Starts drinking later, solitary drinker, unlikely to use alcohol with other drugs
    d. Social drinker, likely to use alcohol with other drugs, drinks to deal with stress

5. Four young men graduate from high school together. Which of them runs the highest risk of abusing alcohol in the next few years?
    a. Wally, who goes to work in the family business in his home town
    b. Pete, who enters religious studies at a small seminary
    c. Tim, who marries his high school girlfriend and goes to night school for a technical degree
    d. John, who enrolls at the university and joins a fraternity

6. Which of the following best describes recent trends in the treatment of alcohol dependence?
    a. Increasing number of programs, more outpatient than inpatient, more brief than long-term
    b. Increasing number of programs, more inpatient than outpatient, more brief than long-term
    c. Stable number of programs, more inpatient than outpatient, more long-term than brief
    d. Decreasing number of programs, more outpatient than inpatient, more long-term than brief

7. Which of the following is true of smokeless tobacco products?
   a. They are a safe, nicotine-free alternative to smoking.
   b. While not nicotine-free, they are medically safe when used by adults.
   c. They are associated with the occurrence of throat and mouth cancer.
   d. There is no medical evidence on their safety one way or the other at this time.

8. Which of the following is an accurate statement concerning the history of drug use in the United States?
   a. For college students, drug use declined during the 1980s but increased again around 1990.
   b. At the beginning of the twentieth century, heroin and morphine were unknown in this country.
   c. When alcohol became illegal in the early part of this century, opiates became legal.
   d. There has been a steady increase in drug use among college students from 1970 until now.

9. If you were outlining this chapter, which of the following substances would constitute a major heading under which the rest would be subcategorized?
   a. methadone
   b. heroin
   c. opium
   d. morphine

10. When drug combinations show a "synergistic" effect, it means that they
    a. cancel each other out.
    b. have opposite effects that make nervous system response unpredictable.
    c. multiply their effects and produce a very strong reaction.
    d. require larger and larger doses to get the same effect.

11. John is exhibiting symptoms of paranoid schizophrenia, and it is suspected that he has been abusing drugs. If John is not really a schizophrenic, which drug is he likely using?
    a. amphetamines
    b. one of the opiates
    c. cocaine
    d. barbiturates

12. PCP use has declined since the late 1970s because
    a. it has become prohibitively expensive for street use.
    b. it is not as effective as LSD.
    c. law enforcement agencies have all but wiped out its availability.
    d. it produces such dangerous effects that even hard-core drug users avoid it.

13. Which of the following is true?
    a. Marijuana is medically useful in treating glaucoma and the side effects of cancer drugs.
    b. The legal availability of drugs is rationally based on their usefulness or dangerousness.
    c. The federal government approves the medicinal use of marijuana, but no states have yet done so.
    d. All of the above are true.

14. Jacques feels himself under a lot of pressure to excel as a member of his high school wrestling team. Which class of drugs is he most likely to use to improve his chances of success?
    a. Anabolic steroids to improve his physical strength and stamina
    b. Non-barbiturate sedatives to calm his nerves and let him concentrate
    c. Amphetamines to help him lose weight and be more trim
    d. Endorphins to enable him to withstand greater punishment in training

15. Current behavioral treatment programs for alcoholism put emphasis on

    a. aversion conditioning that pairs alcohol with nausea.
    b. both ways of avoiding drinking and coping with stress.
    c. reducing unrealistic expectations for what alcohol can provide.
    d. improving self-awareness of guilt and power issues.

16. Henggeler and his associates have pioneered a home-based family treatment program for substance-abusing teens, that involves not only the family but all the other institutions that touch the teen's life. This approach is called

    a. multi-system treatment.
    b. Project Match.
    c. the abstinence violation effect (AVE).
    d. FRAMES.

17. Estimates of relapse rates for clients undergoing substance-dependence treatments average around

    a. 0 to 10%.
    b. 10 to 50%.
    c. 50 to 90%.
    d. 90 to 100%.

18. Cognitive theorists have identified three categories of factors that are related to relapse. Which of the following is NOT one of these three?

    a. individual
    b. interactional
    c. environmental
    d. physiological

19. Malcolm is what some researchers would call a Type 2 alcohol dependent. It is likely that Malcolm

    a. has suffered from child abuse and a neglectful mother.
    b. began drinking heavily as an aggressive and rebellious adolescent.
    c. is a shy, quiet-living person.
    d. has only a weak genetic vulnerability coupled with severe environmental stress.

20. The concept of *harm reduction* deals with

    a. stricter law enforcement to keep drug users and dealers out of drug-free communities.
    b. incarcerating drug-dependent individuals to dry up the market for illegal drugs.
    c. trying to make drug dependency less harmful to people if it cannot be eliminated entirely.
    d. creating ghettos to keep drug-dependent people segregated from non-users.

ANSWERS

Guided Self-Study (p. 182)

1. psychological (313)

2. a. psychological
    b. physiological
    c. substance dependence (313)

3. a. preoccupation   e. control
    b. unintentional   f. abandonment
    c. tolerance   g. drug-related (314)
    d. withdrawal

4. any three (314)

5. a. abuse
    b. responsibilities
    c. dangerous
    d. legal
    e. interpersonal (314)

6. a. slows
    b. higher
    c. The first things that are depressed are a person's (cortical) inhibitions. (316)

7. a. 0.05
    b. 0.10% (316)

8. Your own findings from Table 12.1 (316)

9. a. weight
    b. sex
    c. mass
    d. fluid (316)

10. death—Yes, it has happened. (316)

11. Aside from experiencing the brain's lowered activity level, the person will play out the expectations he/she has about what the alcohol is "supposed" to do to behavior. (317)

12. a. $45 billion (*not m*illion) (315)
    b. $185 billion (315)

13. a. Decreased work productivity
    b. Health problems
    c. Motor vehicle accidents (315)

14. Stomach ulcers, hypertension, heart failure, cancer, cirrhosis of the liver, brain damage, and malnutrition, leading to Korsakoff's psychosis (317)

15. a. fetal alcohol syndrome
    b. mental
    c. delayed
    d. malformations

16. twelve to eighteen years (318)

17. a. spree
    b. bender (318)

18. compulsive gambling (319)

19. a. later
    b. stressful
    c. spouse
    d. alone, close
    e. polydrug (319)

20. a. high education level
    b. high socioeconomic level
    c. native American
    d. men (319–321)

21. peer-group behavior (320)

22. a. variety   e. marital
    b. detoxification   f. relaxation
    c. withdrawal   g. support
    d. fluids   h. nausea (323)

23. a. paradoxical
    b. stimulant
    c. calming
    d. aggressive
    e. elevate
    f. withdrawal
    g. reinforcement
    h. C
    i. stress

    j. addiction
    k. increasing
    l. mild
    m. death
    n. cancer
    o. heart
    p. secondhand
    q. chewing
    r. mouth (326–329)
    e. coping
    f. support
    g. number (326–329)

24. a. motivation
    b. intrinsic
    c. extrinsic
    d. efficacy

25. a. depressants (330)
    b. stimulants (333)
    c. hallucinogens (335)
    d. marijuana/hashish (336)

26. a. Tolerance
    b. Withdrawal
    c. Lowered or decreased (330)

27. synergistic (332)

28. "b" (3323)

29. 7, 3, 6, 4, 1, 5, and 2 (333)

30. Amphetamines—stimulant (315)   Tranquilizers—depressant (332)
    Alcohol—depressant (330)   Caffeine—stimulant (333)
    Opiates—depressant (330)   Cocaine—stimulant (333)
    LSD—hallucinogen (335)   Barbiturates—depressant (332)

31. Opiates—opium (from the opium poppy plant), opium derivatives, and synthetic drugs designed to copy the effects of opium (330)
    Nicotine—tobacco (326)
    Caffeine—found in coffee, tea, cola drinks, cocoa, and chocolate (333)
    Cocaine—from the coca plant (334)
    Marijuana—leaves of the cannabis plant (336)
    Hashish—resin from the cannabis plant (336)
    MDMA—is an illegal synthetic drug (336)

32. a. nicotine (326)
    b. alcohol (314)
    c. marijuana (336)
    d. heroin (331)
    e. MDMA (336)

33. paranoid schizophrenia (333)

34. THC, which stands for delta-9, tetrahydrocannabinol (337)

35. a. accelerated
    b. reddening (337)

36. a. testosterone
    b. immune
    c. lungs
    d. personality (337–338)

37. It refers to a balancing act, a process by which drugs are used to counteract painful emotional states and restore emotional equilibrium. (340)

38. "c" (340)

39. a. tension-reduction
    b. negative
    c. positive
    d. dopamine
    e. endorphins (341)

40. a. aversion
    b. respondently
    c. nausea
    d. shock
    e. suppress
    f. elicit
    g. social
    h. problem-solving
    i. stress (341)

41. a, b, d, and e are true; c is false. (342)

42. Expectancies that alcohol will enhance social and physical pleasure, enhance sexual performance, increase social power, aggressiveness, and assertiveness, and that it will reduce tension (343)

43. This might work for the beginning drinker, but a confirmed drinker ought to know that these expectancies are not being met. (343)

44. a. restructuring
    b. relapse
    c. recovery
    d. planned
    e. thinking
    f. defeatist
    g. total (343)

45. a. intrapersonal
    b. physiological
    c. environmental
    d. intrapersonal
    e. physiological
    f. physiological
    g. environmental (344)

46. a. genetic
    b. autonomic
    c. two
    d. adulthood
    e. sexes
    f. stressor
    g. low
    h. quiet
    i. adolescence
    j. father
    k. son
    l. ninety
    m. nine
    n. personality
    o. driving (345–349)

47. a. endorphins
    b. withdrawal
    c. dopamine (345–349)

48. sociocultural (349)

49. a. dependence
    b. harm
    c. needle
    d. HIV (351)

50. a. one-third (352)
    b. two-thirds
    c. half

Practice Test (p. 191)

1. a. No, it used to do that, but it doesn't now.
   b. Sorry, it's not the drug but what you do with it that counts.
   c. Incorrect. Remember *DSM* diagnoses on the basis of behavior.
   d. Correct!

2. a. Yes!
   b. No. This term is no longer current in the diagnostic literature.
   c. No, substance dependence is more serious than this.
   d. In a loose sense, I suppose, but this is not a term used in connection with drugs.

3. a. Incorrect. Gender has to be taken into account here.
   b. No. Body fat and fluid proportions between the sexes is important.
   c. Unfortunately, they will both be intoxicated.
   d. Right! Males have proportionately more body fluids to dilute the alcohol.

4. a. No. These are just details you have to know. Look on page 302 in the text.
   b. Right!
   c. Incorrect. Women are more likely to be polydrug users.
   d. Sorry, one out of three this time.

5. a. Sorry, a stable situation like this does not present much risk.
   b. No. Religious commitment tends to vary inversely with alcohol abuse.
   c. Incorrect. This is not as risky an environment as one of your other choices.
   d. You got it!

6. a. Right!
   b. Two out of three, but try again.
   c. No. Everything is wrong with this choice.
   d. This time one of the three is correct. See page 307 in the text.

7. a. Wrong on both counts.
   b. Half right, but the dangerous half is incorrect.
   c. Correct!
   d. Sorry, there is a lot of evidence on this.

8. a. Yes!
   b. No, in fact, they were commonly used and sold over the counter.
   c. No, they were both illegal at that time.
   d. Too pessimistic, but not entirely wrong.

9. a. No. In fact this would probably be the last one on the list, since it is synthetic.
   b. Sorry. This is a derivative of one of the others.
   c. Right!
   d. Incorrect. This is a derivative of the one we want here.

10. a. Unfortunately, no. There is still an effect, but what kind?
    b. No. This vaguely reminds me of something called "reverse tolerance," but it is not a drug interaction effect, and the book does not go into it.
    c. Right!
    d. No, this is called the tolerance effect.

11. a. Right!
    b. No. These tend to lower activity level and decrease worries and cares.
    c. Sometimes, but there is a better choice.
    d. Incorrect. Like the opiates, they tend to lower activity and decrease worries.

12. a. No, expense is not the big issue.
    b. If anything, it produces a more dramatic reaction.
    c. Sorry, but law enforcement is not that effective with any drug.
    d. Correct!

13. a. Yes!
    b. Unfortunately, it is often based on economic and political concerns first.
    c. No, just the other way around; the federal government is blocking state initiatives.
    d. Incorrect.

14. a. Correct!
    b. No. These will calm him all right, to the point where he will be an ineffective wrestler.
    c. No. Strength-dependent athletes do not want to lose weight.
    d. No. Endorphins are naturally occurring brain chemicals similar to the opiates.

15. a. Sorry, this was an early emphasis that turned out to be insufficient.
    b. Right!
    c. No, this is a more cognitive approach.
    d. No, this would be a psychodynamic approach.

16. a. Correct!
    b. Sorry. This was a study in pairing people with the most effective treatment program.
    c. No. This is what happens when a drug user relapses.
    d. Incorrect. This is an acronym used in motivational interviews.

17. a. No. Way too low.
    b. Sorry. This would be excellent results, but unfortunately things aren't that good.
    c. Right!
    d. Too pessimistic.

18. a. No. This is one of the factors.
    b. Correct! Nothing like this is mentioned.
    c. Incorrect. This is one of the factors, a very important one.
    d. Incorrect. This is a factor that would include things like withdrawal symptoms.

19. a. No. He could have, of course, but for a Type 2 it would not make that much difference.
    b. Right!
    c. Just the opposite. This is more characteristic of Type 1.
    d. Just the opposite. The genetic component is far more important here.

20. a. No. Harm reduction is not a brute-force approach to prevention in the traditional sense.
    b. Sorry. This is advocated by some, but it is not what we mean by harm reduction.
    c. Right!
    d. Nobody serious about the drug issue proposes this.

CHAPTER 13
SEXUAL DYSFUNCTIONS, PARAPHILIAS, AND GENDER IDENTITY DISORDERS

LEARNING OBJECTIVES

By the time you have finished studying this chapter, you should be able to do the following:

1. Discuss the difficulties involved in defining normal and abnormal sexual behavior, using historical and cultural factors and the issue of homosexuality as examples. (356–358)

2. Define sexual dysfunction, and describe the dysfunctions grouped under each of three phases of the sexual response cycle. (358–361)

3. Describe two sexual pain disorders, and discuss the issues surrounding the diagnosis of sexual dysfunctions, distinguishing among lifelong, acquired, generalized, and situational dysfunctions. (362)

4. Summarize statistics on the distribution of sexual dysfunction by gender, education, ethnicity, and income. (363–364)

5. Explain the psychodynamic perspective on sexual dysfunction, and then describe behavioral and cognitive approaches that have largely displaced the psychodynamic viewpoint. (364–367)

6. Summarize multifaceted treatment of sexual dysfunction, making reference to the family systems approach and to Kaplan's theory involving immediate and remote causes. (367–369)

7. List and describe possible organic causes of sexual dysfunction, and describe treatments for dysfunction based on the neuroscience perspective. (369–370)

8. Define paraphilias according to *DSM-IV-TR,* define fetishism, transvestism, exhibitonism, and voyeurism, describe the persons likely to engage in each, and explain how each one presents problems for the client and/or interferes with the rights of others. (370–374)

9. Define sadism, masochism, frotteurism, pedophila, and incest, describe the persons likely to engage in each, and explain how each one presents problems for the client and/or interferes with the rights of others. (374–377)

10. Explain the psychodynamic perspective on the paraphilias, with special emphasis on the role of Oedipal fixation. (379–380)

11. Explain the behavioral and cognitive understandings of the paraphilias, and give examples of learning-based treatment strategies. (380–381)

12. Explain the neuroscience view of and treatment for the paraphilias. (381–383)

13. Define gender identity disorder, describe three patterns in which this disorder manifests itself, and give examples of treatment for gender identity disorder from the psychodynamic, behavioral, and neuroscience perspectives, including sex reassignment surgery. (383–386)

KEY TERMS

The following terms are in bold print in your text and are important to your understanding of the chapter. Look them up in the text and write down their definitions.

acquired dysfunction (362)

autogynephilia (373)

dyspareunia (362)

exhibitionism (371)

female orgasmic disorder (361)

female sexual arousal disorder (360)

fetishism (371)

frotteurism (371)

gender dysphoria (383)
gender identity disorders (GID) (383)
gender reassignment (383)
generalized dysfunction (362)
hypoactive sexual desire disorder (358)
incest (377)
lifelong dysfunction (362)
male erectile disorder (360)
male orgasmic disorder (361)
masochism (371)
paraphilias (371)
pedophilia (371)

premature ejaculation (362)
rape (371)
sadism (371)
sadomasochistic (375)
sexual aversion disorder (360)
sexual dysfunctions (358)
situational dysfunction (362)
spectator role (365)
transsexual (383)
transvestism (371)
vaginismus (362)
voyeurism (371)

IMPORTANT NAMES

Identify the following persons and their major contributions to abnormal psychology as discussed in this chapter.

Magnus Hirschfield (356)
Virginia Johnson (358)
Helen Singer Kaplan (361)
Alfred Kinsey (357)

Richard von Krafft-Ebing (356)
William Masters (358)
Leopold von Sacher-Masoch (375)
Marquis de Sade (375)

GUIDED SELF-STUDY

Defining Sexual Abnormality

1. In this chapter you will not be asked to note your own personal experiences to facilitate your memory for chapter information. What do you think is the explanation for this obvious change in approaching the chapter?

2. Fill in the following blanks to complete the three categories of sexual disorders.

    a. _____ Sexual disorder term meaning "doesn't work"

    b. _____ Sexual disorder term meaning "likes weird things"

    c. _____ _____ _____ Sexual disorder whereby you want to have your genitalia changed to that of the opposite sex

3. _____ Term meaning penile-vaginal intercourse

4. a. What is the name of the Irish island where people have as little sex as possible?

    b. What is the name of the Polynesian island where people past the age of puberty seem to have sexual interactions as their primary activities?

5. How you personally "characterize" these vastly different attitudes will depend on your own ideas about sex. Why the difference between these two societies' sexual practices?

6. a. Whose famous research report pointed out that traditionally accepted norms for sexual behavior in the United States were quite different from what people actually did?

    b. What is the name of the improved survey that found Americans to be more sexually conservative than the earlier survey led us to believe?

7. Here are some of the benefits of the current, more open approach to sexuality.

    a.   Increased flow of _____ about sex

    b.   Better _____ between partners on sexual matters

    c.   Less anxiety and _____ over harmless sexual practices

8. The down side of the new focus in sexuality is anxiety about one's sexual _____.

Sexual Dysfunction

9. Sexual dysfunction means either a disruption of the sexual response cycle or pain during intercourse. There is either pain or repeated failure in the sexual response cycle. Failure problems are grouped according to the part of the sexual response cycle in which they occur. Here are descriptions of the three phases of the sexual response cycle that Kaplan used to organize sexual dysfunctions. Give the name of each phase.

    a.   _____ The want-to

    b.   _____ Physiological responses of want-to

    c.   _____ Moving to completion on the want-to and the physiological arousal

10. Name the problems seen in the desire stage.

    a.   _____ _____ _____ _____ Lack of interest in sex

    b.   _____ _____ _____ Negative emotions about sex

11. Identify the specific nature of the dysfunction in each of the following arousal stage disorders:

    a.   Female sexual arousal disorder:

    b.   Male erectile disorder:

12. In the third and last stage, orgasm, the male problem is likely to be one of timing; the most common sexual dysfunction for men is what?

13. The female orgasm issue is more debated.

    a.   What was Freud's opinion about female orgasms? What kinds? What was the "normal," desirable one?

    b.   What is the current attitude on female orgasms, neurologically and psychologically?

14. Two sexual dysfunctions that are not categorized by phase of arousal are instead associated with pain. Identify the following two disorders:

    a.   _____ Either sex can experience it; it can be biogenic or psychogenic

    b.   _____ Involuntary vaginal contractions against penile penetration

15. Sexual dysfunction has two more elements, or descriptors. Complete the concepts:

    a.   First, there is lifelong dysfunction versus _____ dysfunction.

    b.   Second, there is _____ dysfunction versus situational dysfunction.

16. The term "sexual dysfunction" is applied *ONLY* to sexual problems that persist over time. Occasional, random episodes of sexual failure are normal. List at least five reasons that occasional, random episodes of sexual failure can happen.

   - ·   ·
   - ·   ·
   - ·

17. Why, when discussing sexual dysfunction, does a distinction need to be made between individuals who are fairly inexperienced sexually and those who have established regular patterns of sexual activity?

Psychodynamic Perspective

18. a. What is key to adult sexuality from a Freudian point of view?

   b. What is the current psychodynamic focus?

Behavioral Perspective

19. Identify the following concepts in connection with behaviorism.

   a. _____ One word that underlies all behaviorism

   b. _____ Type conditioning assumed to underlie sexual dysfunction

   c. _____ Term for the role one takes on when "watching" one's own sexual performance and anticipating failure

   d. _____ "Petting" exercise

   e. _____ Instruction in the direction opposite the desired goal

Cognitive Perspective

20. The focus of the cognitive perspective is always *thinking!* What thinking can cause problems in sexual functioning?

21. Beyond the first level of thinking listed in the previous question, what can a couple's mutual exploration of their mental processes produce?

22. Helen Singer Kaplan addressed the question of whether to treat the symptoms (obvious dysfunction) or to look for deep psychic causes. What is Kaplan's term for

   a. therapy that addresses dysfunction from a variety of different approaches.

   b. causes that behaviorists and cognitive therapists would want to address.

   c. causes that psychodynamic therapists would want to address.

   d. causes Kaplan would address first to see if they alone are causing the difficulties.

   e. the therapy used to address immediate causes.

23. Mark each of the following as an *immediate* or *remote* cause for sexual dysfunction, according to Kaplan.

a. _____ Deep-seated guilt

b. _____ Intrapsychic conflicts about infantile needs

c. _____ Lack of communication between partners

d. _____ Poor technique

e. _____ Marital conflict

f. _____ Overconcern about pleasing one's partner

g. _____ Performance anxiety

h. _____ Unresolved Oedipal struggles

Interpersonal Perspective

24. In interpersonal theory, an analysis of the relationship looks at the interlocking (a)_____ of each of

the partners. The therapist must discover what the secret (b)_____ are for each of the partners in each

of the areas of dysfunction. Since the dysfunctions do serve purposes, the couple will unconsciously

(c)_____ change. If the systems therapist tries to remove the dysfunctions without seeing that the

needs of each individual are met in a satisfactory manner, the couple will experience emotional chaos.

Neuroscience Perspective

25. From the neuroscience perspective, what is a primary question about sexual dysfunctions?

26. List five physical problems that can cause erectile dysfunction.

- •   •
- •   •
- •

27. List four physical problems that can cause female dyspareunia.

- •   •
- •   •

28. What are some more subtle organic problems that could be present in some cases of sexual dysfunction where there is no known physical cause?

29. What does NPT "stand for?" How does it help?

Paraphilias

30. List what brings sexual gratification in each of the following deviations.

    a. Fetishism:

    b. Transvestism:

    c. Exhibitionism:

    d. Voyeurism:

    e. Sadism:

    f. Masochism:

    g. Frotteurism:

    h. Pedophilia:

31. How are transvestites and transsexuals alike, and how are they different?

32. What is a common difficulty seen in men who are transvestites?

33. What are the two sex offenses most often reported to the police?

34. Typically, exhibitionists and voyeurs are not dangerous, *but* (a)_____% of child molesters started out as exhibitionists, (b)_____% of rapists began as exhibitionists, and (c)_____ to _____% of voyeurs go on to rape the women they covertly watch.

35. Here are the terms to complete the blanks about the typical exhibitionist:

    masculinity   *masturbation*   *puritanical*   *inadequacy*

    The typical exhibitionist is likely to be a shy, submissive, immature man who has very (a)_____ ideas about sex, particularly about (b)_____. He may experience feelings of social or sexual (c)_____ and have serious doubts about his (d)_____.

36. When dealing with an episode of exhibitionism, what are some other factors that may need to be considered as possible explanations?

37. What is the more realistic portrait of a pedophile instead of the mythological "dirty old man" from Somewhere Else? Circle the most common profile.

Age:	20	30	40	50	60	70

    Marital status: single / married / divorced

    Parental status: has children / has none

    Relation to victim: known / unknown to the victim

38. There are at least four possible reasons why a person becomes a pedophile:

   a. The person has arrested emotional development, so that the individual is more _____ relating to a child.

   b. The person is too _____ to establish adult sexual relationships, so turns to children as substitutes.

   c. Because of early sexual experience with other _____, the individual may have fixated on children and still experiences arousal with children.

   d. The perpetrator was molested as a child and now replays the scene as the adult in the control role to _____ the feelings of being the helpless victimized child.

39. Complete these five factors that contribute to the psychological damage done to a child by a molester.

   a. If begun at an _____ age

   b. If there are _____ episodes over time

   c. If _____ or _____ is involved

   d. If the molester is _____ to the child (particularly father or stepfather)

   e. If the child feels he/she _____ in any way

40. Identify the two distinct types of child molesters.

   a. _____ molesters have a more or less normal, heterosexual history and prefer adults but as a stress reaction impulsively molest a child and then feel disgust at their behavior.

   b. _____ molesters are not married, are attracted to children, particularly boys, use pedophilia as a planned, regular sexual outlet, and don't think their behavior is abnormal.

41. The typical incestuous father is likely to be a man who limits his extramarital sexual contact to his daughters; he is likely to be highly (a)_____ and devoutly attached to (b)_____ _____ doctrines. His relationship with his wife is (c)_____.

Perspectives on the Paraphilias

42. Identify the psychodynamic term for the following concepts:

   a. _____ Diffuse sexual preoccupations like that of a child

   b. _____ The pregenital stage where paraphilias are seen to have fixated

   c. _____ The anxiety that is seen as the major source of trouble

   d. _____ Disorder seen as a confusion of sexual and aggressive impulses

43. Identify the behavioral term for the following concepts:

   a. _____ The mechanism underlying all behaviorism

   b. _____ Conditioning pairs sexual response to an unconventional stimulus

   c. _____ Overdoing something until you don't want to do it anymore

   d. _____ Directing a deviant fantasy to the worst possible outcome

   e. _____ Being required to rehearse one's paraphilia in the therapist's office in front of the therapist and one's spouse

44. Identify the term from the cognitive perspective for the following concepts:

a. _____ Always the basis of behavior from a cognitive perspective

b. _____ Common attitude of sex offenders whereby victims are seen only as sources for gratification for the perpetrator instead of human beings with their own feelings

c. _____ Cognitive therapy that identifies deviant beliefs, challenges them, and replaces them with more adaptive beliefs

d. _____ Cognitive therapy to counteract objectification of victims by having offenders consider things from the victim's viewpoint

e. _____ Cognitive therapy whereby the therapist pretends to be the offender and the real offender takes the role of the authority figure arguing against a sexually aggressive belief system

45. Identify the following concepts from the biological perspective:

a. _____ Hormone reduced by castration and antiandrogen drugs

b. _____ Psychotropic medications that have proved effective in the treatment of paraphilias

c. _____ Technique to measure erection

46. Identify the following concepts for gender identity disorders:

a. _____ Term meaning unhappiness

b. _____ Native American role where men dress and act as women

c. _____ Person who wants to change his/her gender

d. _____ Men who become aroused while imagining themselves as women

e. _____ Process of changing one's gender

47. Complete the steps in the gender reassignment process.

a. _____ months of psychotherapy to consider gender options

b. _____ therapy to initiate physical changes

c. _____-_____ one-year test to see if living in the opposite gender is satisfactory

48. Identify the perspective for the explanations of gender identity disorders.

a. _____ Abnormality in the EEG, particularly temporal lobe

b. _____ "Blissful symbiosis" with opposite-sex parent

c. _____ Gender fixation resulting from reinforcement during a critical period

49. Over the past decade, considerable progress has been made in developing biological treatments for erectile disorder. List three techniques and medications currently used.

-
-
-

50. Discuss whether you think rape is as a result of a psychological disorder or our cultural emphasis on sex and violence.

HELPFUL HINTS

1. Students sometimes assume homosexuality is synomous with pedophilia. This is an incorrect assumption. Homosexuality is not a disorder. Research finds no justification for considering it as a pathological disorder, and it was completely removed from the *DSM* in 1986. Homosexuality and pedophilia are unrelated topics. Pedophiles may be heterosexual, homosexual, or bisexual. The pattern of pedophilia that is likely to be homosexual is preference molestation. The preference molester does prefer male children, and they average seven times as many victims as those who prefer girls.

2. For those of you who are uninformed on the subject, baby boys sometimes have erections; it's a perfectly normal autonomic nervous system arousal. It does not mean they are going to grow up to be "perverts." Little boys engaging in any exciting activity may experience some degree of erection.

PRACTICE TEST

Use the following test questions to check your knowledge of the material in this chapter. You may want to write the answers on a separate sheet of paper so you can take the test more than once.

1. What is the current status of homosexuality in the *DSM-IV-TR*?
   a. *DSM-IV-TR* makes no direct reference to homosexuality at all.
   b. *DSM-IV-TR* considers homosexuality to be a mental disorder worthy of treatment.
   c. *DSM-IV-TR* considers homosexuality a validation of the concept of polymorphous perversity.
   d. *DSM-IV*-TR concerns itself only with "ego-dystonic" homosexuality, that is, homosexuality not in keeping with the person's self-image.

2. A recent 1994 survey of sexual attitudes and practices in the United States found that
   a. 75 to 85% of married persons have cheated on their spouses.
   b. the prevalence of homosexuality is about 15% for men and 7.1% for women.
   c. masturbation is engaged in primarily by those who no other sexual outlets.
   d. the average age for loss of virginity has dropped by about half a year over the past several decades.

3. Which of the following is an orgasmic disorder?
   a. premature ejaculation
   b. dyspareunia
   c. erectile disorder
   d. vaginismus

4. Which of the following is the most reasonable description of a sexual dysfunction?
   a. a lifelong, residual problem
   b. an acquired, lifelong problem
   c. an acquired, situational problem
   d. a generalized, situational problem

5. Statistical research tabulated in your text indicates that the most common sexual dysfunction complained of by men is
   a. pain during sex.
   b. sex not pleasurable.
   c. premature ejaculation.
   d. anxiety about performance.

6. Assuming the "spectator role" in sex means that one
   a. is preoccupied with watching one's own sexual performance, looking for signs of inadequacy.
   b. watches sexually explicit behavior modeled in videos to promote the learning of better technique.
   c. engages in voyeurism as a means of sexual gratification.
   d. first learns about sexuality in adolescence by viewing sexual magazines and movies.

7. According to Kaplan's approach to sex therapy, "remote causes" call for _____ treatment, and "immediate causes" call for _____ treatment.
   a. psychodynamic; behavioral
   b. cognitive; medical
   c. individual; couple-oriented
   d. outpatient; inpatient

8. Today, many researchers in the area of sexual dysfunction believe that the causes of such dysfunctions are
   a. primarily psychological.
   b. primarily physiological.
   c. both psychological and physiological.
   d. neither psychological nor physiological.

9. According to *DSM-IV-TR*, the term *paraphilia* denotes a pattern of sexual activity that deviates from the standard of
   a. heterosexual interaction capable of resulting in reproduction.
   b. nondestructive interplay between consenting adults.
   c. voluntary interactions between any individuals.
   d. legally permitted activities between married partners.

10. According to the text, which of the following is true of transvestism?
    a. Transvestites usually have a successful marital sexual relationship.
    b. Transvestites appear to be no more prone to mental disturbance than the general population.
    c. Transvestism is unrelated to homosexuality and gender identity disorder.
    d. Transvestism and voyeurism usually occur together.

11. Arnold has the habit of going about the house nude with the curtains open. He feels sexual excitement at the idea of being at the window just as the lady next door passes by. Arnold may be classified as a(n)
    a. fetishist.
    b. exhibitionist.
    c. transvestite.
    d. transsexual.

12. Exhibitionism and voyeurism are the two paraphilias most often reported to the police. How dangerous are these offenders?
    a. Most of these offenders will eventually commit serious sex crimes.
    b. About half these offenders will eventually be convicted of rape.
    c. A minority of these offenders are likely to commit more serious sex crimes.
    d. Virtually none of them will commit other sex crimes because their paraphilias serve as an escape valve for their impulses.

13. Sadism is to _____ as masochism is to _____
    a. children; adults
    b. "peeping;" exposing
    c. inflicting pain; being abused
    d. being abused; inflicting pain

14. Frotteurism is defined as

    a. reliance on inanimate objects or on some body part for sexual gratification to the exclusion of the person as a whole.
    b. sexual gratification through dressing in the clothes of the opposite sex.
    c. sexual gratification through pain and/or humiliation inflicted on oneself.
    d. sexual gratification through touching and rubbing against a nonconsenting person.

15. Which of the following statements about pedophiles is true?

    a. Most pedophiles use physical violence in their sexual encounters with children.
    b. Most pedophiles appear to be law-abiding and may be respected members of the community.
    c. Most pedophiles molest children they do not know.
    d. It is rare for a pedophile to be under 50 years old.

16. Which of the following sexual activities is almost universally condemned an all cultures, worldwide?

    a. pedophilia
    b. sadism
    c. frotteurism
    d. incest

17. Freud believed that in the developing years, sexual interest takes many forms and that as the child matures, society forces him/her to narrow those interests down to an acceptable few. The technical term for the child's wide-ranging interests is

    a. polymorphous perversity.
    b. endogenous deviance.
    c. dissociative attraction.
    d. sublimated eroticism.

18. Which of the following is a true statement regarding the biological perspective on paraphilias?

    a. Brain structure abnormalities have been clearly associated with at least three serious paraphilias.
    b. Hormone imbalances are known to cause sadism and pedophilia.
    c. Neurotransmitter imbalances are involved with rape and incest.
    d. While biological causes are not clear, biological intervention can be useful in treatment.

19. Which of the following is true of gender identity disorder?

    a. It is another term for transvestism.
    b. It is a variety of fetishism.
    c. It is an early stage of homosexuality.
    d. It is a case of being in a body that doesn't match one's mental sex.

20. In connection with the therapeutic outcome of gender reassignment, research indicates that

    a. male-to-female reassignment seems to produce better outcomes than female-to-male.
    b. social support does not seem to be a factor, because clients have had so little of it all their lives.
    c. the longer the client prepares for reassignment by role-playing in real life, the better the outcome.
    d. psychological health does not seem to influence outcome because this is a medical procedure.

ANSWERS

Guided Self-Study (p. 200)

1. We have a very strong cultural norm that says we do not publicize the details of our sexual experiences (*unless* you've been with famous people—movie stars, politicians, or royal families. Then you can tell all and make big money!).

2. a. dysfunction
    b. paraphilias
    c. gender identity disorder (383)

3. coitus (356)

4. a. Inis Beag
    b. Mangaia (356)

5. Sex drive is inborn, but how it is acted on is determined by the society. (356)

6. a. Alfred Kinsey [1953] (357)
    b. Sex in America (359)

7. a. information
    b. communication
    c. guilt (358)

8. performance (358)

9. a. desire (358)
    b. arousal (358)
    c. orgasm (358)

10. a. hypoactive sexual desire disorder
    b. sexual aversion disorder (358–360)

11. a. lack of vaginal lubrication (360)
    b. lack of an erection (360)

12. premature ejaculation

13. a. There were two kinds—clitoral and vaginal. According to Freud, the vaginal orgasm was the "normal," psychologically mature one. (361)
    b. Neurologically, all orgasms are the same, regardless of what stimulation elicits them. If a woman finds her sexuality satisfying, then she has no reason to seek professional help looking for "the normal" female pattern. (361)

14. a. dyspareunia (362)
    b. vaginismus (362)

15. a. acquired (362)
    b. generalized (362)

16. Possible reasons for transient sexual failures: fatigue, illness, emotional upset, mental distraction, performance anxiety, too much to drink. (That is something else psychoactive depressant drugs take down besides higher cortical functions.) (362–363)

17. Contrary to myths, sexual expertise does not just come naturally to men or women. Until skills have been perfected, there are likely to be performance difficulties and anxieties that practice will eventually eliminate. Remember when your parent would tell you to practice, practice, practice in order to get a thing right? Well, it applies to sex too! (363)

18. This chapter covers the psychodynamic perspective in a rather cursory manner because the effectiveness of psychodynamic treatment for sexual dysfunction has not been proved. (364–365)
    a. In basic Freudian theory, the only way to reach the adult sexual function is to progress successfully through all the psychosexual stages of development so that the genital stage can manifest at the time of puberty. If all the psychosexual stages of development are not successively navigated, then the therapist will help the patient uncover and "work through" the unconscious conflicts that prevented normal development. The patient can then approach the conflicts from an adult level instead of from the position of the very young child that he/she was when the problem first arose.
    b. Current psychodynamic approaches are more likely to look at disturbances in object-relations. Object-relations is the psychodynamic term for early human bonds, usually with the mother as the primary caretaker. Look back to Chapter 5 for more on psychodynamic theory.

19. a. LEARNING! (365)
    b. respondent (365)
    c. spectator role (365)
    d. sensate focus (366)
    e. paradoxical (366)

20. Sexual beliefs, sexual attitudes, any thoughts that take away from the immediate mood of the moment (concerns about bodily appearance, performance, the environment, intrusive thoughts from the past, outside worries about job, kids, etc.) (367)

21. Beyond increasing a flow of intimate knowledge with each other, partners can build or restore a trusting belief in each other as suitable, compatible partners. (367)

22. a. multifacted (367)
    b. immediate (367)
    c. remote (367)
    d. immediate (367)
    e. direct (368)

23. a, b, and h are remote causes; all others are immediate causes. (367)

24. a. needs
    b. benefits
    c. resist (368)

25. Is it organic or is it psychological? There is still much debate about the underlying causes of sexual dysfunctions. Researchers are examining whether the causes are not either/or but a very intricate pattern of both psychological and physiological components. (369)

26. Diabetes, heart disease, kidney disease, alcohol problems, medication side effects (369)

27. Vaginal infections, ovarian cysts, lacerations or scar tissue resulting from childbirth, hormonal deficiencies (369)

28. Hormonal deficiencies, neurological impairment, or low levels of neurotransmitters are all possibilities. (369)

29. Nocturnal penile tumescence. Since men have erections during REM sleep cycles several times a night, checking to see if the penis is physiologically working is a simple matter. (369)

30. a. Fetishism—inanimate object or bodily part to exclusion of person as a whole
    b. Transvestism—dressing in clothes of opposite sex
    c. Exhibitionism—exposing one's genitals to an unwilling viewer
    d. Voyeurism—clandestine viewing of body parts or sexual activity without the consent of those being viewed
    e. Sadism—inflicting pain on others
    f. Masochism—experiencing pain or humiliation oneself
    g. Frotteurism—touching and rubbing a nonconsenting person
    h. Pedophilia—sexual contact with children (371)

31. Both wear women's clothing; transvestites are sexually aroused by wearing women's clothes, but transsexuals are not; transsexuals wear women's clothes just because they find the role of a woman comfortable. (372–373)

32. Marital problems if the cross-dressing is discovered, unless the wife is tolerant or even willing to include the cross-dressing into the couple's sexual activities (372–373)

33. exhibitionism and voyeurism (373–374)

34. a. ten
    b. eight (374)
    c. 10–20

35. a. puritanical
    b. masturbation
    c. inadequacy
    d. masculinity (373–374)

36. schizophrenia, psychomotor epilepsy, senile brain deterioration, or mental retardation (374)

37. A man in his twenties, thirties, or forties; married or divorced; with children of his own; and who is acquainted with the victim and/or the victim's family (376)

38. a. comfortable
    b. shy
    c. children
    d. counter (376–377)

39. a. early
    b. repeated
    c. violence, penetration
    d. closely related
    e. cooperated (377)

40. a. Situational
    b. Preference (376)

41. a. moralistic
    b. fundamentalist religious
    c. unsatisfactory (377)

42. a. polymorphous perverse (379)
    b. oedipal (379)
    c. castration (379)
    d. sadism (374–375)

43. a. LEARNING!! (380)
    b. respondent (380)
    c. stimulus satiation (380)
    d. covert sensitization (380)
    e. shame aversion (380)

44. a. THINKING!! (381)
    b. objectification (381)
    c. restructuring (381)
    d. empathy training (381)
    e. role reversal (381)

45. a. testosterone (382)
    b. antidepressants (382)
    c. penile plethysmography (383)

46. a. dysphoria (383)
    b. berdache (383)
    c. transexual (383)
    d. autogynephilia (373)
    e. reassignment (383–384)

47. a. Three
    b. Hormonal
    c. Real-life (385)

48. a. neuroscience (385)
    b. psychodynamic
    c. behaviorism

49. Viagra, injection of a vascular dilation agent, testosterone supplementation (360–361)

50. Rape is a common crime. Some rapists may have antisocial personalities, while others may be compelled to rape as a result of the cultural emphasis on sex and violence. (378)

Practice Test (p. 207)

1. a. Correct!
   b. No. The earliest editions took this position, but it is not current.
   c. Incorrect. Freud might find this to be true, but the *DSM* tries to avoid theory.
   d. No. This is a position taken between the original pathology viewpoint and the current one.

2. a. Actually, just the other way around; 75 to 85% did *not* cheat.
   b. No. Actually the results were about half that.
   c. Wrong. It is common among those who have partners.
   d. Correct!

3. a. Right!
   b. No, this is a pain disorder.
   c. No, this is an arousal disorder.
   d. Sorry, this is a pain disorder.

4. a. Incorrect. No such category as a residual disorder.
   b. No, this is a contradiction—if it is lifelong, when was it acquired?
   c. Right!
   d. Sorry, but this is a contradiction—an across-the-board problem is not situational.

5. a. No, this is much more common in women.
   b. Sorry, but this is more a women's complaint.
   c. Yes!
   d. No. This is fairly common, but there is one even more common.

6. a. Correct!
   b. This is sometimes done, but it is not what is meant by the spectator role.
   c. No. This is a paraphilia; spectator role has to do with dysfunction.
   d. Sorry, but this has nothing to do with the term; the concept deals with dysfunction.

7. a. You got it!
   b. No. Remote means long ago. Which perspective deals a lot with the past?
   c. No. Totally unrelated concept—besides, nearly all sex therapy is couple therapy.
   d. Incorrect. Totally unrelated. The terms have to do with a time frame, not a place.

8. a. No. This was the Masters and Johnson assessment, but that was nearly thirty years ago.
   b. No. An extreme position that is not borne out by the facts.
   c. Correct!
   d. Incorrect. If not these two, then what do you have left?

9. a. No. This is a very rigid, essentially religious position that the *DSM-IV* does not hold.
   b. Right!
   c. No, too general. Children are the exception here.
   d. Sorry, too narrow. Just because something is illegal, doesn't make it a mental health issue.

10. a. No. The partners of these people often take exception to their activities.
    b. True!
    c. Sorry, but there is some overlap between these behaviors.
    d. No, there is no connection here.

11. a. No. Fetishism is dependence on objects or parts of the person for arousal.
    b. Yes!
    c. Hardly. Nude is not crossdressing!
    d. No. Nothing is said here about Arnold being unhappy with his gender.

12. a. Too alarmist. The evidence does not support this.
     b. Too high. These folks may disturb others, but their dangerousness is overrated.
     c. Correct!
     d. Sorry, this is too optimistic, but it is closer to the truth than a or b.

13. a. No. You have to know your definitions here. Look on page 371 of the text.
     b. No, these relate to voyeurism and exhibitionism.
     c. Correct!
     d. Sorry, you got it backward.

14. a. Incorrect. This alternative has to do with fetishism.
     b. No, that would be transvestism.
     c. No, that would be masochism.
     d. Yes!

15. a. Not really. They tend to control verbally rather than physically.
     b. Right!
     c. No. Actually, it is most often a neighbor or a relative.
     d. No. The "dirty old man" stereotype is false—they come in all ages.

16. a. Incorrect. This is found worldwide.
     b. No. Hint: Which one tends to threaten the culture by producing genetic problems?
     c. Sorry, but this is very common.
     d. Correct!

17. a. You got it!
     b. No. Big words do not a right answer make. (Endogenous went with depression, remember?)
     c. Wrong. You've seen dissociative before, but not in this chapter.
     d. No. Sublimation is a Freudian term (a defense mechanism), but not the one we need.

18. a. No. This has not been demonstrated.
     b. Sorry, there is no clear evidence of this.
     c. Incorrect. This is not known to be true.
     d. Right!

19. a. No. Cross-dressing may be involved, but for a completely different reason.
     b. Incorrect. There is no fetish object here.
     c. Homosexuality may be involved in GID, but GID is not a "stage" in homosexual development.
     d. Yes!

20. a. No, just the other way around.
     b. Sorry, it is a big factor in how well people adjust to their reassignment.
     c. Correct!
     d. On the contrary, the better the mental health, the better the outcome.

CHAPTER 14
SCHIZOPHRENIA AND DELUSIONAL DISORDER

LEARNING OBJECTIVES

By the time you have finished studying this chapter, you should be able to do the following:

1. Define *psychosis*, and list three varieties of psychosis referred to in the text. (390)

2. Summarize the history of the disorder now called *schizophrenia*, summarize population data on schizophrenia, and distinguish schizophrenia from brief psychotic disorder and schizophreniform disorder. (390–391)

3. Define and give examples of the following cognitive symptoms of schizophrenia: delusions, loosened associations, poverty of content, neologisms, clanging, word salad. (391–396)

4. Define the perceptual symptoms of schizophrenia (breakdown in selective attention, hallucinations), and summarize the disorders of mood, behavior, and social interaction that can accompany schizophrenia. (396–399)

5. Describe the course of schizophrenia, defining the prodromal, active, and residual phases of the disorder. (399)

6. Describe three classic subtypes of schizophrenia and explain the process-reactive, positive-negative symptoms, and paranoid-nonparanoid dimensions of schizophrenia. (400–403)

7. Define delusional disorder, distinguish it from paranoid personality disorder and paranoid schizophrenia, and describe five categories of delusional disorder contained in *DSM-IV-TR*. (405–406)

8. Discuss why schizophrenia is difficult to diagnose, and describe difficulties encountered in the study of a disorder like schizophrenia. (406–407)

9. Summarize genetic research on schizophrenia, citing the results of family studies, twin studies, adoption studies, and high-risk research. (407–412)

10. Describe brain structure abnormalities and evidence of prenatal brain injury found in some schizophrenics. (413–414)

11. Explain the suspected role of neurotransmitters in schizophrenia, describe the relationship of dopamine to Type I and Type II schizophrenia, and discuss the pros and cons of chemotherapy for schizophrenia. (416–417)

12. Summarize the cognitive perspective's ideas on the role of attention problems as a factor in schizophrenia, and describe cognitive treatments for this disorder. (418–422)

13. Summarize the role of pathological interpersonal relationships in the development of schizophrenia according to the interpersonal approach, and describe family-based therapies that have been applied to this disorder. (422–425)

14. Summarize the behavioral and sociocultural positions on the causes and treatment of schizophrenia. (425–427)

15. Summarize the diathesis-stress theory of schizophrenia. (427–428)

16. Summarize the current research in the prevention of schizophrenia (schizophrenic prodrome). (428)

KEY TERMS

The following terms are in bold print in your text and are important to your understanding of the chapter. Look them up in the text and write down their definitions.

active phase (399)
anhedonia (397)
antipsychotic drugs (417)
behavioral high-risk design (412)
blunted affect (397)
catatonic schizophrenia (401)
catatonic stupor (401)
clanging (395)
communication deviance (CD) (424)
deficit symptoms (404)
delusional disorder (406)
delusions (391)
dementia praecox (390)
diathesis-stress model (407)
differential deficits (407)
disorganized schizophrenia (400)
dopamine hypothesis (416)
echolalia (406)
expressed emotion (EE) (422)
flat affect (397)
genetic high-risk design (411)
good-poor premorbid dimension (403)
hallucinations (396)

inappropriate affect (397)
loosening of associations (393)
negative symptoms (404)
neologisms (395)
paranoid-nonparanoid dimension (405)
paranoid schizophrenia (402)
phenothiazines (417)
positive-negative symptoms dimension (404)
positive symptoms (404)
poverty of content (394)
process-reactive dimension (403)
prodromal phase (399)
psychoses (390)
residual phase (399)
schizoaffective disorder (397)
schizophrenia (390)
social-skills training (426)
stereotypy (398)
tardive dyskinesia (416)
token economy (426)
Type I schizophrenia (404)
Type II schizophrenia (404)
word salad (396)

IMPORTANT NAMES

Identify the following persons and their major contributions to abnormal psychology as discussed in this chapter.

Eugen Bleuler (390)
Loren and Jean Chapman (407)
Emil Kraepelin (390)

Sarnoff Mednick (412)
Milton Rokeach (391)
The Three Christs of Ypsilanti (391)

GUIDED SELF-STUDY

1. Both schizophrenia and delusional disorder are called _____, which means the sufferer has difficulty in perceiving, processing, and responding to environmental stimuli in an adaptive manner.

2. List the three main groups of psychoses.

   a.

   b.

   c.

Schizophrenia

3. Schizophrenic disorders are characterized by three major types of symptom patterns:

   a. _____ behavior,

   b. social _____; and

   c. distortion in th_____, per_____, and m_____.

4. In 1896, Kraepelin called schizophrenia (a)_____ _____, which means premature mental deterioration. In 1911, Bleuler said that in some cases the dementia was not premature, and it was obviously not a permanent deterioration because some people recovered. So Bleuler called the disorder (b)_____, which means "split-mind." Split-mind described the separation of (c)_____ processes within one personality.

5. According to statistics, what are the chances that you will ever have a schizophrenic episode in your life?

6. One- (a)_____ of all beds in mental hospitals are occupied with someone who has schizophrenia; as many as one- (b)_____ of all homeless people are schizophrenic.

7. Fill in the following list of the five characteristic symptoms of schizophrenia.

   a. de_____

   b. hall_____

   c. disorganized s_____

   d. disorganized b_____, which includes cat_____ behavior

   e. ne_____ symptoms

8. What is a negative symptom?

9. If a person has two or more of these characteristic symptoms for

   a. less than one month, the diagnosis is _____ _____ _____.

   b. for at least one month but less than six months, the diagnosis is _____ _____.

   c. at least six months, the diagnosis is _____.

10. Write in the correct term describing the following disorders of thought and language in schizophrenia.

    a. Firmly held beliefs that have no basis in reality:

    b. Thoughts that are related but that stray from the original direction of thinking:

    c. Language used grammatically correctly, yet conveying little or no meaning for the hearer:

    d. "New words"—using parts of existing words or using existing words in new ways:

    e. Speech based more on the sound of words than on their meaning:

    f. Utterances where words seem to have no connection to one another:

11. List the seven types of delusional thought described in your text.

 - _____   - _____
 - _____   - _____
 - _____   - _____
 - _____

12. Apply the information from the previous question and write in the name of the delusional pattern that goes with each description.

 a. _____   My mother-in-law is trying to poison me.

 b. _____   I feel myself slipping away. Some days I just don't exist.

 c. _____   My boss at the store where I work is having me followed by the CIA.

 d. _____   It was so terrible. I caused that last earthquake in California.

 e. _____   The national news reporters always smile at me; they know when I am watching the TV.

 f. _____   My husband won't let me spend any money. When I try to, he paralyzes me by remote control.

 g. _____   I'm your guardian angel, and I'm writing this exercise just for you because I can read your mind and I know what you don't understand in this chapter.

 h. _____   My bladder doesn't work because I have rust in my pipes.

 i. _____   I can't talk on the telephone while the television is on because my voice goes out through the TV antenna.

13. List two manifestations of disordered perception in schizophrenia.

14. (a)_____ hallucinations are most frequently experienced, and (b)_____ hallucinations are the second most frequently occurring type.

15. By definition, the mood symptoms are considered secondary in schizophrenia because otherwise schizophrenia would be in the diagnostic category of mood disorders where emotion is the primary problem. Identify the following concepts associated with the disorders of mood seen in schizophrenia.

 a. _____   Patient shows little emotion

 b. _____   Patient shows no emotion

 c. _____   Term for reduced experience of pleasure

 d. _____   Term for mood that seems unsuitable to the situation

 e. _____   Diagnosis citing both affective and cognitive symptoms

16. Typically, people with schizophrenia show (a)_____ physical activity. If this trend is carried to the

 extreme, the individual may lapse into a catatonic (b)_____.

17. _____ is the purposeless repetitive activity that some people with schizophrenia may engage in for hours at a time.

18. If you sit and observe a schizophrenia ward for an hour, you may see many normal, many unusual, and maybe many inappropriate behaviors. The one thing that will be noticeably lacking is normal

_____ interaction.

19. List the three phases of schizophrenia, in order, from beginning to end.

a.

b.

c.

20. Match each of the following patterns of behaviors seen in catatonic schizophrenia to its definition.

negativism   *stupor*   *echopraxia*
rigidity   *mutism*   *echolalia*
posturing   *waxy flexibility*

a. _____ Complete immobility

b. _____ Cessation of speech

c. _____ Assuming a pose and remaining in that pose for hours at a time.

d. _____ Staying in whatever pose someone arranges

e. _____ When a pose resists attempts of others to change it

f. _____ Doing the opposite of what is being asked

g. _____ Imitating movements of others

e. _____ Parroting what is said by others

21. Position yourself in front of a clock, standing with your arms held straight out to the sides. How long could you stand there without moving? Did you find the experience more exhausting than you would have imagined? This experience makes clear the intense amount of energy that is utilized as the catatonic individual poses immobile, appearing to be doing nothing at all.

22. You enter a room and find four people there. Determine which one most represents each of the following categories of schizophrenia: *catatonic, paranoid, disorganized*, and *residual*.

a. _____ One claims to be the President of the United States and says an assassin is looking for him.

b. _____ When I introduce myself, one of them responds quite appropriately; she is clearly the most normal person in the group.

c. _____ One sits at attention, staring out the window with one hand held up in the "live long and prosper" salute.

d. _____ One wanders about the room singing a nonsense rhyme and occasionally hopping as though he is playing a childhood game.

23. List the three pairs that have been defined as dimensions of schizophrenia.

a. _____ vs. _____

b. _____ vs. _____

c. _____ vs. _____

24. Now take those dimensions of schizophrenia and arrange them so each part is under the proper heading of "good prognosis" or "poor prognosis."

	Good Prognosis	Poor Prognosis
a.		—
b.		—
c.		—

25. Circle the "positive" symptoms" in the following list of behaviors.

delusions   *speech with little meaning*   *social withdrawal*

hallucinations   *flat affect*   *bizarre behavior*

apathy

26. What impact has the discovery of these patterns and correlations (things that go together) had on our understanding of schizophrenia?

27. Name the two new patterns of schizophrenic disorders.

28. Answer the following questions about the long-term outlook for patients with schizophrenia.

    a. What percentage of schizophrenics continue to be schizophrenic?

    b. What percentage alternate between residual and active phases?

    c. What percentage return to and maintain normal functioning?

Delusional Disorders

29. Identify the category for each of the following delusions:

erotomanic type   *jealous type*   *somatic type*
grandiose type   *persecutory type*

    a. _____ My teacher hates me. No matter what I do in this class, she is going to fail me.

    b. _____ Don't worry, Mom. I don't have to study. I've got this term under control.

    c. _____ My girlfriend (who's been in the coma ever since the accident) is cheating on me with her doctor. I can tell by that sneaky look on her face when I visit.

    d. _____ Michael Jackson is in love with me. He is doing all those hang-ups on my telephone. He's just too shy to speak to me.

    e. _____ The cafeteria food is causing my guts to rot.

30. Even though delusional disorder is a popular topic in story lines, it is really extremely rare, occurring

    in (a)_____ individuals per thousand. Schizophrenia occurs in one or two people out of every

    (b)_____.

Biological Perspective

31. Biological research on schizophrenia is currently one of the most (circle the best answer) *underrated / exciting / disappointing / simplistic* areas in abnormal psychology.

32. List five topics discussed under the biological perspective on schizophrenia.

- •
- •
- •

- •
- •

33. List six different areas of genetic research on schizophrenia.

- •
- •
- •

- •
- •
- •

34. Family studies have revealed that the closer you are related to a person with schizophrenia the more likely you are to have a schizophrenic episode yourself. Fill in the following statistics on your risk for schizophrenia. If you have

   a. no relatives with schizophrenia, your risk is _____ in a hundred.

   b. one parent with schizophrenia, your risk is _____ in a hundred.

   c. two parents with schizophrenia, your risk is _____ in a hundred.

   d. a MZ twin with schizophrenia, your risk is _____ in a hundred.

35. Twin studies support the hypothesis that there are two different types of schizophrenia; Type I is

   characterized by (a)_____ symptoms, and Type II typically has (b)_____ symptoms. The

   one with the greater genetic component is (c)_____.

36. Use the following terms to complete the four advantages that longitudinal "high-risk" studies offer in research about the development of schizophrenia. (Mednick's list summarizes these nicely.)

   bias   *confounding*   *control*   *memories*

   a. Data is collected before the _____ effects of hospitalization and medications have occurred.

   b. It eliminates the _____ of using data from patients whose clinical outcome is already known.

   c. Data is collected on an ongoing basis instead of depending on people's _____.

   d. This approach provides two _____ groups: the low-risk children and the high-risk children who did not develop schizophrenia.

37. Studies using genetically high-risk subjects are used to increase the odds that researchers will eventually

   have a group of schizophrenics large enough to make the study worthwhile. If researchers chose a random

   sample of children from the population, they would get only (a)_____ or _____ with

   schizophrenia for every hundred children they followed. By using a group that is more at risk, the researchers

   know they will get more cases of schizophrenia. When one parent has schizophrenia, the person's chances

   increase to about (b)_____ in a hundred. Thus, the number that is going to develop schizophrenia

   has increased by (c)_____ times.

38. Use the following terms to complete the five critical differences found in Mednick's study for the high-risk children who did become mentally ill.

complications   distractions   separated   troubled   unmanageable

   a.   Home life and family relationships were more _____.

   b.   They were more likely as infants to have been _____ from their mothers.

   c.   These children were more likely to have displayed extremely _____ behavior in school.

   d.   These children were more vulnerable to _____ from the environment.

   e.   The children were much more likely to have experienced _____ during pregnancy or childbirth.

39. What other high-risk research, besides genetic research, does your book mention? What does this research study?

40. What are some of the high-risk behaviors thought to be associated with schizophrenia?

41. Identify the areas of the brain affected in each type of schizophrenia.

   a.   A person with Type I (positive symptom) schizophrenia is likely to show abnormalities in

   b.   A person with Type II (negative symptom) schizophrenia is likely to have enlarged

   c.   A person with Type II schizophrenia shows abnormally low activity in

   d.   Both Type I and Type II schizophrenias are characterized by abnormalities in

42. Use the following terms to complete this summary of prenatal brain injury:

asymmetrical   discordant   flu   gliosis   second   fingerprints

Prenatal brain injury during the (a)_____ trimester of pregnancy seems to be more common in

schizophrenia patients. In normal prenatal brain development, the two halves of the brain become different

from each other. The brains of people with schizophrenia do not show this (b)_____ pattern. Brain

injuries usually produce evidence of (c)_____, which is the brain's healing process; however, this

process does not start to operate until the third trimester. Autopsies on the brains of people who had

schizophrenia show brain damage that does not have this healing process. Identical twins who are

(d)_____ for schizophrenia (one has it, one does not) also have more variation between their

(e)_____, which also develop during this time. Another bit of support for this being a critical period

is research showing that women who had (f)_____ during their second trimester of pregnancy had

offspring who were more likely to develop schizophrenia in later life.

43. Fill in the following blanks with concepts associated with biochemical research and therapies for schizophrenia.

a. _____ The theory that has dominated biochemical research for the last three decades

b. _____ Another name for antipsychotic drugs

c. _____ Class of antipsychotic drugs that reduce dopamine activity

d. _____ Stimulant drug that increases dopamine activity

e. _____ Neuropsychological disorder at least partially caused by dopamine deficiency

f. _____ Side effect of antipsychotic medications which is uncontrollable facial grimacing and lip smacking

g. _____ New antipsychotic medication that primarily acts on the serotonin receptors with only a weak effect on dopamine receptors

h. _____ Possible clozapine side effect which is a potentially life-threatening blood disorder

i. _____ Neurotransmitter system that has become the newest area of biochemical research

j. _____ Type of schizophrenia that tends to respond best to phenothiazine medications

k. _____ Type of schizophrenia that tends to respond best to the nonphenothiazine medications

44. The ultimate shortcoming of antipsychotic medications is that they do not _____ schizophrenia.

Cognitive Perspective

45. Fill in the following concepts from the cognitive perspective.

a. _____ Ultimate cause of schizophrenia

b. _____ Psychological function most impaired by the underlying cause

c. _____ The "problem" in Type I schizophrenia

d. _____ The "problem" in Type II schizophrenia

e. _____ Response expected when a person is surprised by a stimulus

f. _____-_____ Task to see if second stimulus can make one forget first stimulus

g. _____ Cognitive therapy to address irrational thoughts and experiences

h. _____ Therapy to repair deficits by instructions training, prompting, and rewards.

46. Choose the correct answer: In backward-masking paradigm research, Type II schizophrenia patients

a. need more time to mentally process the masking stimulus.
b. need more time to mentally process the target stimulus.
c. can remember the target stimulus for only a short time.
d. can remember the masking stimulus for only a short time.

Family Theories

47. List the two main problems seen in families in which there is schizophrenia.

48. List the two factors that are considered in an expressed-emotion rating.

49. Identify the following communications patterns:

    a. Mom has written to a college-aged child to say that she and Dad love the child very much, but they are sorry that they both are going to miss her graduation day. Each parent has appointments "that can't be missed."

    b. Mom and Dad tend to be perfectionists and want the very best from their children. They have encouraged their children to participate in many extracurricular activities. The parents are always right there with "helpful criticism" (with the emphasis on criticism), telling the children how to improve their performances.

    c. Dad: "Here today, gone tomorrow."
        Son: "Could we?"
        Dad: "I've been planning . . . "
        Son: "You never listen to me!!"

Behavioral Perspective

50. Identify the following concepts

    a. _____ The ultimate cause of schizophrenia according to behaviorists

    b. _____ Behavior that may be learned to tune out a chaotic environment

    c. _____ Reason bizarre behaviors would be maintained

    d. _____ Basis of all behavioral therapies

    e. _____ Kind of reinforcement when payment is the actual reinforcer

    f. _____ Reinforcement when a conditioned reinforcer is used as payment

    g. _____-_____ Area of training that most all schizophrenics need

51. List social skills that would be involved in social skills training.

52. Identify the following concepts from the sociocultural perspective.

    a. _____ Alternative treatment approach to hospitalization

    b. _____ Term meaning treatment taking place in the patient's real-life world

    c. _____ Program that makes frequent contacts with released patients to keep them well in touch with whatever services they may need

    d. _____ One-to-one case-management that focuses on control of emotions, identifying developing stress, coping with stressors, and avoiding emotional escalation that could lead to a relapse

Diathesis-Stress Model

53. Researchers in the field of schizophrenia do not believe there is only one single determining factor for schizophrenia. Most researchers use a diathesis-stress model whereby

    a. _____ is the genetically inherited degree of predisposition toward schizophrenia and

    b. _____ is the environmental element.

54. The diathesis-stress model is seen currently as the most productive approach to finding the "causes" of schizophrenia. What further important questions does it raise?

Implications for Prevention

55. The costs of treatment and lost productivity owing to schizophrenia place a huge burden on family caregivers and the community at large. Consequently, the prevention of schizophrenia is an important public health goal. Discuss the research focused on the schizophrenic prodrome.

HELPFUL HINTS

1. *Do not confuse "split-mind" (schizophrenia) with split (multiple) personality.* Other than the use of the term "split," they are totally unrelated concepts! Review multiple personality in Chapter 8 if this is not perfectly clear.

2. Beware of the five characteristic symptoms of schizophrenia versus the five general categories of dysfunction for schizophrenia. They are not the same although they are conceptually overlapping in content.

3. To recall the seven patterns of delusions use the word *perishing* and delete the vowels. The remaining letters are the first letters of each type of delusion.

4. Be alert that in the schizophrenic disorders, those that are reactive (acute, good premorbid, positive symptoms, Type I) are *more* responsive to medication. That is just the reverse of the mood disorders, where reactive depression is *less* responsive to medication.

5. Beware of people who throw around the terms "schizo" and "paranoid." By now I hope you know that those terms relate to several different diagnoses that encompass a wide variety of behavioral abnormalities.

6. Ask your instructor to what extent you are required to know the drug categories and specific drugs (generic and /or brand names) for each category.

7. Review the parts of Chapter 3 (Research Methods in Abnormal Psychology) that relate to research methodology with schizophrenia patients. It is advantageous to refresh the learning that you have already done on that material. The most directly related materials in Chapter 3 are "Correlational Research Designs" and "Longitudinal or Prospective Studies," which includes genetic and behavioral high-risk designs.

PRACTICE TEST

Use the following test questions to check your knowledge of the material in this chapter. You may want to write the answers on a separate sheet of paper so you can take the test more than once.

1. What percentage of the U.S. population has had or will have a schizophrenic episode?
   a. 1–2%
   b. 3–6%
   c. 7–12%
   d. 13–20%

2. The major difference between brief psychotic disorder and schizophreniform disorder is that
   a. brief psychotic disorder is Type I and schizophreniform disorder is Type II.
   b. brief psychotic disorder lasts longer than schizophreniform disorder.
   c. brief psychotic disorder is biogenic and schizophreniform disorder is psychogenic.
   d. brief psychotic disorder does not last as long as schizophreniform disorder.

3. The main type of delusion exhibited by the "Three Christs of Ypsilanti" is
   a. delusion of control.
   b. delusion of grandeur.
   c. nihilistic delusion.
   d. hypochondriacal delusion.

4. Which of the following is the best illustration of clanging?

    a. Don't run, have fun, be a bun in the sun.
    b. I'm getting better now; I have overfinished my most terminal score.
    c. Don't say something good about somebody if you can't say anything at all.
    d. Remember, any is too far into nowhere traded homecoming at least to conquer.

5. According to clinical observations, the most common mode of hallucination is

    a. auditory.
    b. tactile.
    c. visual.
    d. olfactory.

6. A woman with schizophrenia screams at her sister for bringing her flowers, yet giggles uncontrollably when talking about her mother's funeral. She is displaying

    a. anhedonia.
    b. word salad.
    c. loosening of associations.
    d. inappropriate affect.

7. Prodromal is to _____ as residual is to _____

    a. neurosis; psychosis
    b. full-blown symptoms; left-over symptoms
    c. emotional disturbance; cognitive disturbance
    d. going downhill; getting better

8. Which of the following is true of the typical "reactive" schizophrenia patient?

    a. Premorbid adjustment is good, onset is sudden, and good recovery is likely.
    b. Premorbid adjustment is good, onset is slow, and good recovery is likely.
    c. Premorbid adjustment is poor, onset is slow, and good recovery is unlikely.
    d. Premorbid adjustment is poor, onset is sudden, and good recovery is unlikely.

9. Negative symptoms in schizophrenia are defined as

    a. the absence of things that should be there.
    b. the presence of things that should not be there.
    c. a pessimistic or depressed outlook on life.
    d. what used to be called reactive disorder.

10. The major difference between delusional disorders and schizophrenia is that

    a. schizophrenia lasts longer than delusional disorder.
    b. schizophrenia is a psychosis but delusional disorder is not.
    c. delusional disorder has fewer symptoms than schizophenia.
    d. delusional disorder is more handicapping than schizophrenia.

11. When researchers look at diagnosed schizophrenia patients in an institutional setting, the behaviors they see are likely to be the result of

    a. the schizophrenic disorder itself.
    b. medication side effects.
    c. living in an institutional environment.
    d. possibly all of the above.

12. It is fairly clear that there is a genetic component in schizophrenia. But exactly what is it that is being inherited?

    a. the disease itself
    b. a potentially stressful family environment
    c. a lower than average IQ
    d. a diathesis

13. Why is there excitement about the finding that many schizophrenia patients cannot visually track objects smoothly?

    a. It is believed that eye problems cause hallucinations.
    b. It is believed that this is a genetic marker for the disorder.
    c. It is believed that eye problems identify those who can benefit from psychotherapy.
    d. It is believed that those with eye problems are prone to positive symptom schizophrenia.

14. Studies on brain asymmetry, fingerprint patterns in twins, and a brain-repair process called *gliosis* all are aimed at investigating whether schizophrenia can be connected to

    a. abnormalities on chromosome 11.
    b. brain damage in the teenage years.
    c. oxygen deprivation during the birth process.
    d. brain trauma in the second trimester of pregnancy.

15. Phenothiazines used to reduce schizophrenic symptoms seem to have their effect by

    a. blocking dopamine receptor sites in the brain.
    b. imitating the effects of dopamine in the brain.
    c. decreasing the production of dopamine in the brain.
    d. increasing the production of dopamine in the brain.

16. Joel has tardive dyskinesia. We should expect that

    a. the problem will be resistant to treatment.
    b. the problem will disappear as soon as he stops taking antipsychotic medications.
    c. he is more likely to have developed schizophrenia due to inheritance than as a result of stress.
    d. he is a recently diagnosed schizophrenia patient who has not yet been given medications.

17. Cognitive theorists suggest that if we are to identify children at risk for schizophrenia, it will be by

    a. noting problems in long-term memory.
    b. listening to the unusual dreams of such children.
    c. focusing on the attention deficits of such children.
    d. reviewing the reasons these children got into trouble at school.

18. Which of the following is the best example of double-bind communication?

    a. A father is highly critical yet overly emotionally involved with his child.
    b. A mother tells her child to show more initiative in doing housework but then criticizes the child when she does so, saying she was acting without permission.
    c. A mother is so overinvolved in her child's life that she refuses to allow the child to make any decisions.
    d. A father refuses to communicate directly with his child and makes all requests of the child through the mother.

19. The token economy approach to treatment of schizophrenia involves

    a. immediate food reinforcers for appropriate behavior.
    b. primarily the extinguishing of unwanted behavior through nonreinforcement.
    c. forcing the patient to get a job in order to promote responsible living.
    d. symbolic reinforcers that can be traded in for other wants at a later time.

20. In the diathesis-stress model of disorder, the diathesis is
    a. the severity of symptoms.
    b. a biological predisposition.
    c. the level of premorbid adjustment.
    d. an indicator of environmental pressure.

ANSWERS

Guided Self-Study (p. 216)

1. *psychoses* (390)

2. a. mood disorders
   b. schizophrenia
   c. delusional disorder (390)

3. a. bizarre
   b. withdrawal
   c. thought, perception, mood (390)

4. a. *dementia praecox* (390)
   b. *schizophrenia* (390)
   c. mental (An individual who has schizophrenia may have experiences of the world, thought patterns, and emotional reactions that are totally unrelated to one another.) (391)

5. between one and two chances out of a hundred (391)

6. a. half
   b. third (390)

7. a. delusions
   b. hallucinations
   c. speech
   d. behavior; catatonic
   e. negative (391) (see Helpful Hints #3)

8. Reduction or loss of normal behaviors such as language or goal-directed behavior (391)

9. a. brief psychotic disorder
   b. schizophreniform disorder
   c. schizophrenia (391)

10. a. delusions (391)   d. neologisms (395)
    b. loosening of associations (392)   e. clanging (395)
    c. poverty of content (394–395)   f. word salad (395)

11. delusions of persecution   hypochondriacal delusions
    delusions of control or influence   nihilistic delusions
    delusions of reference   delusions of grandeur (392)
    delusions of sin and guilt

12. a. persecution   f. control or influence
    b. nihilistic   g. grandeur
    c. persecution   h. hypochondriacal (392)
    d. sin and guilt   i. control (thought broadcasting) (392)
    e. reference

13. breakdown of selective attention and hallucinations (396–397)

14. a. Auditory
    b. visual (396–397)

15. a. blunted affect
    b. flat affect
    c. anhedonia
    d. inappropriate affect
    e. schizoaffective disorder (397–398)

16. a. decreased
    b. stupor (398)

17. Stereotypy (398)

18. social (398)

19. a. prodromal (399)
    b. active (399)
    c. residual (399)

20. a. stupor   e. rigidity
    b. mutism   f. negativism
    c. posturing   g. echopraxia
    d. waxy flexibility   e. echolalia (401–402)

21. Your time and experience. This activity was to make you aware of how much energy a catatonic posture requires.

22. a. paranoid
    b. residual
    c. catatonic
    d. disorganized (400–402)

23. process vs. reactive (also called good-poor premorbid) (403)
    positive vs. negative symptoms (404)
    paranoid vs. nonparanoid (405)

24. a. Reactive: good / Process: poor
    b. Positive symptoms: good / Negative symptoms: poor
    c. Paranoid: good / Nonparanoid: poor (403–405)

25. delusions, hallucinations, bizarre behavior (404)

26. Researchers now propose that there may be two different disorders. (404)

27. Type I and Type II schizophrenia (404)

28. a. 10%
    b. 50–65%
    c. 25% (404)

29. a. persecutory type
    b. grandiose type
    c. jealous type
    d. erotomanic type
    e. somatic type (405–406)

30. a. 3
    b. 100 (406)

31. exciting (407)

32. genetic studies (407)
    brain imaging studies (413–414)
    investigation of prenatal brain injury (414)
    biochemical research (416)
    chemotherapy (417)

33. family studies (407)
   twin studies (408)
   adoption studies (409–410)
   studies looking for the specific nature of the genetic transmission (410)
   genetic high-risk studies (410–412)
   behavioral high-risk studies (412–413)

34. a. 1 to 2
    b. 13
    c. 46
    d. 48 (407–408)

35. a. positive
    b. negative
    c. Type II/negative (408–409)

36. a. confounding
    b. bias
    c. memories
    d. control (412)

37. a. 1 or 2
    b. 13
    c. 6 to 13 (410–412)

38. a. troubled
    b. separated
    c. unmanageable
    d. distractions
    e. complications (412)

39. Behavioral high-risk research studies people who have demonstrated thoughts and behaviors thought to be associated with schizophrenia. (412–413)

40. perceptual abnormalities and magical thinking (412–413)

41. a. the temporal lobes or limbic structures.
    b. the ventricles.
    c. the frontal lobes.
    d. the basal ganglia. (413–414)

42. a. second
    b. asymmetrical
    c. gliosis
    d. discordant
    e. fingerprints
    f. flu (414–415)

43. a. dopamine hypothesis
    b. neuroleptics
    c. phenothiazines
    d. amphetamine or methylphenidate)
    e. parkinson's disease
    f. tardive dyskinesia
    g. clozapine
    h. agranulocytosis
    i. glutamate
    j. Type I
    k. Type II (416–418)

44. cure (418)

45. a. biological (418)
    b. attention (418)
    c. overattention (419–420)
    d. underattention (420–421)
    e. orienting (420)
    f. backward-masking (421)
    g. questioning (422)
    h. cognitive rehabilitation (421)

46. "b" (421)

47. expressed emotion and communication deviance (422)

48. level of criticism and level of emotional overinvolvement (422)

49. a. double-bind communication—We love you, but you are not very important to us. (423)
    b. expressed emotion—overinvolvement with child and very critical (422)
    c. communication deviance—fragmented, incomplete non sequiturs (423)

50. a. biology (425)
    b. unresponsiveness (425)
    c. reinforcement (425)
    d. relearning (425)
    e. direct reinforcement (425–426)
    f. token economy (426)
    g. social-skills (426–427)

51. eye contact, smiling, appropriate physical gestures, conversation skills, improved speech intonation (426–427)

52. a. community
    b. in vivo
    c. assertive community treatment (ACT)
    d. personal therapy (427)

53. a. diathesis
    b. stress (427)

54. What is the specific nature of the genetic defect that leads to the biological predisposition for schizophrenia? (427–428)
    What stressors are most likely to cause (trigger) schizophrenia to develop? (427–428)

55. Preventing schizophrenia requires being able to predict illness, so that clinicians can identify individuals at risk and in need of early treatment. Therefore, research focuses on the stage of the illness that begins with the first changes in behavior and lasts until the onset of psychosis. (428)

Practice Test (p. 225)

1. a. Correct!
   b. No. Too high.
   c. Incorrect. Way too high.
   d. Sorry. Way, way too high!

2. a. Sorry. These distinctions are not applied in these two cases.
   b. No, you have it backward.
   c. No. These two problems are both generally seen as reactive (psychogenic).
   d. Right!

3. a. Sorry. No mention is made of their feeling controlled in this case.
   b. Yes!
   c. No. Nihilistic delusions are the belief that nothing is real ("nil" means nothing).
   d. Incorrect. This would be the belief that they were afflicted by a bizarre disease.

4. a. Right!
   b. No. This would be an example of neologism.
   c. Sorry, this is just a mixed-up statement.
   d. Incorrect. This is an example of word salad.

5. a. You got it!
   b. No, this one is somewhat down the list.
   c. Sorry, this is second.
   d. Incorrect. This one happens, but it is not the most common.

6. a. No. Anhedonia is the inability to enjoy anything.
   b. No. Word salad is just jumbled words with no meaning.
   c. Wrong. This is the inability to follow a train of thought to its conclusion.
   d. Yes!

7. a. No, we are not looking for degrees of seriousness, but stages in a process.
    b. Sorry, you're on the right track, but not the right ideas.
    c. Incorrect. Prodromal and residual are steps in a process.
    d. Right!

8. a. Correct!
    b. No. Lots of stuff to know here, and you got two out of three.
    c. Sorry. Zero for three on this try.
    d. Incorrect. You have one of the three right.

9. a. Correct!
    b. No, these would be positive symptoms.
    c. Incorrect. People who are pessimistic are negative, but this is a different concept.
    d. Not at all. In fact negative symptoms are more associated with process disorder.

10. a. Incorrect. Each may last a long time.
    b. No, they are both psychoses.
    c. Yes!
    d. No, with fewer symptoms, it actually interferes less.

11. a. This is entirely possible, because treatment isn't always effective, but read on.
    b. Definitely a possibility, but don't stop here.
    c. This can be a big factor; but it is not the only one.
    d. Correct!

12. a. No. If that were true there would be 100% concordance in identical twins.
    b. Sorry, you can be born into such a situation, but you didn't "inherit" it.
    c. There is a genetic component to IQ, and there is a negative correlation between IQ and the occurrence of schizophrenia, but there is a better, more direct answer.
    d. Right!

13. a. No. You are confusing a correlation with causation here.
    b. Right! The genetic problem that is associated with one disorder is probably close to the genetic problem associated with the other—this makes it easier to find the gene.
    c. No. Therapy has nothing to do with this.
    d. No evidence was presented for this much of a conclusion—much more basic than this.

14. a. Sorry. Chromosome 11 has been implicated in mood disorder but not schizophrenia.
    b. No, this is way too late in the developmental process.
    c. You are on the right track, but the time frame is wrong.
    d. Right!

15. a. Correct!
    b. No, the problem is apparently too much dopamine activity already.
    c. No. You are on the right track, but this is the wrong mechanism of action.
    d. Incorrect. This would just make things worse.

16. a. Right, unfortunately.
    b. Unfortunately not.
    c. No. Tardive dyskinesia is a side effect of drug treatment.
    d, Incorrect. It is the medications that produce the problem.

17. a. Not really. Remember the major focus of the cognitive people in this chapter.
    b. No. This would be far too symbolic for a cognitive theorist.
    c. Right!
    d. No. This sounds more like a behavioral approach.

18. a. No, this is EE, or expressed emotion.
    b. Correct!
    c. No, this is a set up for learned helplessness, but not really for schizophrenia.
    d. Incorrect. This is just a distant parent—not helpful, but not what we are talking about here.

19. a. No. Remember, a token is something you cash in later.
    b. No, this would be a direct extinction procedure.
    c. Incorrect. If the patient has schizophrenia, this just won't work. Reality contact can't be forced.
    d. Right!

20. a. Incorrect. We are talking about causes in this question.
    b. Yes!
    c. No. This is a factor in the disorder, but a diathesis is a more basic causal factor.
    d. Sorry, this would be the stress side of the equation.

CHAPTER 15
NEUROPSYCHOLOGICAL DISORDERS

LEARNING OBJECTIVES

By the time you have finished studying this chapter, you should be able to do the following:

1. Define acquired brain disorder or neuropsychological disorder, and discuss the problems involved in identifying organic causation and in specifying the nature and site of the damage. (432–433)

2. Describe seven common signs of acquired brain disorder, and define delirium, dementia, aphasia, apraxia, and agnosia. (434–435)

3. Name and describe seven disorders listed in the text under the category of cerebral infection, identify those at risk for these disorders, and describe common treatments. (436–438)

4. Name and describe three types of traumatic brain injury discussed in the text, identify those at risk for these problems, and describe common treatments. (439–441)

5. Identify and describe the effects of two types of cerebrovascular accidents, identify those at risk for these disorders, and describe common treatments. (441–444)

6. Describe the effects of brain tumors on mental and behavioral processes, identify risk factors associated with brain tumors, and describe common treatments. (444)

7. Describe the following degenerative brain disorders: age-related dementia, Alzheimer's disease, Lewy body disease, vascular dementia, Huntington's chorea, and Parkinson's disease. Identify those at risk for these disorders, and describe common treatments. (444–451)

8. Describe the causes and effects of Korsakoff's psychosis. (451)

9. Name and describe two thyroid syndromes and two adrenal syndromes discussed under the heading of endocrine disorders. (451–452)

10. Name and describe the effects of five substances that can lead to toxic disorders. (452–453)

11. Distinguish between symptomatic and idiopathic epilepsy, distinguish among simple partial, complex partial, absence, and tonic-clonic seizures, identify those at risk for these disorders, and describe common treatments. (453–455)

KEY TERMS

The following terms are in bold print in your text and are important to your understanding of the chapter. Look them up in the text and write down their definitions.

absence seizures (454)
acquired brain disorders (432)
acute confusional state (440)
agnosia (435)
Alzheimer's disease (445)
amnesia (434)
aphasia (435)
apraxia (434)
brain tumors (444)
cerebral abscess (436)
cerebrovascular accident (CVA) (441)
complex partial seizure (453)

concussion (440)
contusion (440)
degenerative disorders (444)
delirium (434)
dementia (435, 445)
embolism (442)
encephalitis (436)
endocrine glands (451)
epilepsy (453)
frontotemporal dementia (447)
general paresis (437)
generalized seizures (454)

hemorrhage (442)
Huntington's chorea (448)
idiopathic epilepsy (453)
infarction (442)
Korsakoff's psychosis (451)
lead encephalopathy (452)
Lewy body disease (447)
Lyme disease (438)
mad cow disease (438)
meningitis (437)
metastatic brain tumors (444)
neurosyphilis (437)

Parkinson's disease (448)
partial seizures (453)
penetrating head injury (440)
primary brain tumors (444)
simple partial seizure (453)
stroke (441)
symptomatic epilepsy (453)
thrombosis (442)
tonic-clonic seizures (454)
traumatic brain injury (439)
vascular dementia (447)

IMPORTANT NAMES

Identify the following persons and their major contributions to abnormal psychology as discussed in this chapter.

Phineas Gage (440–441)   James Parkinson (448)

GUIDED SELF-STUDY

1. To make the concepts of this chapter concrete and more relevant to you, list the people that you know who have had an organic brain disorder. Ask older family members about your family tree to increase your number of examples and to further provoke your interest. When you know some disorder is in your biological family, the text material about which disorders are genetically based becomes interesting! (Also add to your list the famous people mentioned in this chapter.)

    Cerebral infection (abscess, encephalitis, meningitis, neurosyphilis):

    Brain trauma (concussion, contusion, laceration):

    Cerebrovascular accidents (strokes):

    Brain tumors:

    Degenerative disorders (Huntington's chorea, Parkinson's disease, Alzheimer's, vascular dementia):

    Nutritional deficiency (Korsakoff's psychosis [Alcoholics]):

    Endocrine disorders

    Thyroid (Graves' disease [hyperthyroidism] and myxedema [hypothyroidism]):

    Adrenal (Addison's disease and Cushing's syndrome):

    Toxic disorders (heavy metals, psychoactive drugs, carbon monoxide):

    Epilepsy:

Problems in Diagnosis

2. Use the following terms to fill in the blanks on the three reasons that biogenic problems are discussed in a psychology textbook: *differential, physical,* and *psychological.*

    a. Organically caused behavior problems can look just like _____ behavior problems, so the first issue is making a _____ diagnosis between organic cause and psychological cause.

    b. How a _____ disease affects a person's behavior is influenced by the person's personality, experiences, and environment, which are all _____ factors.

    c. Onset of organic brain disorders can cause the person to have secondary _____ problems as a reaction to the primary physical problem.

3. Organic brain disorders are a major health problem in the United States; one _____ of all first admissions to mental hospitals turn out to be _____ _____ _____.

4. What are the four major questions to be answered in diagnosing an organic brain disorder?

   a.

   b.

   c.

   d.

5. What are the seven major symptoms of organic brain disorder?

   a.   e.

   b.   f.

   c.   g.

   d.

6. Using the following terms, fill in the blanks to form a list of information sources used to make a differential diagnosis.

   brain wave   history   neurological
   cerebrospinal   interviews   neuropsychological
   emission   magnetic   observation
   x-rays

   a.   Direct _____ of the patient

   b.   Detailed _____ of the onset and progress of the symptoms

   c.   _____ with the patient's family and physician

   d.   A series of _____ tests to assess reflexes

   e.   EEGs (electrical _____ _____ readings from the face and scalp)

   f.   Brain CT scans (a series of _____-_____ of the brain)

   g.   Chemical analyses of _____ fluid

   h.   _____ tests such as the Halstead-Reitan Battery

   i.   PET (positron _____ tomography)

   j.   MRI (_____ resonance imaging)

7. Beyond determining organicity, more difficulties are encountered in diagnosing specific organic brain disorders. Complete the following summary of the difficulty of symptom overlap:

   (a)_____ disorders sometimes have same symptoms, and

   (b)_____ _____ disorder can have different symptoms in different patients.

8. Name seven factors that determine which symptoms a patient will manifest with an organic brain disorder.

   •   •

   •   •

   •   •

   •

9. What is the difference between a disorder that is *diffuse* and one that is *localized*?

10. What does the symptom pattern of an organic disability often indicate?

11. Write the name of the problem next to the appropriate symptoms.

apraxia   *fluent aphasia*   *nonfluent aphasia*   *visual agnosia*

a. _____   Unable to make sense out of visual perceptions

b. _____   Great difficulty initiating speech and enunciating words

c. _____   Unable to perform ordinarily simple voluntary tasks

d. _____   Can form words but does so with a lack of meaning

12. Name the lobe of the brain and the region of the lobe that would be affected if the average right-handed person has

a. fluent aphasia:

b. nonfluent aphasia:

Types of Acquired Brain Injuries

13. Identify the following types of cerebral infection mentioned in your text: AIDS dementia, general paresis, cerebral abscess, meningitis, Creutzfeldt-Jacob, and encephalitis.

a. _____   Infection encapsulated by connective tissue

b. _____   Infection that inflames the brain

c. _____   Infection that inflames the covering of the brain and spinal cord

d. _____   Brain deterioration as a result of untreated syphilitic infection

e. _____   Encephalopathy that is the human equivalent of mad cow disease

f. _____   Brain deterioration resulting from acquired immunodeficiency syndrome

14. What fraction of AIDS patients will experience neuropsychological difficulties?

15. Identify the three kinds of brain trauma: *penetrating head injury, concussion,* and *contusion*.

a. _____   Exterior head trauma causes brain to slosh against inside of skull, causing neural bruising, coma, and possibly convulsions or delirium

b. _____   Injury from a foreign object entering the brain and destroying brain tissue

c. _____   Brain is jarred with brief loss of consciousness

16. Write the correct terms in front of their definitions.

a. _____ _____ is a state of disorientation that sometimes occurs when a person awakens from a coma after a contusion

b. _____ _____ is the common term for *dementia pugilistica*.

17. Organize the three types of brain trauma from least serious to most serious.

Least serious — _____ / _____ / _____ — Most serious

18. Serious head trauma, the leading cause of death among children and young adults, occurs at a rate of about

    (a)_____ people per 100,000. That means your chances of serious head trauma are about

    (b)_____ in 1,000. However, if you are a young (c) *male / female*, between the ages of

    (d)_____ and _____ years old, you are in the highest risk group. The nature of the accident is

    likely to concern a(n) (e)_____, and (f)_____ intoxication is likely to be involved.

19. Phineas P. Gage is a famous character in psychology books. Would you want his claim to fame? Why or why not?

20. Identity the following CVA-related concepts.

    a. _____   is the common term for a CVA.

    b. _____   is what CVA stands for.

    c. _____   is the area of dead brain tissue damaged by reduced blood supply.

    d. _____   is bulging in the wall of a blood vessel.

    e. _____   is rupturing of a blood vessel.

    f. _____   is a big factor that contributes to the possibility of brain hemorrhage.

    g. _____   is when a floating ball lodges in a vessel which is too narrow for it to pass.

    h. _____   is the gradual build up of fatty material slowly blocking off the blood vessel.

    i. _____   is the term for a small CVA that goes unnoticed in a less critical brain area.

21. Identify the term for the following definitions that classify brain tumors.

    a. _____   tumors grow within the brain, destroy normal brain tissue, and replace it with abnormal tumor cells.

    b. _____   tumors grow outside the brain, but inside the skull.

    c. _____   tumors develop in some other area of the body and travel to the brain via body fluids.

    d. _____   tumors are original sites of disease development.

22. Give examples of degenerative brain disorders with deterioration in the following locations.

    a. Cerebral cortex:

    b. Subcortical areas:

    c. Both cortical and subcortical regions:

23. Use terms from the degenerative disorders to identify the following concepts.

   a. _____ is severe general mental deterioration.

   b. _____ down is a normal central system change expected with aging.

   c. _____ is the term for severe organic deterioration not part of normal aging.

   d. _____ _____ are twisted, distorted nerve fibers found in Alzheimer's disease.

   e. _____ _____ are microscopic lesions in neurons.

   f. _____ is a damaged area.

   g. _____ are the hidden victims of dementia.

24. Identify the degenerative disorder(s) associated with each of the following concepts.

   a. Most common form of dementia: _____ disease

   b. Second most common degenerative brain disease: _____ _____ disease

   c. Down syndrome victims will develop this if they live past age forty: _____ disease

   d. Dominant gene disorder (either parent to either gender child): _____ _____

   e. Shows tremor that can be controlled for short periods of time: _____ disease

   f. Psychological distress: _____

   g. Neurotransmitter acetylcholine is involved: _____ disease

   h. Major risk factor is high blood pressure: _____ dementia

25. Why is a correct dementia diagnosis very important when the prognosis is ultimately the same?

26. Identify the following concepts associated with nutritional deficiencies.

   a. _____ Disorder caused by thiamine deficiency

   b. _____ Disorder caused by niacin deficiency

   c. _____ _____ Another thiamine-deficiency disease commonly seen in the United States

   d. _____ _____ Inability to develop new memories

   e. _____ Tendency to unknowingly fill memory gaps with fantasized "memories"

27. List the disorders resulting from overactivity and underactivity for these two glands.

Gland	Underactivity	Overactivity
Thyroid:		
Adrenal:		

28. What are some toxic agents that can affect the brain and, as a result, one's psychological health?

29. Lead poisoning, called (a)_____ _____, causes an accumulation of (b)_____ in the brain. The most frequent victims of lead poisoning are (c)_____, who may become mentally (d)_____ as a result of the poisoning. Lead is in the environment in the forms of (name at least four) (e)_____ _____ _____ _____.

30. Mercury and manganese poisoning are seen most often in people who (a)_____with these on a daily basis. Other people may suffer from these toxins as a result of industrial waste contamination, such as by eating (b)_____ from polluted waters.

31. A failed suicide attempt with carbon monoxide may leave a person (a) *ap_____*, (b) *con_____* and with (c)_____ deficits, in addition to the issues that were involved in the suicide attempt. These symptoms may clear up within (d)_____ years; however, for some people they are permanent.

The Epilepsies

Use the following terms to complete the next two questions about epilepsy:

absence seizure	*idiopathic*	*tonic-clonic*
complex partial	*simple partial*	
disruption	*symptomatic*	

32. Epilepsy is a (a)_____ in the normal electrical activity of the brain. Epilepsy that has a known cause is classified as (b)_____, and epilepsy that has no known cause is classified as (c)_____.

33. Identify each of the following types of epileptic seizures:

    a.   _____ _____   Loss of contact with reality for a brief time while engaging in mechanical behavior

    b.   _____-_____   Loss of consciousness and convulsions

    c.   _____ _____   Brief loss of awareness

    d.   _____ _____   Muscle spasms in part of the body

34. Number the events for a tonic-clonic epileptic seizure in the correct temporal order.

    _____ Confused and sleepy

    _____ Aura phase

    _____ Clonic phase

    _____ Tonic phase

35. Although there is no particular personality type and no mental illness associated with epilepsy, a person

with epilepsy may experience a secondary psychological disturbance because of the loss of _____

_____ that goes with being temporarily unable to control one's own body.

36. Lagniappe—a little something extra—just in case it's on the test. Match the following terms to the appropriate phrases.

absence seizure	*differential diagnosis*	*lability*
aura	*encephalitis*	*meninges*
automatisms	*executive function*	*threshold model*
Cushing's syndrome	*head-hunter*	
delirium	*hypertension*	

a. _____ Term meaning high blood pressure

b. _____ Genetic risk factors plus additional risk factors that cause the disorder to develop

c. _____ Moving from one emotion to another quickly and inappropriately

d. _____ Choice between disorders when there is overlap of symptoms

e. _____ Sleeping sickness

f. _____ Membrane covering brain and spinal cord

g. _____ Particularly responsible for head injuries in football

h. _____ Ability to plan, initiate, sequence, and monitor complex behaviors

i. _____ Acute confusion (not "a cute confusion") (see Helpful Hint 2)

j. _____ Possible diagnosis for an abnormally emotional, obese young woman

k. _____ Repetitive, purposeless movements of a complex partial seizure

l. _____ A strange sensation that warns a seizure may be coming

m. _____ Same as petit mal

HELPFUL HINTS

1. *Beware*—do not "confuse" *delirium* and *dementia*. They both mean confused. But if you had to be one, which one would you rather be?

2. Remember that acquired brain disorders, as their name tells us, are by definition biological. This may help you to keep them separate from other disorders.

PRACTICE TEST

Use the following test questions to check your knowledge of the material in this chapter. You may want to write the answers on a separate sheet of paper so you can take the test more than once.

1. Neuropsychological disorders differ from other types of mental disorders in that
   a. they are unrelated to age.
   b. emotions are not involved in the symptoms.
   c. they are, by definition, biogenic.
   d. judgment is rarely impaired.

2. Which of the following is a problem in the diagnosis of neuropsychological disorders?

    a. The symptoms of a given problem often overlap with the symptoms of other problems.
    b. A given problem may produce different symptoms in different patients.
    c. A variety of circumstances in the patient's life may affect his/her pattern of symptoms.
    d. All of the above can be true.

3. A woman who has suffered a stroke has difficulty speaking. When asked how she feels, she says, "Uh, . . . I, . . . I, . . . ah . . . bad. Uh, . . . feel bad." This illustrates

    a. nonfluent aphasia.
    b. agnosia.
    c. fluent aphasia.
    d. apraxia.

4. Agnosia patients display an impairment of

    a. voluntary movement.
    b. comprehension of spoken language.
    c. sensory perception.
    d. recognition of common objects.

5. Creutzfeldt-Jakob disease is related to

    a. general paresis.
    b. mad cow disease.
    c. sleeping sickness.
    d. AIDS dementia.

6. Which of the following is classified as a brain trauma?

    a. meningitis
    b. contusion
    c. infarction
    d. thrombosis

7. Jarring the brain and short-term unconsciousness are to _____ as bruising the brain and coma are to _____.

    a. concussion; contusion
    b. apraxia; agnosia
    c. traumatic delirium; delirium tremens
    d. contusion; laceration

8. A problem characterized by blockage of arteries carrying blood to the brain is called

    a. a cerebral hemorrhage.
    b. senility.
    c. Korsakoff's psychosis.
    d. a cerebral infarction.

9. The term for a brain tumor that is the result of cancer originating in another part of the body and spreading to the brain is

    a. metastatic tumor.
    b. aneurysm.
    c. extracerebral tumor.
    d. cerebral thrombus.

10. Which of the following is a subcortical degenerative disorder?

    a. Parkinson's disease

    b. Alzheimer's disease

    c. Addison's disease

    d. Grave's disease

11. A child has been diagnosed with Down syndrome. Which of the following can be said with greatest certainty?

    a. This is a genetically-based disorder linked to problems on chromosome 11.

    b. This child has a greater than normal risk of developing Korsakoff's pyschosis.

    c. Down syndrome is the end result of untreated syphilis.

    d. If he/she lives long enough, the person will eventually succumb to Alzheimer's disease.

12. Which of the following is true of Lewy body disease?

    a. It is named after Gherick Lewy, a baseball player who died from it.

    b. It is named after the presence of microscopic brain structures called Lewy bodies.

    c. It is the one degenerative disease that strikes younger people more often than the elderly.

    d. Its symptoms include a characteristic 4–8 cycle per second tremor in the extremities.

13. Both _____ and _____ involve damage to the basal ganglia.

    a. Huntington's chorea; Parkinson's disease

    b. vascular dementia; AIDS dementia

    c. Grave's disease; Cushing's disease

    d. dementia; delirium

14. Which of the following disorders is somewhat successfully treated with drugs that increase dopamine levels in the brain?

    a. Lewy body disease

    b. Addison's disease

    c. Parkinson's disease

    d. Grave's disease

15. Aunt Mary has Korsakoff's psychosis. What might we also guess about Aunt Mary?

    a. She has had a drinking problem for some time.

    b. She is in the early stages of Alzheimer's disease.

    c. She is only of borderline intelligence.

    d. She is probably of Eastern European Jewish descent.

16. Grave's disease is to _____ as Addison's disease is to _____.

    a. alcoholism; lead poisoning

    b. the adrenal glands; the pancreas

    c. syphilis; AIDS

    d. the thyroid gland; the adrenal glands

17. Three-year-old Bess complains of stomach pains. She is constipated, is very pale, and constantly pulls at her hair. Her doctor suspects that she has

    a. been eating paint chips containing lead.

    b. been sniffing glue.

    c. an overactive thyroid.

    d. epilepsy.

18. Thousands of Japanese have been paralyzed and brain damaged after eating fish contaminated with

    a. lead.

    b. apolipoprotein E (ApoE).

    c. mercury.

    d. Epstein-Barr virus.

19. Randolph, age ten, has begun suffering from seizures. He passes out and exhibits muscle spasms. His doctor says he has idiopathic epilepsy. The cause of Randolph's seizures is

    a. head injury.

    b. lead encephalopathy.

    c. a toxic reaction.

    d. Cannot tell for sure—idiopathic epilepsy has no certain cause.

20. Both absence ("petit mal") and tonic-clonic ("grand mal") seizures are considered

    a. non-epileptic forms of seizure.

    b. generalized seizures.

    c. non-spreading forms of seizure.

    d. partial seizures.

ANSWERS

Guided Self-Study (p. 236)

1. Cerebral infection (neurosyphilis): Henry VIII, probably Christopher Columbus (437)
Brain trauma: Concussion—Merril Hodge, Al Toon, Steve Young, Troy Aikman (439–440)
                     Laceration—Phineas Gage (440–441)
Brain tumor: George Gershwin (433)
Degenerative disorders: Alzheimer's disease—Former President Ronald Reagan (446)
Endocrine disorder: Graves' disease—Former President and Mrs. Bush and their dog (452)
Epilepsy: Julius Caesar, Fyodor Dostoevsky, and Vincent van Gogh (452)

2.   a. psychological; differential

    b. physical; psychological

    c. psychological (432–433)

3. one-fourth; organic brain disorders (432)

4.   a. Is the disorder organically caused?

    b. If so, what is the nature of the brain pathology?

    c. Where is it located in the brain?

    d. How are psychosocial problems influencing the organic disorder's symptoms, and is psychotherapy needed? (432)

    ("Is it? If so, what kind and where?"—summarizes the first three questions for easy memory facilitation.)

5.   a. impairment of attention and arousal (orientation)

    b. impairment of language function

    c. impairment of learning and memory

    d. impairment of visual-perceptual function

    e. impairment of motor skills

    f. impairment of executive function (ability to plan, initiate, sequence, monitor, and stop complex behaviors)

    g. impairment of higher-order intellectual function (434–435)

6. a. observation
   b. history
   c. Interviews
   d. neurological
   e. brain wave

   f. x-rays
   g. cerebrospinal
   h. neuropsychological
   i. emission
   j. magnetic (432–433)

7. a. Different
   b. the same (777)

8. specific location of the pathology in the brain
   patient's age
   patient's general physical condition
   patient's prior level of intellectual development
   patient's premorbid personality
   patient's emotional stability
   patient's social situation (433–434)

9. *Diffuse* is scattered out over many different areas.
   Localized is clearly affecting specific locations within the brain without affecting other locations. (432–433)
   (for ease of memory: diffuse = scattered; localized = limited)

10. the specific areas of the brain that are affected by the pathology (433)

11. a. visual agnosia (435)
    b. nonfluent aphasia (435)
    c. apraxia (434)
    d. fluent aphasia (435)

12. a. left hemisphere, toward the rear (435)
    b. left hemisphere, toward the front (435)

13. a. cerebral abscess (436)
    b. encephalitis (436–437)
    c. meningitis (437)

    d. neurosyphilis (437)
    e. Creutzfeldt-Jacob (438)
    f. HIV dementia (437–438)

14. 30 to 50% (437)

15. a. contusion (440)
    b. penetrating head injury (440)
    c. concussion (439)

16. a. Acute confusional state (440)
    b. Punch drunk (440)

17. Least serious— *concussion / contusion / laceration* —Most serious (439–440)

18. a. 200
    b. 2
    c. male

    d. 15 and 24
    e. automobile or motorcycle
    f. alcohol (441)

19. No, Phineas's claim to fame is not one to be envied. He had a huge metal rod blown into his skull in the 1840s. His survival of such a trauma would be surprising even with modern medicine, to say nothing of the medicine of the 1840s. His personality was profoundly changed by the head trauma. (440–441)

20. a. Stroke (441–442)
    b. Cerebrovascular accident (441–442)
    c. Infarction (441)
    d. Aneurysm (443)
    e. Hemorrhage (442–443)

    f. Hypertension (442)
    g. Embolism (442)
    h. Thrombosis (442)
    i. Silent (442)

21. a. Intracerebral
    b. Extracerebral
    c. Metastatic
    d. Primary (444)

22. a. Alzheimer's disease (445–446)
    b. Huntington's chorea and Parkinson's disease (447–448)
    c. Vascular dementia and Lewy body disease (447–448)

23. a. Dementia (445)
    b. Slowing (445)
    c. Pathological (445)
    d. Neurofibrillary tangles (445)
    e. Senile plaques (445)
    f. Infarct (447)
    g. Caregivers (446)

24. a. Alzheimer's (445–446)
    b. Lewy body (447)
    c. Alzheimer's (445–446)
    d. Huntington's chorea (448)
    e. Parkinson's (448–449)
    f. All of the disorders (This was to point out the reason these disorders are discussed in this course. Even though these are caused by physical pathology, they involve psychological issues.)
    g. Alzheimer's (445–446)
    h. Vascular (447)

25. There are some medications that help (or at least delay the progression of) some of the degenerative disorders, but much more importantly, there are treatable disorders that mimic dementia (illnesses, reactions to medication, depression). (449)

26. a. Beriberi (451)
    b. Pellagra (451)
    c. Korsakoff's psychosis (451)
    d. Anterograde amnesia (451)
    e. Confabulation (451)

27.

Gland	Underactivity	Overactivity
Thyroid	hypothyroidism, or myxedema	hyperthyroidism, or Graves' disease
Adrenal	Addison's disease	Cushing's syndrome (451–452)

28. Lead, psychoactive drugs, carbon monoxide, heavy metals such as mercury and manganese, psychoactive drugs, and carbon monoxide (452–453)

29. a. lead encephalopathy
    b. fluid
    c. children
    d. retarded
    e. lead-based paints, lead-lined water pipes, old plaster walls, clay pottery, candles with lead-core wicks, exhaust from leaded gasoline in autos, and industrial pollution (452–453)

30. a. work (452–453)
    b. fish

31. a. apathetic
    b. confused
    c. memory
    d. two (453)

32. a. disruption (454)
    b. symptomatic (453)
    c. idiopathic (454)

33. a. complex partial
    b. tonic-clonic
    c. absence seizure
    d. simple partial (454)

34. 4, 1, 3, and 2 (454)

35. self-esteem (454)

36. a. hypertension (442)   h. executive function (435)
    b. threshold model (447)   i. delirium (434)
    c. lability (435)   j. Cushing's syndrome (452)
    d. differential diagnosis (432) k. automatisms (454)
    e. encephalitis (436–437)   l. aura (453)
    f. meninges (437)   m. absence seizure (454)
    g. head-hunter (442)

Practice Test (p. 242)

1. a. Incorrect. Many of them, especially the degenerative disorders, are very age-related.
   b. No. Emotions are affected as well as all other aspects of psychological functioning.
   c. Right!
   d. No. Judgment is affected as well as all other aspects of psychological functioning.

2. a. This is true, but read on.
   b. Yes indeed, but keep going.
   c. This is correct, but look at the others again.
   d. Correct!

3. a. Yes!
   b. No. Agnosia in inability to recognize familiar objects.
   c. Sorry. Fluency relates to smooth talking—she doesn't seem too smooth here.
   d. No. Apraxia is related to motor movements.

4. a. No, that would be apraxia.
   b. No, that would be aphasia.
   c. Sorry. The senses aren't the problem; how that information is interpreted is the issue.
   d. Right!

5. a. This is one you just have to memorize. General paresis relates to syphilis.
   b. You got it!
   c. No, this is epidemic encephalitis.
   d. Sorry, totally different disease.

6. a. No, this is an infection.
   b. Correct!
   c. No, this is a blockage of a blood vessel.
   d. Sorry, this is something that blocks a blood vessel.

7. a. Right!
   b. No. The question is getting at degrees of injury, not types of problem.
   c. Sorry. The word traumatic is related here, but delirium tremens refers to alcoholism.
   d. You're on the right track but we want a different pair in a different order.

8. a. Wrong. A hemorrhage is breaking of a blood vessel.
   b. No. Senility is a general term not used here. We want the term for the specific problem.
   c. No, this has to do with alcohol use, not blood vessel damage.
   d. Right!

9. a. Correct!
   b. No, this is a ballooning weak spot in an artery.
   c. No, this just means a tumor outside the brain (between brain and skull).
   d. Sorry. This is another form of arterial blockage.

10. a. Right!
    b. No. Alzheimer's disease affects higher centers first.
    c. No. This is an endocrine disorder, not a degenerative disorder.
    d. No. This is an endocrine disorder, not a degenerative disorder.

11. a. Half correct, but wrong chromosome; it's chromosome 21.
    b. No. Korsakoff's psychosis is related to alcoholism.
    c. Incorrect. It is a genetic problem.
    d. Right, unfortunately.

12. a. Gotcha! You were thinking of Lou Gherig's disease.
    b. Correct!
    c. Incorrect. It is not significantly different from Alzheimer's disease in this regard.
    d. No, that would be Parkinson's disease.

13. a. Right!
    b. No. These can affect the brain anywhere.
    c. No. These are endocrine disorders that do not specifically target movement centers.
    d. Incorrect. These are terms for decreased cognitive capacities and confusion, not motor problems.

14. a. No. There doesn't seem to be any drug for this one.
    b. No. This seems unaffected by dopamine treatment.
    c. Yes!
    d. No. Dopamine is not mentioned in connection with this.

15. a. Right!
    b. No. Remember, Korsakoff's psychosis is related to one specific thing.
    c. No. Intelligence has nothing to do with it.
    d. No. This would be Tay-Sachs disease, and it's not even in this chapter.

16. a. Incorrect. Hint: the answer has to do with the problematic body part.
    b. Sorry. You're on the right track, but wrong body parts.
    c. No. The ones we are looking for are endocrine disorders.
    d. Right!

17. a. Correct!
    b. No. You just have to know the symptoms here.
    c. No, the one we are looking for is a toxic reaction.
    d. Incorrect. We are looking for a toxic reaction.

18. a. Good guess, but wrong. You are on the right track, though—we are looking for a metal.
    b. No. This is a brain chemical suspected of being connected with Alzheimer's disease.
    c. Correct!
    d. No. This is a source of a cerebral infection

19. a. This is possible, but read on.
    b. Could be, but there are other possibilities.
    c. Perhaps, but think about it some more.
    d. Yes!

20. a. No. They are very epileptic.
    b. Right!
    c. No, actually, they do spread. That's why they are not partial seizures.
    d. Sorry. Just the opposite.

CHAPTER 16
DISORDERS OF CHILDHOOD AND ADOLESCENCE

LEARNING OBJECTIVES

By the time you have finished studying this chapter, you should be able to do the following:

1. Compare and contrast disorders of childhood and adolescence with disorders of adulthood, and summarize information on the prevalence of child psychopathology. (458–461)

2. Explain the classification system *DSM-IV-TR* uses for childhood disorders, describe the degree to which childhood disorders predict adult disorders, and describe the degree to which treatment of childhood disorders can prevent adult disorders. (459–460)

3. Define disruptive behavior disorders, and describe three subtypes of attention deficit hyperactivity disorder. (461–462)

4. Describe two varieties of conduct disorder based on age of onset, and explain how they relate to adult antisocial behavior and antisocial personality disorder. (463–464)

5. Name and describe three varieties of anxiety disorder in children, and summarize information presented in your text on childhood depression. (466–469)

6. Name and describe three varieties of eating disorder in children and adolescents. (469–471)

7. Name and describe two varieties of elimination disorder in children. (471–472)

8. Name and describe four varieties of sleep disorder in children. (473–474)

9. Summarize information presented in your text on learning disorders. (474–476)

10. Summarize information presented in your text on problems with stuttering, and with language articulation, reception, and expression. (476)

11. Summarize explanations of and recommended treatments for the disorders of childhood and adolescence from the psychodynamic, behavioral, and cognitive perspectives. (476–481)

12. Summarize explanations of and recommended treatments for the disorders of childhood and adolescence from the interpersonal, sociocultural and neuroscience perspectives, referring particularly to the biological treatment of attention deficit hyperactivity disorder. (479–482)

KEY TERMS

The following terms are in bold print in your text and are important to your understanding of the chapter. Look them up in the text and write down their definitions.

anorexia nervosa (469)
attention deficit hyperactivity disorder (461)
bulimia nervosa (470)
childhood depression (468)
conduct disorder (463)
disruptive behavior disorders (461)
encopresis (472)
enuresis (472)
generalized anxiety disorder (467)

learning disorders (474)
nightmares (473)
play therapy (480)
self-instructional training (478)
separation anxiety disorder (467)
sleep terrors (473)
sleepwalking (473)
social phobia (467)
stuttering (476)

IMPORTANT NAMES

Identify the following persons and their major contributions to abnormal psychology as discussed in this chapter.

Meichenbaum and Goodman (478)   O. H. Mowrer (477)
T. E. Moffitt (465)

GUIDED SELF-STUDY

General Issues in Childhood Psychopathology

1. Childhood disorders need to be studied separately from adult disorders. In other words, the disorder is particularly noted as part of childhood instead of just included in the regular listing of disorders. This is because

    a. some childhood disorders have no _____ in adult psychopathology.

    b. _____ is a critical issue in determining what is a problem in a child. (Standards of behaviors change with different ages for children.)

    c. Childhood is a time of changes, so even normal children may have _____ psychological problems that will just pass as development continues.

    d. Course and _____ of a disorder is very different in children than in adults.

    e. Children, who by the fact of being children, are little people with limited awareness, knowledge, and resources. They are unable to get help for themselves and their situations and are dependent on adults for _____ for their psychological problems.

2. Complete the following information about the prevalence of childhood disorders.

    a. _____ Estimated number of children and adolescents believed to have some form of moderate to severe psychological disorder

    b. _____ Age at which treatment is often first sought for children

    c. _____ Reason childhood disorder rates rise at that age

    d. _____ Gender that has more problems in childhood

    e. _____ Gender that has more problems in adolescence

3. Complete the following blanks to form the four major categories of childhood and adolescence disorders.

    a. *d*_____ behavior disorders

    b. disorders of *e*_____ distress

    c. *h*_____ disorders

    d. learning and *c*_____ disorders

4. Use the following terms to describe the big questions about the relationship between childhood disorders and adult disorders:

continuity   *reactivity*   *prevent*
predict   *stability*

    a.   Do childhood disorders _____ adult disorders?

    b.   If so, can treatment in childhood _____ adult disorders?

    c.   _____ of disorders: Will a childhood disorder persist into adulthood in a similar form?

    d.   _____ of developmental adaptation: Does having a childhood problem cause later development to be skewed (screwed up) so that eventual normal adult adjustment can never be attained?

    e.   _____ to particular stressors: If a child has had a problem in childhood, will he/she have that same vulnerability (weak spot) in his/her adult emotional life?

Disruptive Behavior Disorders

5. Name the two disruptive behavior disorders discussed in this chapter. After each one list the subtypes into which it is divided.

    a.

    b.

6. List some behaviors that a child must learn in order to evolve from the totally un-self-controlled, impulsive infant to a well-behaved elementary school student.

7. Fill in the following blanks for ADHD:

    a. _____   Term for excessive physical activity

    b. _____   Difference between the high physical activity of a normal child and a child with this disorder

    c. ____ ____ ____   Term for unspecified brain disorder supposed to cause this problem

    d. _____ _____   Term for inability to focus and sustain attention

    e. _____-_____   Percentage of school children believed to have ADHD

    f. _____:_____   Ratio of boys to girls with ADHD

8. Fill in the following blanks to complete the four criteria for conduct disorders.

    a. _____   against people or animals

    b. _____   of property

    c. _____   or theft

    d. Other serious _____ of rules

9. a. _____   Age group when antisocial behavior is most commonly found

    b. _____ _____   Type of conduct disorder most correlated with antisocial personality disorder

    c. _____   Frequent outcome for people who as children had conduct disorders but did not develop antisocial personality disorder

    d. _____   Besides gender, what group of factors definitely play a part in conduct disorders?

Disorders of Emotional Distress

10. In the disorders of emotional distress, the child is not acting out aggressively toward the outside world.

    He/She has turned the stress and conflict (a)_____. This type of disorder includes (b)_____

    disorders and childhood (c)_____. In younger children, these disorders are difficult to diagnose

    because the child does not have the conceptual skills to understand his/her own (d)_____, nor the

    (e)_____ skills to communicate them in order to get help.

11. What two fears are normally experienced by very young children?

12. When do these normal fears become "disorders?"

13. List the three fear disorders discussed in this chapter. (Two of them were already introduced in the chapter on anxiety disorders.)

    -
    -
    -

14. What is the "vicious" cycle in generalized anxiety disorder?

15. Here are words to complete the summary of childhood depression:

accurate	exaggerated	older
altered	interest	
clinging	mood	

    Depressed children do not necessarily act like depressed adults. Depressed adults usually show sad or

    hopeless (a)_____, loss of (b)_____ in usual activities, fatigue, insomnia, and

    (c)_____ (poor or excessive) appetite. Children may or may not show these symptoms of

    depression. Psychologists that deal with depressed children find that children may show depression by

    (d)_____ to parents, refusing to go to school, or by expressing (e)_____ fears, perhaps

    about their parents' deaths. (f)_____ children may seem sulky, withdrawn, or retreat to their rooms.

    They may have school problems, get in trouble, or develop a slovenly manner of self-presentation. Again, an

    (g)_____ diagnosis is very important.

16. Explain how the *warriors* and *worriers* explanation fits the gender patterns seen in both disruptive behaviors disorders and in emotional distress disorders.

Eating Disorders

17. Identify the following concepts associated with eating disorders:

    a. _____ _____   Severe restriction of food intake caused by fear of gaining weight

    b. _____   Percentage of underweightness that *DSM-IV* defines as abnormal

    c. _____-_____   Percentage of eating disorder victims who are female

    d. _____-_____   "Normal" age of onset for an eating disorder

    e. _____   Suspension of menstrual period

    f. _____   Term for type of eating disorder in which there is refusal to eat

    g. _____-_____   Type that eats voraciously and then forces the food out of the body, are abnormally underweight, and without menstrual cycles

    h. _____ _____   Type that eats voraciously and then forces the food out of the body, but does not meet the criteria for anorexia

    i. _____   Term for being 20% or more overweight

    j. _____   Term for syndrome when only some of the criteria for the eating disorders are met

18. List some of the behaviors for girls who may be particularly at risk for developing an eating disorder.

Elimination Disorders

19. Identify the following concepts associated with the elimination disorders.

    a. _____   Term for attainment of major developmental skills

    b. _____   Lack of bladder control

    c. _____   Minimum age when *DSM-IV* will even consider a bladder problem

    d. _____   Term meaning bladder control never developed

    e. _____   Term meaning bladder control developed and lost

    f. _____   Lack of bowel control

    g. _____   Which of the two elimination disorders is more common?

    h. _____   What percentage of boys, aged ten years, have enuresis?

    i. _____   What is the common cause of secondary enuresis?

Childhood Sleep Disorders

20. Identify which childhood sleep disorder terms goes with each of the following phrases:

    a. _____   Difficulty falling asleep or staying asleep

    b. _____   "Normal" scary dreams that happen in dream sleep

    c. _____ _____   Rare kind of scary dream which happen during slow wave sleep

    d. _____ _____   Scary dream that causes intense physiological arousal

    e. _____-_____   Percentage of children who have the rare kind of bad dreams

    f. _____-_____   Percentage of three- to five-year-olds who have "normal" scary dreams

    g. _____ _____   Bad dream whose occurrence is more likely in first hours of sleep

h. _____ Bad dream whose occurrence is more likely closer to morning

i. _____ Another term for sleepwalking

j. _____-_____ Percentage of healthy children who may sleep walk

k. _____ When sleepwalking is most likely to occur

Learning and Communication Disorders

21. Identify the following concepts from the learning and communication disorders:

    a. _____ Reading disorders

    b. _____ Disorder showing inability to enunciate clearly at age-appropriate level

    c. _____ Disorder characterized by a problem of putting thoughts into words

    d. _____ Disorder when there is a problem understanding what others are saying

    e. _____ Interruption of fluent speech because of sound production error

22. List three difficulties involved in making a diagnosis of a learning disorder.

    •

    •

    •

23. List some other problems that must be eliminated to diagnose a learning-based disorder.

24. Use the following terms to fill in the blanks for learning disorders.

birth	*esteem*	*normal*
dietary	*genetics*	*social*
educational	*mathematical*	
environmental	*mentally retarded*	

If a child is professionally diagnosed as being learning disordered, by definition you automatically know that

the child is not (a)_____ _____. Even though the child displays (b)_____

intelligence, the child has a handicapping deficit in reading, written expression, or (c)_____ skills.

The resultant academic problems may cause low self-(d)_____, anxiety, and frustrations, which in

turn compound into problems in (e)_____ relationships. The causes of learning disabilities are not

known: Some of the possibilities are (f)_____, injuries during the (g)_____ process, and

(h)_____ deficiencies. Technically, deficiencies caused by (i)_____ problems and

inadequate (j)_____ opportunities are not supposed to be included in the diagnostic category of

learning disorders; however, the reality is that they often are included since one cannot say with certainty

what the cause of a child's deficiency may be.

The Psychodynamic Perspective

25. *Id, ego, or superego?* The "general rule" for the psychodynamic interpretation of childhood developmental

    disorders is that the child's sexual and aggressive impulses from the (a)_____ are in conflict with

    the parents and the developing (b)_____.

26. Now, match each of the following childhood disorders to those basic psychodynamic explanations for the
    disorders.

    anorexia   *enuresis*
    encopresis   *nightmares and night terrors*

    a. _____ Unconscious conflicts coming out in disguised (latent) form

    b. _____ Expression of hostility toward parents

    c. _____ Regression, likely motivated by envy of a younger sibling

    d. _____ Regression to avoid maturing sexuality in adolescence

27. Since children lack the conceptual and verbal skills to engage in traditional psychoanalytic talk therapy, what
    approach do the psychoanalysts use?

The Behavioral Perspective

28. Behaviorists always look at behavior as a (a)_____ process: The problem is the (b)_____

    to learn a needed skill or environmental (c)_____ of inappropriate behavior. For behaviorism,

    therapy is always a matter of (d)_____.

29. Identify the following learning processes or behavioral treatment techniques.

    a. _____ Using a star chart for "dry" nights to earn a trip to get ice cream

    b. _____ Ignoring obscenities uttered by a three-year-old

    c. _____ Using a Mowrer pad to reduce nocturnal enuresis

    d. _____ Having an older child demonstrate gentle play with the new puppy

    e. _____ Going to visit the new school classroom several times before the first
                            attendance day

The Cognitive Perspective

30. What does the cognitive theorist always "think" the primary problem is?

31. Cognitive therapists try to teach the ADHD student to guide his/her own thinking instead of letting his/her
    thoughts range free at the whim of whatever grabs the attention at any given moment. List self-talk
    statements that an ADHD child might learn in self-instructional training to increase self-direction in a task.
    List at least four.

    •

    •

    •

    •

32. List retraining goals a cognitive therapist would aim for in a depressed child.

    a. Less *in*_____ attributions, less *st*_____ attributions, and less *gl*_____ attributions

    b. Improved _____-solving skills

    c. Increase _____ level

    d. Increase _____ communication

    e. _____ skills training

33. What does the acronym STOP represent?

Interpersonal Perspective

34. The family systems theorist uses the main interpersonal method of therapy which sees the child's developmental disorder as a symptom of a larger problem in the (a)_____. The family systems therapist watches to see how family members (b)_____ with each other. Here, to cure the child, one must cure the (c)_____.

Sociocultural Perspective

35. There is no doubt that there are correlations between the disorders of childhood and adolescence and socioeconomic and cultural factors.

    a. _____-related factors correlate with conduct disorders.

    b. Cultural studies point out how a child displays its dysfunction will be _____ of that particular culture.

    c. _____ disorders are seen in subcultures that idealize hyper-thinness.

Neuroscience Perspective

36. The biological perspective thinks at least some developmental disorders are biological because they tend to be seen in the same (a)_____ and some of them respond to (b)_____.

37. a. What disorder(s) in particular respond(s) to medication?

    b. What medications are used?

38. There are three strong arguments against using drugs to treat psychological disorders in children. What are they?

39. Young people with conduct disorder persistently (a)_____ _____ _____ _____ _____ as well as show (b)_____ tendencies toward people or animals. (c) those diagnosed with this disorder must be under the age of (c)_____.

40. Extensive research on the caused of ADHD focuses on (a)_____ abnormality that accounts for

impaired (b)_____ and (c)_____. The most common form of biological intervention is

doses of (d)_____.

HELPFUL HINTS

1. One of the most common misconceptions among students is that "learning disabled" is a nice way to say mentally retarded. In fact, the professional diagnosis of learning disabilities *guarantees* that the child is *not mentally retarded*. One can find children in gifted programs (programs for high IQs) who are learning disabled.

2. A young child becoming afraid of strangers and becoming afraid of being separated from a primary caretaker reflects no psychological problem at all. These developments are the result of a child getting smarter. Developing thinking skills allows a child to identify a person as "not-my-caretaker" or to realize that separation from primary caretaker is about to happen. Before, the child wasn't afraid because conceptual development was not adequate for realizations and expectations. If you are a parent worried that your child's problem might be serious, seek professional counsel so you will know whether intervention is necessary.

PRACTICE TEST

Use the following test questions to check your knowledge of the material in this chapter. You may want to write the answers on a separate sheet of paper so you can take the test more than once.

1. Clinic admissions for treatment of childhood disorders begin to rise when
   a. puberty occurs.
   b. children begin to go to school.
   c. language development is obviously defective.
   d. children finish the genital stage of development.

2. Outcome studies have found that psychotherapy with children is
   a. about as successful as it is with adults and may head off some problems in adulthood.
   b. more helpful for boys than for girls, which accounts for why girls have more eating disorders.
   c. much less successful than it is with adults, which emphasizes the need for adult treatment later.
   d. helpful for school problems only, and even then success is limited mainly to learning disabilities.

3. Which of the following is a major heading under which the others can be grouped as subheadings?
   a. conduct disorder
   b. disruptive behavior disorder
   c. attention deficit hyperactivity disorder
   d. ADHD

4. The *DSM-IV-TR* divides ADHD into subcategories. Those subcategories are
   a. predominantly inattentive; predominantly hyperactive/impulsive; combined.
   b. early onset; late onset.
   c. associated with conduct disorder; associated with drug abuse; non-associated.
   d. hyperactive; impulsive.

5. Which of the following is a type of conduct disorder?
   a. predominately inattentive type
   b. combined type
   c. childhood onset type
   d. predominately hyperactive/impulsive type

6. Research in New Zealand indicates that there may be two different kinds of antisocial adolescents. On what basis can we differentiate them?
   a. One group abuses drugs in adolescence; the other does not.
   b. One group initiates antisocial behavior in childhood; the other in adolescence.
   c. One group comes from overprotective parents; the other does not.
   d. One group focuses on sexual offenses; the other on offenses against property.

7. The main difference between separation anxiety disorder and social phobia is that in social phobia
   a. the fear generalizes to all social situations, including those involving the parents.
   b. the fear is in response to adults, not same-aged peers.
   c. the fear is in response to same-aged peers, not adults.
   d. the fear is not based on abandonment by the parent; it is just a response to unfamiliar people.

8. Constant worry is to _____ as severe shyness when around strangers is to _____.
   a. separation anxiety disorder; sleep disorder
   b. separation anxiety disorder; social phobia
   c. childhood depression; social phobia
   d. generalized anxiety disorder; social phobia

9. Eating disorders are thought to reflect deep-seated emotional problems because
   a. schizophrenics are known to have a problem with low blood sugar.
   b. eating is connected to feelings about those who are responsible for nurturing us.
   c. some mental patients will respond to primary reinforcers (food) and nothing else.
   d. Western culture emphasizes the social process of eating.

10. Anorexia is often accompanied by suspension of the menstrual period, a symptom called
    a. bulimia.
    b. amenorrhea.
    c. encopresis.
    d. enuresis.

11. Anorexia and bulimia are very similar in some ways. How are they different?
    a. Bulimia usually involves more severe weight loss than anorexia.
    b. Anorexics are more likely to be female, but bulimia is evenly divided between the sexes.
    c. Bulimia is much more common than anorexia.
    d. Anorexia is not as dangerous to the health as bulimia.

12. Enuresis is to _____ as encopresis is to _____.
    a. disruptive behavior; habit disorder
    b. rare; common
    c. males; females
    d. bladder control; bowel control

13. Probably the most common response to stress in early childhood is
    a. eating disorder.
    b. encopresis.
    c. insomnia.
    d. depression.

14. Which of the following is seen almost exclusively in children and rarely in adults?

    a. social phobia
    b. somnambulism
    c. depression
    d. generalized anxiety disorder

15. Eleven-year-old Maureen has been diagnosed with learning disorders. It is likely that she will have trouble
    a. with several perceptual systems (visual, auditory, touch and movement).
    b. remembering academically-relevant information.
    c. with low self-esteem.
    d. All of the above are accurate.

16. Stuttering, articulation disorder, and receptive language delays are all examples of

    a. learning disorders.
    b. communication disorders.
    c. dyslexias.
    d. disruptive behavior disorders.

17. Desiree is five years old and speaks hesitantly. She repeats syllables and whole words. She is diagnosed with stuttering. What is relatively unusual about Desiree's case?

    a. It is relatively unusual for a girl to have stuttering problems.
    b. It is relatively unusual for stuttering to be a problem at age five.
    c. It is relatively unusual for a stutterer to repeat syllables.
    d. It is relatively unusual for a stutterer to repeat whole words.

18. According to psychodynamic therapists, regression best explains which of the following disorders?

    a. secondary enuresis
    b. bulimia
    c. dyslexia
    d. attention deficit hyperactivity disorder

19. David's nocturnal enuresis is being treated by having him sleep on a liquid-sensitive surface connected by a battery to an alarm. If he starts to wet the bed, the alarm will sound to wake him. This technique is called _____ and is an example of the use of _____.

    a. flooding; classical conditioning
    b. punishment; instrumental learning
    c. the Mowrer pad; respondent conditioning
    d. eclectic therapy; operant conditioning

20. Of all the childhood disorders discussed in the text, the disorder that seems most likely to have a biological basis is

    a. articulation disorder.
    b. attention deficit hyperactivity disorder.
    c. separation anxiety disorder.
    d. bulimia nervosa.

ANSWERS

Guided Self-Study (252)

1. a. counterparts
   b. age
   c. temporary
   d. outcome
   e. intervention (459)

2. a. one out of every five
   b. six or seven
   c. school
   d. boys
   e. girls (459)

3. a. disruptive
   b. emotional
   c. habit
   d. communication (459–460)

4. a. predict
   b. prevent
   c. Stability
   d. Continuity
   e. Reactivity (460–461)

5. a. Attention deficit hyperactivity disorder (predominately inattentive type, predominantly hyperactive/impulsive type, combined type)
   b. Conduct disorder (childhood-onset and adolescent-onset type); age ten years is the cutoff point between the two. (461–464)

6. sit still
   direct attention
   wait for turn
   inhibit aggressive behavior
   control temper
   respond to adult supervision—inhibit or exhibit behaviors as directed
   complete tasks
   consider the feelings of others (461)

7. a. hyperactivity
   b. disorganized (seemingly purposeless)
   c. minimal brain dysfunction (MBD)
   d. attention deficit
   e. 3–5%
   f. 9 to 1 (461–463)

8. a. aggression
   b. destruction
   c. deceitfulness
   d. violation (463)

9. a. adolescence
   b. childhood onset
   c. "ordinary" criminals (464)
   d. socioeconomic (465)

10. a. inward
    b. anxiety
    c. depression
    d. emotions
    e. verbal (466)

11. Fear of strangers, beginning about eight months of age and extending to perhaps two and a half years, and separation anxiety, which peaks at about twelve months of age (466–467)

12. If fears persist into school years, or if they disappear as they should but then reappear (466)

13. separation anxiety disorder (466)
social phobia (467)
generalized anxiety disorder (467–468)

14. Fear makes a person less likely to be successful in whatever he/she attempts to do. The failure then leads to more fear, which makes success even less likely on the next attempt. (467–468)

15. a. mood   e. exaggerated
    b. interest   f. Older
    c. altered   g. accurate (466–468)
    d. clinging

16. The warriors are young males acting out emotional distresses in aggressive behaviors, and the worriers are young women acting out emotional distresses in gentler, more nurturing behaviors. This pattern is suggested by the biological and social circumstance that females, as the bearers and nurturers of the very young, must necessarily channel their mental energies in ways that will promote survival of the young and the species. The males' energies can be aggressively expressed and even rewarded, because aggressive behaviors that bring home resources and drive away threatening forces are biologically successful for sustaining the species. (468–469)

17. a. anorexia nervosa   f. restricting
    b. 15%   g. binge/purge (470)
    c. 85–95%   h. bulimia nervosa (470)
    d. 12 and 18   i. obese (470–471)
    e. amenorrhea   j. partial (471)

18. worried about weight
    skips meals, experiencing loss of control while eating
    feels guilty about eating
    believes that others see them as overweight (471)

19. a. milestone   f. encopresis
    b. enuresis   g. enuresis
    c. five years   h. three
    d. primary   i. stress (471–472)
    e. secondary

20. a. insomnia   g. sleep terror
    b. nightmares   h. nightmares (473)
    c. sleep terrors (night terrors)   i. somnambulism (473)
    d. sleep terrors   j. 15–30%
    e. 1–6%   k. first hour or two of sleep (473)
    f. 10–50%

21. a. dyslexia (474)
    b. articulation
    c. expressive
    d. receptive (476)
    e. stuttering (476)

22. No clear definition of learning disorder syndrome
    Term is used to avoid the stigma of mental retardation
    Difficult to separate from other disorders that can interrupt the learning process (474)

23. Impairment in vision or hearing organs
    Perceptual problems (that is seeing and hearing on a brain level)
    Memory problems
    Cognitive problems ordering and organizing thoughts (474)

24. a. mentally retarded
    b. normal
    c. mathematical
    d. esteem
    e. social
    f. genetics
    g. birth
    h. dietary
    i. environmental
    j. educational (474–476)

25. a. id
    b. superego (480–481)

26. a. nightmares and night terrors
    b. encopresis
    c. enuresis
    d. anorexia (480–481)

27. Play therapy, where the child acts out what is in his thoughts (480–481)

28. a. LEARNING!
    b. failure
    c. reinforcement
    d. relearning (477)

29. a. token economy (477)
    b. extinction (477)
    c. classical conditioning
    d. modeling
    e. systematic desensitization (477)

30. THINKING! As always, the cognitive psychologist is going to be looking at the child's thinking, particularly negative beliefs and faulty attributions routinely applied to him/herself in an across-the-board manner. (478–479)

31. Defining the problem—What do I have to do?
    Focusing attention—Keep working at it.
    Guiding performance—Now I have to do thus and so.
    Evaluating performance—Did I do it right?
    Correcting errors—That's wrong; let's go back.
    Rewarding oneself for good performance—I did a good job! (478–479)

32. a. internal, stable, and global
    b. problem
    c. activity
    d. affective
    e. Social (478–479)

33. Stopping *Scary Thoughts*, replacing them with *Other* thoughts, and *Praising* one's self for more effective cognitive coping. (479)

34. a. family
    b. interact
    c. family (479–480)

35. a. Poverty
    b. characteristic
    c. Eating (480)

36. a. families
    b. medications (480)

37. a. attention deficit disorder
    b. amphetamines: Dexedrine or Ritalin (480)

38. Drugs have adverse side effects.
    These medications do not cure the disorder.
    Medicating problems when what is needed is a more appropriate academic challenge, or psychotherapy, or family counseling, would be an abuse of prescribed drugs. (480–481)

39. a. violate the rights of others
    b. aggressive
    c. 18

40. a. neurological
    b. behavioral inhibitions
    c. self-control
    d. amphetamines

Practice Test (p. 259)

1. a. Sorry. Earlier than that.
    b. Correct!
    c. No. In many of these disorders, language is not involved.
    d. No. Actually, the genital stage is the beginning of adulthood.

2. a. Right!
    b. Nonsense answer. Boys have more problems overall than girls.
    c. No. Children can be helped quite successfully.
    d. Incorrect. Many types of problems can be successfully treated.

3. a. No, this is a specific type of problem under a general heading.
    b. Yes!
    c. No, this is a subheading.
    d. No. This is just the abbreviation for attention deficit hyperactivity disorder.

4. a. Correct!
    b. No, this is a way of dividing conduct disorders.
    c. Incorrect. None of these are categories of ADHD.
    d. Half right, but these two types are actually one type in the right answer.

5. a. No. This is a type of ADHD.
    b. No. This is also a type of ADHD.
    c. Right!
    d. No. This is a type of ADHD.

6. a. No, this is not a clear way of differentiating them.
    b. Correct!
    c. Wrong. Parenting style is not mentioned as the critical issue.
    d. No. This is not mentioned as a factor.

7. a. Incorrect. The child is not afraid of the parents.
    b. Incorrect. The child can fear people of any age.
    c. No. The child can fear people of any age.
    d. You got it!

8. a. No. Hint: constant worry is a problem we discussed before under Anxiety Disorders.
    b. Half right, but constant worry is not necessarily a separation issue.
    c. Half right, but worry and depression are different things.
    d. Right!

9. a. Nonsense answer. We know no such thing about schizophrenics.
   b. Right!
   c. Eating disorder in children in a natural setting has nothing to do with mental patients.
   d. No. All cultures emphasize the social aspects of eating.

10. a. No. This is name for the binge-purge problem.
    b. Yes!
    c. No. This is loss of bowel control.
    d. Sorry. This is loss of bladder control.

11. a. Incorrect. Bulimics may not be excessively thin.
    b. No. Both disorders are disproportionately female.
    c. Right!
    d. Actually, just the other way around.

12. a. No. Hint: these are elimination disorders.
    b. Sorry, it would be just the other way around.
    c. No. In reality, both these problems are predominately experienced by males.
    d. Correct!

13. a. No. Anorexia, especially, is relatively rare.
    b. No. This is fairly rare and indicates a serious problem.
    c. Right!
    d. Sorry. Depression isn't rare, but there is another one that is much more common.

14. a. No. Remember, childhood anxiety disorders have largely been merged with adult versions.
    b. Right!
    c. Sorry. This is an anxiety disorder comparable to the adult problem.
    d. Incorrect. This is an anxiety disorder comparable to the adult problem.

15. a. This is true, but keep reading.
    b. Correct, but there's more to consider.
    c. Right, but look at the other choices, too.
    d. You got it!

16. a. No. All of these are speech/language problems. What does that connect with?
    b. Correct!
    c. No. Dyslexia is a reading problem; there is more involved here than reading.
    d. Incorrect. Disruptive behavior is not the issue here.

17. a. Right!
    b. No, this is a prime age for stuttering to occur.
    c. No, they do this all the time.
    d. Incorrect. This is very common in stuttering.

18. a. Right!
    b. Psychodynamic types have an opinion on this, but there is a more obvious choice.
    c. No. Even psychodynamic types see this as being biologically involved.
    d. Incorrect. The text does not even mention the psychodynamic approach in this connection.

19. a. Half right, but the flooding part was just thrown out there for fun.
    b. Wrong on both counts. The wetting is simply being paired with awakening.
    c. Right!
    d. Wrong on both counts. "Eclectic" is not electric, and it is not operant conditioning.

20. a. Incorrect. This one might have a biological basis but there is a better answer.
    b. Right!
    c. No. Separation anxiety is probably built-in, but separation anxiety disorder may not be.
    d. No. Given the demographic pattern with this, it is unlikely to be biogenic.

CHAPTER 17
MENTAL RETARDATION AND AUTISM

LEARNING OBJECTIVES

By the time you have finished studying this chapter, you should be able to do the following:

1. Define mental retardation according to the *DSM-IV-TR*, and describe four levels of retardation, giving IQ scores and representative behaviors for each. (485–486)

2. Summarize the research findings on the genetic causes of retardation. (486–488)

3. Describe prenatal environmental factors that can result in retardation. (488–490)

4. Describe postnatal environmental factors that can result in retardation, making reference to pseudo-retardation and the effects of institutionalization. (490–492)

5. Discuss physical and psychological comorbidity issues related to retardation in adults, making specific reference to Alzheimer's disease. (492–493)

6. Define autism, describe four symptom categories characteristic of this disorder, and relate autism to savant syndrome. (493–497)

7. Summarize research on genetic, congenital, biochemical, and neurological problems related to autism. (497–500)

8. Summarize the cognitive perspective's position on the role of sensory and attention deficits in autism. (499–500)

9. Summarize five basic principles of public policy toward the mentally retarded that have evolved over the past thirty years. (500–501)

10. Summarize changes in attitudes and public policy relating to family support and employment opportunities for retarded and/or autistic individuals. (502–504)

11. Describe primary and secondary prevention, and outline behavioral techniques for improving the adaptive skills of retarded persons and for minimizing maladaptive behavior. (504–506)

12. Describe cognitive, pharmacological, and psychotherapeutic measures that have been useful in the treatment of autistic and mentally retarded persons. (506–508)

KEY TERMS

The following terms are in bold print in your text and are important to your understanding of the chapter. Look them up in the text and write down their definitions.

amniocentesis (488)
brain plasticity (491)
congenital disorders (488)
cretinism (488)
Down syndrome (487)
echolalia (496)
fetal alcohol syndrome (FAS) (489)
fragile X syndrome (487)

infantile autism (493)
mental retardation (485)
phenylketonuria (PKU) (488)
savant syndrome (495)
sheltered workshops (503)
Tay-Sachs disease (488)
theory of mind (499)
trisomy 21 (487)

IMPORTANT NAMES

Identify the following persons and their major contributions to abnormal psychology as discussed in this chapter.

Association of Retarded Citizens (ARC) (500)　　　　　Langdon Down (487)

GUIDED SELF-STUDY

Mental Retardation

1. Complete the following statements to produce the three criteria for mental retardation as defined by *DSM-IV-TR*.

   a. Significantly subaverage general _____ functioning

   b. Related deficits in _____ functioning

   c. Onset before age _____ years

2. Fill in the following chart, describing four traditional levels of retardation based on IQ scores.

Name of Level	IQ Range	Skills Level
a.		
b.		
c.		
d.		

3. The American Association on Mental Retardation (AAMR) argues against a criterion based on

   (a)_____ until deficits in (b)_____ functioning have been established. The AAMR also

   recommends a classification system based on levels of required (c)_____.

4. Why does the AAMR take the position described above?

5. Mental retardation affects about (a)____% of the population. Of those people, (b)____% are only mildly retarded.

6. For each of the following skills, check the level(s) of retardation that would probably permit that skill to be performed reliably with no supervision.

Mild	Moderate	Severe	Profound	
____	____	____	____	Feed ones' self
____	____	____	____	Ride a bike
____	____			Respond to one's own name
____	____	____	____	Swing on a swing
____	____	____	____	Balance a checkbook
____	____	____	____	Brush teeth
____	____	____	____	Tie shoes
____	____	____	____	Buy a month's supply of groceries
____	____	____	____	Buy a list of five items

____	____	____	____	Dial a telephone number
____	____	____	____	Cross a residential street alone
____	____	____	____	Plan a budget
____	____	____	____	Work as a grocery store bagger
____	____	____	____	Work carrying out scrap lumber
____	____	____	____	Sort two sizes of nails

7. As usual, for effective treatment of any problem, correct differential diagnosis is necessary. List three conditions *besides* mental retardation that also impair behavior and development. Then keep in mind that a person may have more than one of *these* conditions, and that will make differential diagnosis even more difficult.

8. a. How many organic disorders have been associated with mental retardation?

   b. What two categories of organic disorders are discussed in your text?

   c. List the examples given for each of these two categories.

9. Fill in the blanks to complete the following description of fragile-X syndrome.

   The person usually is in the (a)_____ mentally retarded range; has large, prominent

   (b)_____; (c)_____ face; (d)_____ testicles in males; (e)_____ activity

   level; and somewhat autistic-like—(f)_____ biting, (g)_____ speech, and (h) poor eye

   _____. The disorder will be more severe in males because they have only one (i)_____-

   _____, whereas women have two.

10. Fill in the blanks to complete the following description of Down syndrome.

    Most people with Down syndrome have (a)_____ mental retardation; a (b)_____

    _____ head; eyes with an extra fold of skin on the upper (c)_____; (d)_____ nose;

    mouth with down-turned (e)_____; a thick protruding (f)_____; fingers usually

    (g)_____ and stubby; poor body (h)_____ _____; increased risk of

    (i)_____ and (j)_____ problems.

11. Langdon Down first described the syndrome named after him in (a)_____, but not until

    (b)_____ did Lejeune find that Down syndrome was almost always correlated with having an

    (c)_____ chromosome on chromosome pair number (d)_____. This is called

    (e)_____-_____. The mother's age is a major factor: For women twenty to twenty-four

    years old, the likelihood of having a Down syndrome child is one in (f)_____; for women thirty to thirty-nine, one in (g)_____; for women aged forty, one in (h)_____; and for those aged forty-five, one in (i)_____. This is why (j)_____ is routinely recommended for pregnant women over the age of thirty-five.

12. Down syndrome and fragile X syndrome are both the result of (a)_____ abnormalities. (b)_____ (PKU) and (c)_____-_____ disease are both the result of recessive genes. Remember, for a recessive gene to show itself, both parents must contribute that same recessive gene. This is where genetic counseling is of tremendous value to people who know they are at risk for carrying certain "problem" genes.

13. Disorders that occur during prenatal development but are not the manifestation of chromosomal anomalies or undesirable genes are called (a)_____ disorders. Three common congenital causes of mental retardation result from the mother contracting (b)_____ (German measles) or (c)_____, or having a (d)_____ imbalance during the pregnancy. These are not common now because of immunizations against (e)_____ and penicillin for (f)_____. Availability of iodized salt remedies the thyroxine deficiency, (also called (g)_____). The new common congenital factor for mental retardation comes from transmission of the (h)_____ virus, contracted in utero from the infected mother, leading to brain degeneration.

14. Name two other prenatal circumstances that interfere with normal brain development.

15. What is environmentally based cultural/familial mental retardation, and where does it come from?

16. The fact that early experiences in life can alter the structure and functioning of the brain illustrates a brain characteristic called

    a. pseudo-development.
    b. brain plasticity.
    c. postnatal encephalopathy.
    d. cerebral atrophy.

17. Just from what you have read in this chapter, if you were designing an institution for children or picking out day-care for your own child, what features would you want to counter the effects of institutionalization?

18. a. What disorder that we studied in the chapter on organic brain problems is associated with Down syndrome?

    b. Mentally retarded adults are also generally susceptible to an emotional problem we discussed in another chapter. What is it?

Autism

19. Autism occurs in about (a)_____ of every (b)_____ births. Traditionally known as

(c)_____ _____, "autism" comes from the Greek word *autos,* meaning

(d)"_____."

20. Describe why prevalence figures for autism vary and why there is considerable disagreement to what should be called *autism*.

21. Complete the following blanks to form a list of the four basic symptoms of autism.

    a. Social _____

    b. Mental _____

    c. _____ deficits

    d. _____ behaviors

22. Identify the following types of autistic "social interaction."

    a. The _____ type will respond only to human approach to get his/her needs met.

    b. The _____ type does not initiate contact but will respond in very simple ways.

    c. The _____-_____-_____ type approaches others, but in strange, unusual ways.

23. a. What percentage of autistic children have an IQ lower than 70?

    b. Describe the difference between a "normal" retarded pattern of cognitive impairment and the retardation seen in autism.

    c. What is the term for autistic people who are mentally retarded yet have above-average ability in one limited area?

    d. What have researchers found about the relationship between the symptoms of autism and savant abilities?

24. Let's discuss some of the peculiarities seen in the speech of autistic children. Less than (a)_____ of

all autistic children speak at all. Some whine, scream, or repeat fragments of overheard dialogue. This

meaningless repetition is called (b)_____. Some have unusual use of pronouns, referring to

themselves as (c)"_____" or "_____/_____." Autistic children generally cannot

engage in (d)_____ (give and take) conversation.

25. A child's level of (a)_____ development is a good indicator of prognosis. If speech is used

    meaningfully by age (b)_____ years, prognosis is more positive.

26. List some patterns of seemingly purposeless, repetitive motor behaviors of autistic children.

27. At what age do normal children tend to insist on an unvarying environment?

28. For two decades, the (a)_____ perspective had proposed that autism was caused by cold, rejecting

    parents. Today, however, the two dominant lines of research are in the (b)_____ and _____

    perspectives.

29. List four different topics the biological perspective has focused on in studying autism.

    a. _____/_____ research
    b. _____ research
    c. _____ disorders and complications in _____ and _____
    d. _____ studies

30. When doing twin studies (comparing concordance rates for DZ and MZ twins), researchers are looking for a

    (a)_____ component in autism. One of the difficulties with twin studies in autism is the statistical

    (b)_____ of the disorder. Despite these difficulties, genetic research has concluded that there (c) *is /*

    is not some genetic component to autism. There may be more than one variety of the disorder. One type,

    with severe retardation, is correlated with having siblings who are (d)_____ or _____, and

    another type, typically with the better functioning patients, is associated with a family history of

    (e)_____ _____.

31. Many autistic children respond positively to medications affecting two neurotransmitters. What are they?

32. What six pieces of evidence presented in your text (pages 498–499) support the idea that whatever the
    problem is in autism, it is within the central nervous system?

    a.

    h

    c.

    d.

    e.

    f.

33. Obtaining EEGs for autistic children is very difficult because

    a. they usually come from very dysfunctional families.

    b. they have very few brain waves.

    c. they are very fearful about electrical equipment.

    d. they cannot cooperate well enough for testing.

34. Cognitive theorists say that _____ problems are primary in autism and cause the social problems that go along with the disorder.

35. Cognitive researchers have defined four areas of cognitive function that are difficult for the person who has autism. Identify each of these areas.

    a. _____ _____ involves planning, problem solving, and self-control.

    b. _____ and _____ involve forming new concepts and long- and short-term retention.

    c. _____ _____ means the understanding of emotions and facial expressions.

    d. Lack of _____ _____ _____ _____ refers to the inability to be aware of the perspective of others.

36. The doll-hiding-the-marble experiment demonstrated that the large majority of autistic children cannot imagine another person's perspective.

    a. Give the sequence of events that makes up the experiment.

    b. Explain what the results suggest.

Society, Mental Retardation and Autism

37. Fill in the following blanks to list the current issues for society in regard to people with developmental disabilities.

    a. Public _____

    b. Community _____

    c. Quality of _____

    d. Support for the _____

    e. _____

38. Explain why society must address each of the preceding issues. In other words, what's the big deal? If you are an "average" American and do not have a friend, neighbor, or family member with a special circumstance, you may never have considered some of these issues.

    a.

    b.

    c.

    d.

    e.

39. What five principles have been established to guarantee full citizens' rights to mentally retarded people?

a.

b.

c.

d.

e.

40. These principles are designed to bring an end to the (a)_____ (or separation) of services that kept

retarded citizens from participating in life as fully as they might. The principle of community

(b)_____ says the retarded should live life right along with everyone else to the extent they are

capable. They now go to school in their (c)_____ schools. Some of the mildly retarded are

(d)_____ in that some of their classes are with non-retarded children when appropriate.

41. What does IEP mean? What is the cascade system?

42. While many mildly retarded adults are self-supporting and live independently, there are a variety of levels of supervised living circumstances. Identify the type of living circumstance represented by each description. Your choices are *supported living arrangement (SLA), community living facility (CLF),* and *intermediate care facility (ICF).*

a. _____ (Ideally) a closely supervised environment for the severely retarded

b. _____ Small group home with supervision provided in the evenings for the mildly mentally retarded

c. _____ Medium-sized residential center with round-the-clock supervision for the moderately retarded and the mildly retarded with emotional and/or behavioral problems

43. Where parents were encouraged in the past to institutionalize mentally retarded children, today they are

encouraged to raise their child in the (a)_____ environment. These parents will need supportive

(b)_____ and _____.

44. What are some issues that parents of mentally retarded children have to cope with more than the parents of nonretarded children? (There are at least five.)

•

•

•

•

•

45. State and federal laws mandate opportunities for useful "employment" for the retarded. What does "employment" encompass in connection with mentally retarded citizens?

46. What does research indicate about the employment record of mentally retarded people? What factor seems most influential when a mentally retarded person loses a job?

Prevention, Education, and Treatment

47. What are some of the methods of primary prevention (those that actually prevent mental retardation)?

48. What are some of the secondary prevention methods (those which use early interventions to reduce the severity of retardation in children who are already affected)?

49. What are infant stimulation programs about, and why are they important?

50. Behavior therapy has been quite (a) *successful / unsuccessful* in a variety of settings for teaching skills and

    for (b)_____ management with both retarded children and adults.

51. Identify each of the following three basic techniques for behavior therapy.

    a. _____ Reinforcing successive approximations of desired behavior

    b. _____ Linking a series of simple tasks together to form a more complex one

    c. _____ _____ Teaching which behaviors should occur in which situations

52. Which behavior therapy listed in the preceding question would be correctly applied in each of the following situations?

    a. Terry is taught not to undo her clothing until she is inside the bathroom door. There are places where undoing one's clothing is appropriate and places where it is not.

    b. Now that Terry has mastered making peanut butter sandwiches, the next challenge will be to pack those sandwiches in a bag and add some fruit and a drink.

    c. Terry is very socially withdrawn. She comes in late and lingers in the locker room. Her supervisor makes a point of reinforcing any inclination toward social interaction on her part. With gradual improvements, Terry now spends less time in the locker room.

53. Two of the most important skills for a mentally retarded person to develop are (a)_____ training

    and (b)_____ skills.

54. (a)_____ (ignore it and it will go away) and (b)_____ are used to reduce inappropriate

    behaviors. Behavior can be maintained by either external or internal reinforcers. When behaviors are

    maintained by (c)_____ rewards, they are very difficult to suppress.

55. Cognitive therapy applies self-instructional training to teach a person to _____ him/herself through a task, to manage his own behavior, and to wait for gratification.

56. Complete the following blanks about pharmacological therapies used for retardation:

    a. _____% take psychotropic drugs for _____ problems

    b. _____% take anticonvulsive drugs for _____ problems

57. For years psychotherapy was overlooked as a therapy for mentally retarded individuals because psychotherapy requires some intellectual skills to successfully gain insight into one's thoughts, feelings, and social interactions. However, areas of benefit from psychotherapy for retarded individuals and their families have now been discovered and developed. List some of the areas of psychotherapy that are beneficial for retarded individuals and their families.

HELPFUL HINTS

1. I find likening the severely mentally retarded adult individual to the mental age of a five- or six-year-old very helpful for understanding what can be expected from an individual at this level. If you are experienced with children and not with mentally retarded individuals, you can still quickly grasp the level of behavioral expectations.

2. Inappropriate orientation to the present is an excessive focus on here and now with none of the future-based consideration that is required for any planning (even planning for ten minutes from now).

3. Autism refers to self-absorption or aloneness. If it helps you to remember, cars are called *auto*mobiles because they are *self*-propelled vehicles.

4. Just in case I need to say this—notice the difference between autistic and artistic. They are very different concepts! And to confuse matters a little more—there are extremely rare autistic children who have an extraordinary *artistic* ability. See the focus box on savant syndrome. (495)

5. I hope you remember from the chapter on organic brain disorders that two major issues are locating the site of dysfunction and determining exactly what kind of pathology exists in that area. As you can see, autism is still very much a mystery. Neither the exact pathology nor the site of the pathology is known.

6. If you do not know the word "cascade," connect it with the common idea of the "cascading waterfall." That is an excellent concrete example of a step-wise sequential gradation.

7. An autistic child learns that the letter D written on the classroom blackboard says a "d" sound, but he is unable to carry that over to the letter D printed in a book. Or if he/she learns it for the letter D on a printed page in a particular book at school, that fact has no connection with the letter D in a book at home. The child is learning to discriminate between situations where no discrimination is appropriate.

PRACTICE TEST

Use the following test questions to check your knowledge of the material in this chapter. You may want to write the answers on a separate sheet of paper so you can take the test more than once.

1. The largest number of mentally retarded individuals fall into the category of _____ retardation.
    a. mild
    b. moderate
    c. severe
    d. profound

2. Dennis has an IQ of 45. He has learned to care for himself, and he currently lives in a group home. He does repetitive work in a sheltered workshop, can carry on a simple conversation, and can read a few basic words. What level of retardation does Dennis demonstrate?
    a. mild
    b. moderate
    c. severe
    d. profound

3. Which of the following is true of Down syndrome?

   a. There are three chromosomes in pair 21 instead of two.
   b. There is an abnormality in the sex chromosomes.
   c. There is an XXY chromosome pattern.
   d. Chromosome pair 21 is missing.

4. Rubella, HIV infection, and syphilis are discussed in the text under the heading of

   a. chromosome anomalies.
   b. metabolic disturbances.
   c. congenital disorders.
   d. toxic reactions.

5. *Pseudo-retardation* is a term for

   a. retardation resulting from genetic inbreeding.
   b. poor IQ performance due to consciously faking a retarded condition.
   c. apparent retardation caused by poverty and lack of environmental stimulation.
   d. autistic behavior in the face of family conflict and domineering parents.

6. A child has a normal IQ. His parents die suddenly and he is placed in an traditional institutional setting. Based on research cited in the text, his IQ will most likely

   a. increase at the normal rate.
   b. decrease.
   c. stay the same.
   d. decline initially, then increase as the child becomes accustomed to the new surroundings.

7. A clinician treats his client's intellectual deficits but virtually ignores the depression the patient also feels. The clinician is demonstrating

   a. diagnostic overshadowing.
   b. inverted treatment priorities.
   c. symptomatic eclipsing.
   d. transparent comorbidity.

8. Willie is autistic. He makes no attempt to initiate contact with others, but when approached, he reacts, answering questions minimally, but generally making sense. Willie seems to have which type of autism?

   a. Aloof
   b. Passive
   c. Passive-aggressive
   d. Active-but-odd

9. The best predictor of recovery from autism is

   a. the child's facility with language.
   b. the amount of stereotyped behavior observed.
   c. whether the child comes from a single-parent household.
   d. whether the child shows the aloof or passive subtype of autism.

10. A child appears severely autistic but has the ability to play, on the piano, any piece of music he has heard once. This ability extends. to very complicated compositions. This is an example of

    a. autistic schizophrenia.
    b. savant syndrome.
    c. psi ability.
    d. left brain / right brain asymmetry.

11. Chuckie has been diagnosed as suffering from autism. He would be expected to have all the following symptoms EXCEPT

    a. stereotyped behaviors.
    b. severe language deficits.
    c. significant cognitive impairment.
    d. an obsessive need to rearrange his living space over and over.

12. Biochemical studies have indicated that autistic symptoms can be alleviated by drugs that

    a. increase norepinephrine levels.
    b. decrease dopamine levels.
    c. increase endorphin levels.
    d. decrease thorazine levels.

13. Cognitive theorists believe that the primary defect in autistism is

    a. the inability to interact with other people.
    b. a reduced ability to comprehend, imitate, be flexible, and use information.
    c. inadequate parenting involving cold and detached modeling of social interactions.
    d. inadequate reinforcement of basic life skills.

14. Which of the following is LEAST useful in predicting the occurrence of autism?

    a. gender
    b. socioeconomic status
    c. presence of the disorder in siblings
    d. family history of serious mood disorder

15. Public Law 94–142, passed in 1975, was a landmark piece of legislation that

    a. gave free public education to every citizen under twenty-one, appropriate to his/her needs.
    b. allowed each state to decide if public school education is practical for retarded children.
    c. required separate special education programs for retarded students in every school district.
    d. mandated handicapped access to all public buildings supported by federal money.

16. According to the text, one of the most complex issues to deal with a mentally retarded adult is

    a. sexuality.
    b. employment.
    c. social adjustment.
    d. money management.

17. Amniocentesis, genetic counseling, and drug treatment for crack-addicted women of childbearing age are all _____ efforts to reduce mental retardation.

    a. secondary intervention
    b. primary prevention
    c. educational
    d. self-instructional

18. An autistic child's therapist has advised his parents to ignore him whenever he throws a tantrum. The behavioral technique being used is

    a. direct reinforcement.
    b. symptom substitution.
    c. extinction.
    d. punishment.

19. Cognitive training in self-management and self-monitoring is designed to
    a. keep clients on task by giving them self-talk statements that control their actions.
    b. help clients make their verbal statements and their actions parallel with each other.
    c. teach clients to regulate and evaluate their own behavior.
    d. train the client in waiting for delayed gratification.

20. For years it was believed that people with mental retardation could not benefit from psychotherapy. Why?
    a. Because most mentally retarded clients are nonverbal and therefore could not participate.
    b. Mentally retarded clients respond well to psychodynamic therapy
    c. It was believed that mentally retarded clients could not benefit from psychotherapy beacused they lacked the intellectual sophistication.
    d. Most mentally retarded clients are institutionalized, and so this form of therapy is not an option.

ANSWERS

Guided Self-Study (p. 268)

1. a. intellectual
   b. adaptive
   c. 18 (485)

2. | Name of Level | IQ Range | Skills Level |
   | --- | --- | --- |
   | a. mild | 50–55 to 70 | Productive and perhaps independent living |
   | b. moderate | 35–40 to 50–55 | Can do self-care but not live independently |
   | c. severe | 20–25 to 35–40 | Some self-care and simple skills in sheltered setting |
   | d. profound | 20–25 and below | Requires extensive supervision; little or no speech (485–486) |

3. a. IQ
   b. adaptive
   c. assistance (486)

4. The AAMR points out that there is not a precise correlation between IQ and adaptive functioning. (486)

5. a. 2 (485)
   b. 85 (485)

6. Feed one's self—yes for each category except profound
   Ride a bike—yes for mild
   Respond to own's name—yes for everyone except profound
   Swing on a swing—yes for everyone except profound
   Balance a checkbook—probably none
   Brush teeth—yes for mild and moderate
   Tie shoes—yes for mild and moderate
   Buy a month's supply of groceries—none
   Buy a list of five items—yes for mild
   Dial a telephone number—yes for mild and possibly moderate
   Cross a residential street alone—yes for mild and moderate
   Plan a budget—none
   Work as a grocery store bagger—yes for mild
   Work carrying out scrap lumber—yes for mild and moderate
   Sort two sizes of nails—yes for everyone except profound
   If there is debate over categorizing some of these skills, it is probably a matter of how well the task is structured. For instance, carrying scrap lumber between two boxes in a clearly laid-out, well-supervised, safe environment is a task that some severely retarded individuals could perform. (485–486) (See Hint 1.)

7. autism, emotional disturbance, and learning disabilities (486–487)

8. a. 300 (486)
   b. chromosomal abnormalities and metabolic disturbances (487–488)
   c. Examples of chromosomal abnormalities are Down syndrome (trisomy 21) and fragile X. Examples of metabolic disturbances are PKU and Tay-Sachs disease. Each of these causes damage by a failure of the body to regulate one of its chemicals, which then builds up in the brain and causes damage. (487–488)

9. a. moderately
   b. ears
   c. elongated
   d. enlarged
   e. hyperactive
   f. hand
   g. limited
   h. contact
   i. X-chromosome (487)

10. a. moderate
    b. small, round
    c. eyelid
    d. flat
    e. corners
    f. tongue
    g. short
    h. muscle tone
    i. heart (or respiratory)
    j. respiratory (or heart) (487)

11. a. 1866
    b. 1959
    c. extra
    d. 21
    e. trisomy 21
    f. 1400
    g. 900
    h. 100
    i. 25
    j. amniocentesis (487)

12. a. chromosomal (487)
    b. Phenylketonuria
    c. Tay-Sachs (488)

13. a. congenital
    b. rubella
    c. syphilis
    d. hormonal (thyroxine)
    e. German measles
    f. syphilis
    g. cretinism
    h. HIV (487–490)

14. The use of drugs such as thalidomide, alcohol, and cocaine affects brain development. Malnutrition, alone or in combination with other detrimental conditions, interferes with genetically programmed brain development. (487–490)

15. It is a phenomenon that looks like mild retardation and is measurable on intelligence tests, but it is assumed to be more emotional than intellectual, the result of an impoverished environment rather than an organic deficit. (490)

16. "b" (490)

17. An environment that is varied and stimulating without being noisy. An environment where there is an abundance of verbal interaction with the children on a one-to-one basis with adults who "believe in" children (giving them respect and dignity) and have adequate vocabulary themselves. These adults should recognize the importance of enrichment and be eager to provide it. (490–492)

18. a. Alzheimer's disease (492)
    b. depression (492)

19. a. 5
    b. 10,000
    c. infantile autism
    d. "self" (493)

20. The figures vary largely because there is a great deal of variation in symptoms and therefore considerable disagreement as to what is called "autism" as opposed to "autistic-like" conditions. (493)

21. a. isolation
     b. retardation
     c. Language
     d. Stereotyped (494–497)

22. a. aloof
     b. passive
     c. active-but-odd (494)

23. a. 76–89% of autistic people have IQs below 70. (494)
     b. Autistic children have a distinctly uneven pattern of capabilities compared to the "ordinary" retarded child who shows cognitive function fairly evenly depressed across all capabilities. (494)
     c. savants (495)
     d. Savant abilities sometimes decline as symptoms of autism become less severe. (495)

24. a. half
     b. echolalia
     c. you, he/she
     d. reciprocal (496)

25. a. language
     b. 5 (496)

26. twirling, tiptoeing, hand flapping, rocking, tensing parts of the body, head banging, self-hand biting, chewing fingers (496)

27. two and one-half years (496)

28. a. psychodynamic
     b. biological and cognitive perspective (497–500)

29. a. genetic/chromosome research
     b. biochemical research
     c. congenital disorders and complications in pregnancy and birth
     d. neurological studies (497–500)

30. a. genetic
     b. rarity (2/1000; when combined with the rarity of twinning, this make twins with autism very hard to find)
     c. is
     d. retarded, autistic
     e. mood disorder (497–499)

31. serotonin and dopamine (498)

32. a. Most characteristic signs of autism involve central nervous system activity. (498)
     b. Many autistic children develop seizure activity in adolescence. (498)
     c. Neurological exams of autistic kids often find other evidence of central nervous system dysfunction. (498)
     d. Abnormal EEGs and ERPs have been recorded for autistic children. (498)
     e. Autopsies reveal damage in the limbic system and cerebellum. (498)
     f. Some correlations have been reported between megalencephaly and autism. (498)

33. "d" (478)

34. THINKING! (If that answer was a surprise to you, you need h-e-l-p at this point, serious help!) (499)

35. a. Executive function (499)
     b. Categorization, memory (499)
     c. Social understanding (499)
     d. theory of the mind (499)

36. a. The children watch the following scene played out with dolls: Sally puts her marble in the basket and leaves the scene. Ann then takes it out of the basket and hides it. The child is then asked where Sally will look for the marble when she returns.
    b. Most normal and retarded children say "in the basket" because they realize that although they saw Ann hide the marble, Sally did not see Ann hide the marble. The autistic child fails to realize that Sally did not see Ann hide the marble as he/she did, so his/her response is that Sally will look for it in the hiding place. (499)

37. a. policy
    b. integration
    c. life
    d. family
    e. Employment (500)

38. a. There is a need to make society more responsive to all segments of the population. (500–504)
    b. Segregation leads to restriction from areas of a society's resources. (502)
    c. Individual choice leads to quality of life because choice allows that individual to tailor his/her own life to suit his/her likes and value system. (502–503)
    d. Families with special needs can function if they have access to the resources that fit their needs. (503)
    e. Opportunities for productive employment are beneficial to the employee and for the society in which she/he participates as a contributing member. (503)

39. a. They are entitled to a free and appropriate education.
    b. Services should be individualized (IEP =individualized education program). (501)
    c. Progress should be evaluated regularly.
    d. Lives should be integrated into the community.
    e. They should be protected from abuse and deprivation. (500)

40. a. segregation
    b. integration
    c. local
    d. mainstreamed (501–502)

41. a. IEP = individualized education program (plan) (501)
    b. Cascade system = nine levels of education to address special needs from regular classroom to the most restrictive, which is a hospital setting (501)

42. a. intermediate-care facility (ICF)
    b. supported living arrangement (SLA)
    c. community living facility (CLF) (502)

43. a. home
    b. training, counseling (502)

44. These children learn more slowly and benefit from whatever enhanced teaching skills the parents can give.
    In addition to mental handicaps, they may also have physical disabilities.
    They have to cope with being "different."
    They will have to cope with their peers leaving them behind cognitively.
    Two major topics of adolescence for any teen are growing independence and developing sexuality. These topics are going to be more complicated if the individual has fewer cognitive skills to bring to bear on trying to cope with these teen challenges. (504)

45. Their daytime activities are to have some purpose for them. "Employment" varies according to the needs and capabilities of each retarded individual. For the more severely impaired "employment" may be a planned daytime program. For the mildly retarded and some moderately retarded, it may be employment in the more traditional sense; they may have paying jobs in the competitive work market or in sheltered workshops that are special work centers tailored to meet the capabilities of their employees. (503–504)

46. Studies indicate that when mentally retarded citizens are properly placed in work that is appropriate to their skill levels, they make good employees. Research indicates that when they are fired, the reason is more likely that they lack the social skills related to the job rather than the ability to do the job itself. (503)

47. Genetic counseling and improved prenatal care
Some blood tests can identify carriers for some disorders. Genetic analyses can be done on the developing fetus. (504)

48. Low-phenylalanine diets for PKU children
Thyroid medications for children with damaged or missing thyroid glands
Stimulation therapy for babies at increased risk for mental impairment, such as Down syndrome children, infants of poverty and mothers with low IQs (504)

49. Infant stimulation programs take advantage of the fact that the brain is plastic, or flexible, in early development. (504) Some aspects of such programs are
   a. language acquisition (talking to and making eye contact).
   b. problem-solving experience with a variety of sensory stimuli (sounds, colors, shapes, textures, and tastes, fine and gross motor manipulation of objects).
   c. achievement motivation.
   d. teaching mothers to help infant with stimulation, exercise, and encouragement. (504)

50. a. successful
   b. behavior (505)

51. a. shaping
   b. chaining
   c. stimulus control (505)

52. a. stimulus control
   b. chaining
   c. shaping (505)

53. a. toilet (505)
   b. language/communication (505)

54. a. Extinction
   b. punishment
   c. internal (505–506)

55. talk (506)

56. a. 30–50; behavior
   b. 25–35; seizure

57. Supportive psychotherapy; group psychotherapy; family therapy; client-centered; changing family dynamics

Practice Test (p. 276)

1. a. Correct!
   b. No. The percentages decrease as seriousness goes up.
   c. Sorry.
   d. Incorrect. The most serious cases are on the smallest end of the distribution.

2. a. Incorrect. Mild means an IQ above 50.
   b. Correct!
   c. No, too pessimistic.
   d. No. Individuals with profound retardation are not nearly this capable.

3. a. Yes!
   b. No. Down syndrome is unrelated to the X or Y chromosomes.
   c. Sorry. X and Y are the sex chromosomes, and Down syndrome is not sex-related.
   d. Just the opposite. There are too many, not too few.

4. a. No. Examples of chromosome anomalies are Down syndrome and fragile X.
   b. No. Examples here would be Tay-Sachs disease and PKU.
   c. Right!
   d. No. Examples here would be lead poisoning and fetal alcohol syndrome.

5. a. Incorrect. That would be biologically based retardation.
   b. No. Malingering is not an issue here.
   c. You got it!
   d. Incorrect. Autism is a separate issue and is not mentioned in this connection.

6. a. No. Remember, institutions are often less stimulating than a more natural setting.
   b. Correct!
   c. Sorry, this is too optimistic.
   d. No. This is half right, however.

7. a. Right!
   b. No such term. Hint: Retardation is usually much more obvious than other problems.
   c. Sorry. You're on the right track, but the terminology is incorrect.
   d. No. Comorbidity is going on, but this is not the term.

8. a. Incorrect. Aloof means the child neither initiates *nor* responds to initiatives from others.
   b. Yes!
   c. No such type—this is an old personality disorder concept.
   d. No. This type initiates but the interaction is not normal.

9. a. Right!
   b. No. There is a better alternative.
   c. Incorrect. This does not seem to be a factor.
   d. No. Hint: what is the most important aspect of social interactions?

10. a. No. Hint: When someone is particularly smart about something, we say he/she is "savvy."
    b. Correct!
    c. Sorry, psi has to do with ESP and related topics.
    d. Incorrect. This does not seem to be an issue.

11. a. This is one of the symptom patterns, not an exception.
    b. Sorry, this is also one of the major problems with autism.
    c. No, this is a problem with autism; we are looking for an exception.
    d. Right! They value sameness and stability.

12. a. Sorry, this just makes things worse.
    b. Right!
    c. No. Endorphins are not mentioned in connection with autism.
    d. No. In fact, Thorazine is one of the drugs that might work—it decreases dopamine activity.

13. a. No. This would be a manifestation of the problem, not the root of it from a cognitive view.
    b. Yes!
    c. Incorrect. This is more psychodynamic or sociocultural in focus.
    d. No. This would be a behavioral position.

14. a. No. There is a definite bias in favor of males.
    b. Right!
    c. No. This can be a valuable predictor.
    d. Sorry, there is in fact a correlation between autism and mood disorder in the family.

15. a. You got it!
    b. No. PL 94–142 was designed to end this kind of inconsistent approach.
    c. Sorry. Think of the concept of "mainstreaming" here.
    d. No. This is an unrelated concept.

16. a. Yes!
    b. No. This is a problem, but there is another one that strikes a lot closer to home.
    c. No. The biggest issue is a lot more personal than this.
    d. Sorry. This is an issue, but the one we're looking for is biological.

17. a. No. The approach we're looking for attacks the problem *before* it occurs.
    b. Correct!
    c. No. Some of these are educational, but others are not.
    d. Incorrect. Amniocentesis is not self-anything. These are all professional services.

18. a. Incorrect. Remember, reinforcement *increases* behavior.
    b. No. This is when removal of one problem results in the appearance of another one.
    c. Yes!
    d. Sorry, the goal is the same, but the process is different.

19. a. No, this is self-instructional training.
    b. No, this is correspondence training.
    c. Right!
    d. No, this is training in self-control.

20. a. Incorrect.
    b. No. Psychodynamic therapy focuses on the unconscious determinants.
    c. Correct! However, we now have less insight-oriented therapies.
    d. Incorrect. Most mentally retarded persons are not institutionalized.

CHAPTER 18
LEGAL AND ETHICAL ISSUES IN ABNORMAL PSYCHOLOGY

LEARNING OBJECTIVES

By the time you have finished studying this chapter, you should be able to do the following:

1. Explain the purpose of the insanity defense, describe four tests for legal insanity, and explain why one of them is now preferred over the others. (511–513)

2. Summarize the procedural and ethical controversies surrounding the insanity defense, making reference to the case of John Hinckley, and discuss the concept of "guilty but mentally ill" as an alternative to "not guilty by reason of insanity." (513–515)

3. Define the purpose of competency proceedings in criminal cases, and discuss the controversies surrounding these proceedings, particularly the use of antipsychotic medications to produce competence. (515–516)

4. List four rights guaranteed to persons accused of a crime, and discuss how these rights either apply or do not apply in civil commitment proceedings. (518–519)

5. Describe four "standards of proof" that could be used in civil commitment proceedings, and explain why one of them may be more appropriate than the others. (519–521)

6. Explain "dangerousness" and the "thank-you" proposition as standards for civil commitment, and discuss the controversy surrounding these standards. (522–525)

7. Discuss the role of expert testimony in civil commitment, the issue of whether commitment should be made easier or more difficult, and the argument over whether civil commitment should be used at all. (525–527)

8. Summarize the cases of *Wyatt v. Stickney*, *O'Connor v. Donaldson*, *Youngberg v. Romeo*, and *Washington v. Harper*, and discuss their impact on a patient's right to treatment and on the right to refuse treatment. (527–529)

9. List ten rights of mental patients relating to a humane treatment environment, and discuss the potential conflict between the desire to protect patients' rights and the need to provide effective treatment. (529–531)

10. Describe how recent legal decisions relating to abnormal psychology have affected client-therapist confidentiality and the power of the mental health profession. (532–534)

11. Describe the general principles of the Ethical Principles of Psychologists and Code of Conduct. (532)

KEY TERMS

The following terms are in bold print in your text and are important to your understanding of the chapter. Look them up in the text and write down their definitions.

civil commitment (518)
false negative (519)
false positive (519)

indeterminate sentences (516)
insanity defense (512)
standard of proof (519)

IMPORTANT NAMES

Identify the following persons and their major contributions to abnormal psychology as discussed in this chapter.

Kenneth Donaldson (511)   Nicholas Romeo (528)
Walter Harper (529)   Thomas Szasz (522)
John Hinckley (513)   Ricky Wyatt (527)
Daniel M'Naghten (512)

GUIDED SELF-STUDY

1. What are the three major areas where mental health and legal issues overlap?

   a.

   b.

   c.

2. Of course, the law gets involved when a crime has been committed or when somebody's rights have been violated, but why does the law have anything to do with civil commitment?

Psychological Disturbance and Criminal Law

3. Psychologists debate the issue of free will, but where does the criminal justice system stand on this subject?

4. Is there any exception to the law's view on free will?

5. What do we mean by a "legal test of insanity?"

6. Briefly name, date, and summarize the cases that have established the following important legal tests of insanity.

   a. The "Irresistible impulse" decision:

   b. The M'Naghten rule:

   c. The Durham test (no date given):

   d. The ALI's Model Penal Code:

7. Which test of insanity is used by each of the following?

   a. Federal courts:

   b. The majority of state courts:

   c. The rest of the state courts (except N.H.):

   d. New Hampshire:

8. As far as expert testimony by mental health professionals is concerned, the ideal test of insanity should be worded so as to put the burden of decision fully in the hands of the (a)_____, because they, not the (b)_____ _____ professionals, are the ones who are legally empowered to make the judgment about responsibility for the crime.

9. What incident led to a radical rethinking of the insanity defense, and why?

10. List three legal changes that have occurred as a result of the case referred to in question 9.

    a.

    b.

    c.

11. List three criticisms of the insanity defense.

    a.

    b.

    c.

12. Statistically, there are more people in mental hospitals who were in trouble with the law but who never went to trial than people who went to trial and were acquitted on insanity defenses. How did all these other people get put away?

13. What is the primary difference between the use of the insanity defense and competency to stand trial?

14. Of what importance is the defendant's state of mind at the time of the trial?

15. Who brings up this competency question, and how can it be abused?

16. How is what now happens to a person who is judged incompetent to stand trial different from what used to happen?

17. By what means may people be *made* competent to stand trial?

18. Summarize some controversial issues surrounding the use of antipsychotic medications to make people competent to stand trial.

Civil Commitment

19. The textbook compares the rights of an individual in a civil commitment proceeding to the rights of a defendant in a criminal trial. What similarity is there between these two situations?

20. What percentage of admissions to public mental hospitals are involuntary?

21. Use the following words to fill in the blanks (one is used twice):

advocate   guardian   time-consuming
counsel   jury
expensive   silence

Fifteen states allow a person to have a (a)_____ trial in civil commitment hearings. The argument

against this is that jury trials are too (b)_____ and (c)_____ and that mentally ill people

will be harmed by having their mental health issues debated openly. In most states, the defendant in a civil

commitment hearing has a right to (d)_____. The question then becomes: Should the lawyer act as

a(n) (e)_____ and pursue what is in the best interest of the client (whether he/she wants it or not) or

act as a(n) (f)_____, working for what the client wants (even if it is "crazy")? Most lawyers usually

end up acting as a(n) (g)_____. In criminal trials, (h)_____ cannot be held against a

defendant. This protection against self-incrimination (i) *is / is not* clearly established for persons in civil

commitment hearings.

22. What three traditional standards of proof might be used in commitment decisions, and what level of certainty
    does each require?

    a.

    b.

    c.

23. Which of the following is a *false positive*, and which is a *false negative*?

    a.   The test says you are pregnant when you are not.

    b.   The test says you are not pregnant when you really are.

24. Which type of error do criminal courts want to avoid, and why?

25. Which type of error do doctors want to avoid, and why?

26. How do the courts weigh the two types of errors in the case of civil commitment? What are the issues, and
    what are the priorities?

27. As a result of the issues raised in the preceding question, what standard of proof for involuntary civil
    commitment was established by the U.S. Supreme Court? How does it compare to the criminal and medical
    standards?

28. In the past, what were grounds for committing someone to a mental institution?

29. What circumstance is *currently* required for a person to be committed to a mental institution?

30. What are some debatable issues in this approach to involuntary mental hospital commitment?

    a.

    b.

    c.

31. Give examples of the following types of dangerousness.

    a. Physical threat to self or other:

    b. Financial threat to self or others:

    c. Psychological threat to others:

32. The following factors tend to swell the number of false positives in the determination of dangerousness:

    a. _____ of the legal definition from state to state leaves mental health professionals shooting for a moving target when trying to determine dangerousness.

    b. _____ _____ to the predictor, because locking up non-dangerous people results in much less bad publicity than freeing someone who is dangerous.

    c. _____ of dangerousness literature, making it difficult to apply the best methods for the diagnosis of dangerousness.

    d. Judgmental _____ on the part of clinicians, who may base their judgments on unproven assumptions.

33. The "thank-you" proposition states that if a seriously disturbed person is forced into treatment against his/her will, that person will eventually be (a)_____ for the treatment after recovery from the problem. This is not always the case, but at least this reason for involuntary commitment has the advantage of stressing the *patient's* (b)_____, which is not the case in decisions based on the criterion of (c)_____.

34. As in the case of the insanity defense, civil commitment rules have varied over the years. In the decade of the (a)_____, laws were changed to make it harder to commit someone. In the (b)_____, it became easier again. Now, in some states, one can be committed for making (c)_____ of violence against someone, and in some cases, even dangerousness to (d)_____ as well as people is sufficient. Regardless of the rule changes, however, the type and number of people committed has (e) *increased / decreased / stayed about the same*. People who ultimately make the decisions in a given case seem to operate as much on the basis of (f)_____ as they do in response to the rules then in force.

35. Respond *true* or *false* to the following statements.

   a. Patients involuntarily committed to a mental hospital are there because they cannot function on their own, and therefore their civil rights are no longer in effect.

   b. In Alabama, a federal court rules that if someone is committed to a mental hospital because he/she needs treatment for a problem, then treatment must be provided to address that problem.

   c. If civil commitment is deemed necessary, simple custodial care meets the legal requirement for treatment since it prevents the person from harming him/herself or others.

   d. The Supreme Court has laid down rules for the general treatment of mental patients, but the judgment of mental health professionals is still presumed to be valid when it comes to the details of therapy.

36. If a patient has a right to treatment; does he/she have the right to refuse treatment? If so, under what conditions?

37. A mental patient also has a right to a humane environment. Included in this right are the following factors.

   dignity   *one's own clothes*   *religious worship*
   exercise   *opposite sex*   *telephone*
   mail   *personal belongings*   *toileting*
   meals   *privacy*

   a. The right to privacy and _____

   b. An opportunity for voluntary _____ _____

   c. The right to nutritionally adequate _____

   d. The right to sleeping area providing _____, a comfortable bed, a place for _____
      _____, a chair, and a bedside table

   e. The right to privacy in _____ and showering areas

   f. The right to wear _____ _____ _____ and use personal possessions

   g. The right to visitation and _____ communication

   h. The unrestricted right to send and receive _____

   i. The right to regular _____ and to be out of doors regularly

   j. Opportunity to interact with members of the _____ _____

38. Which of the preceding rights may be abridged if the mental health professionals believe such abridgment is in the patient's best interest?

39. How can behavior therapy conflict with the patients' rights mentioned above?

40. In view of the *Wyatt v. Stickney* decision, when can electric shock treatment be used as a "punishment" for a mental patient?

41. List four reasons why behavioral treatment techniques have been singled out for court scrutiny in connection with patients' rights.

    a.

    b.

    c.

    d.

Ethics and the Mental Health Profession

42. Mental health professionals are powerful in that they define what behavior is normal and (a)_____

    and who should be (b)_____ and for how long. The people who are in this position are not

    representative of the population as a whole; they are most commonly (c)_____ _____. The

    public are now trying to become informed consumers by insisting they have information to make decisions

    for themselves, which is called (d)_____ _____.

43. The American Psychological Association adheres to its Ethical Principles of Psychologists and Code of Conduct. List the five general principles.

44. A number of court cases were presented in this chapter. Just in case your instructor wants you to know them by name and issue, explain what is significant in each of the following precedent-setting cases. I'm giving you page numbers after the dates to make things a little easier.

    a. *Jones v. United States* (1983) [516]:

    b. *Jackson v. Indiana* (1972) [517]:

    c. *Addington v. Texas* (1979) [520]:

    d. *Wyatt v. Stickney* (1972) [529]:

    e. *O'Connor v. Donaldson* (1975) [528]:

    f. *Youngberg v. Romeo* (1982) [528]:

    g. *Tarasoff v. Regents of California* (1976) [523]:

    h. *State v. Soura* (1990) [530]:

    i. *State v. Summers* (1993) [530]:

    j. *Knecht v. Gillman* (1973) [531]:

HELPFUL HINTS

1. Clarify with your instructor how much detail you need to know about the legal cases discussed in this chapter. Do you need to know the names of the cases to go with the principles they established, dates of the cases, and/or the individual details associated with each?

2. Shock used as aversive stimulation, or as punishment to suppress a behavior, has nothing to do with shock therapy, which is an electrochemical therapy used to reduce severe depression.

3. In connection with behavior modification and patients' rights, remember that behaviorists believe in the importance of *learning* as the way of acquiring behavior. B. F. Skinner once said: "People who help those

who can help themselves can work a sinister kind of destruction by making the good things in life no longer contingent upon behavior." *Learning* requires a connection between what you do and what happens afterward.

PRACTICE TEST

Use the following test questions to check your knowledge of the material in this chapter. You may want to write the answers on a separate sheet of paper so you can take the test more than once.

1. Which of the following is true of the insanity defense?
    a. It assumes that all behavior is irrational.
    b. It is necessary only if free will is assumed to be responsible for normal behavior.
    c. It applies only to people who have been previously diagnosed as psychotic.
    d. It is intended to replace the concept of "guilty but mentally ill."

2. Which of the following expresses the criterion of the M'Naghten rule? A person is not to be held responsible for a crime if he/she
    a. cannot resist the impulse to do wrong.
    b. does not know what he/she is doing, or does not know that the action is wrong.
    c. commits the act as a result of mental illness or defect.
    d. is already under treatment for a disorder that causes the behavior he/she is accused of.

3. The major problem of the Durham Test is that
    a. the jury seldom agrees on when the test is to be used.
    b. it does not apply to many individuals who commit crimes.
    c. it does not hold for the truly insane.
    d. it requires expert evaluation of the accused by a mental health professional.

4. Which of the following is a change that occurred after the Hinckley insanity verdict?
    a. The prosecution now has to prove that the defendant is sane.
    b. The defense now has to prove that the defendant is insane.
    c. Most states have eliminated the insanity defense altogether.
    d. Federal rules were changed to accept only "guilty, but mentally ill" pleas.

5. All the following statements are valid criticisms of the insanity defense EXCEPT
    a. the jury must often make its decision based on contradictory expert testimony.
    b. the successful defendant may be worse off than if he or she had been convicted of a crime.
    c. the jury must make a retrospective judgment.
    d. the insanity defense equates mental disorder with criminality but most mentally ill persons are not criminals.

6. An actively psychotic person has been committed to a hospital for the criminally insane following his alleged commission of a bizarre, violent crime. He will stand trial for that crime
    a. when he can understand the proceedings and can assist in his defense.
    b. within the six-month time limit after the grand jury has filed an indictment against him.
    c. when he is no longer dangerous.
    d. when he has improved enough to be given release time from the hospital.

7. The insanity defense is to _____ as a competency hearing is to _____.
    a. malingering; genuine disorder
    b. criminal law; civil commitment
    c. moral responsibility; intellectual capability
    d. psychological disorder; organic disorder

8. Christopher has committed no crime but is so severely disturbed and potentially dangerous to himself that his parents want to institutionalize him. Christopher, however, does not want to go to an institution. A court will now decide the issue. Christopher is facing

   a. an insanity defense case.
   b. a hearing to see if he is competent to defend himself.
   c. civil commitment proceedings.
   d. a Tarasoff decision.

9. All the following are unresolved questions about the role of counsel at a commitment hearing EXCEPT whether the attorney should

   a. act as a guardian.
   b. act as an advocate.
   c. rely on the judgment of expert witnesses.
   d. worry about whether the client is guilty or innocent.

10. In medicine, it is considered a terrible error to miss a diagnosis of cancer; it is not such a bad error to incorrectly diagnose cancer and discover that the problem was minor. This means that, in medicine, diagnosticians want to avoid

    a. a false positive.
    b. a true negative.
    c. a false negative.
    d. an error of commission.

11. Which of the following standards of proof can be said to require accuracy about 75% of the time?

    a. The medical standard
    b. The civil standard of "preponderance of evidence"
    c. The criminal standard of "beyond a reasonable doubt"
    d. The standard of "clear and convincing evidence"

12. In criminal cases, the standard of proof is _____; after the *Addington v. Texas* (1979) ruling, the standard of proof in civil commitment cases is _____.

    a. 51% certainty; 75% certainty
    b. "preponderance of evidence"; "clear and convincing evidence"
    c. "beyond a reasonable doubt"; "clear and convincing evidence"
    d. 95% certainty; 51% certainty

13. If a person was not institutionalized and then committed a violent crime, there would probably be a great deal of bad publicity about the case. If the same person, with little tendency to be violent, was institutionalized there would be little, if any, bad publicity. These factors

    a. explain why therapists criticize the Tarasoff decision.
    b. illustrate the problem of low interjudge reliability in commitment cases.
    c. contribute to the high rate of false negatives in commitment cases.
    d. explain the large number of false positives when predicting dangerousness.

14. The "thank-you" proposition states that

    a. a person committed involuntarily will thank you for it after being cured.
    b. patients must be treated politely and with respect or commitment decisions may be reversed in court.
    c. society's gratitude for the removal of dangerous individuals justifies their commitment.
    d. once institutionalized, most patients can be treated in ways that will minimize complaints.

15. Which of the following is the LEAST appropriate question to ask a mental health professional serving as an expert witness in a civil commitment proceeding?

    a. How dangerous is this patient?
    b. Is the patient too dangerous to be released?
    c. What is the probability that treatment will be effective?
    d. What is the probability that the patient will later be grateful for treatment?

16. The case of *Wyatt v. Stickney* is a precedent-setting case in the area of

    a. patient's rights.
    b. competency to stand trial.
    c. the insanity defense.
    d. civil commitment criteria.

17. The case of *Harper v. Washington*, a 1990 Supreme Court case, involved a prison inmate who argued that a judge should determine if he must take antipsychotic drugs against his wishes. The court ruled that

    a. prisoners have no rights when it comes to refusing medication.
    b. prisoners can make the decision about medication for themselves.
    c. health professionals should make decisions about the need for treatment.
    d. judges can overrule the authority of mental health professionals.

18. All the following are part of patients' rights to a humane environment EXCEPT a right to

    a. privacy and dignity.
    b. wear one's own clothes.
    c. leave the institution at any time.
    d. send and receive mail.

19. In 1990, the Supreme Court ruled that a mentally retarded woman was competent to have marital sex but was incompetent to agree to extramarital sex. What was the reasoning here?

    a. Marital sex is legal, but extramarital sex is illegal.
    b. Marital sex is morally approved of, but extramarital sex is adultery.
    c. Marital sex is fair to both partners, but extramarital sex is unfair to the woman's husband.
    d. Marital sex is safe, but extramarital sex is unsafe, and the woman was incapable of appreciating the dangers.

20. The power of the mental health profession to pass judgment on the behavior of people has been challenged on which of the following grounds?

    a. Largely white, upper-middle-class therapists are not in touch with the realities of life in the rest of the world.
    b. It smacks of paternalism and violates the right of people to lead their own lives.
    c. Many problems that people are stigmatized with are not problems with individuals but with the culture.
    d. All of the above

ANSWERS

Guided Self-Study (p. 288)

1. a. psychological disturbance and criminal responsibility
    b. civil commitment
    c. patients' rights (511)

2. Civil commitment means that the state takes action to insist that a person be hospitalized for mental health care against his/her wishes. In this case, a person is losing his/her freedom, so civil commitment is very much a question of a person's legal rights. (518)

3. It assumes all persons have free will, and therefore a person can be blamed, held accountable, and punished for a behavior that society has defined as intolerable. (511)

4. The insanity defense is the exception for those people who, because of mental disturbance, are not judged to have free choice about their actions. (511)

5. A "legal test of insanity" is the set of criteria that a defendant must meet in order to be declared not responsible for his/her actions. These criteria have been established in earlier, precedent-setting cases in which an insanity defense was attempted. (512)

6. a. "Irresistible impulse" (1834): Person could not make him/herself do the right thing or prevent him/herself from doing the wrong thing.
   b. M'Naghten rule (1843): Person either didn't know what he/she was doing or didn't know the action was wrong.
   c. Durham test: Excused an unlawful act that was the result of a mental problem
   d. American Law Institute's (ALI) Model Penal Code of 1962: Person is not guilty if he/she lacks ability to understand the criminality of his/her behavior, or to act within the law. This does not include repeated criminal behavior and antisocial conduct. (512–513)

7. a. A test similar to M'Naghten
   b. ALI test
   c. M'Naghten, some with irresistible impulse, some without
   d. Durham test (512)

8. a. jury
   b. mental health (512)

9. The Hinckley verdict—acquitting someone by reason of insanity who did not appear sufficiently psychotic—brought the insanity defense to the forefront of public attention. (513)

10. a. The development of a new verdict, "guilty but mentally ill," in some jurisdictions. It is an intermediate position between not guilty by reason of insanity and guilty. It is for the person who has a mental illness but *does* know what he/she was doing and that the behavior was wrong. (513)
    b. Another change involves the question of which side has the responsibility to prove sanity or insanity. Since the Hinckley verdict many jurisdictions have changed the rules so that now it is up to the defense to prove insanity. Before, the burden fell on the prosecution to prove sanity. (515)
    c. Prior to the 1970s, a person acquitted by reason of insanity was automatically committed to a mental hospital. In the 1970s, mental health laws were changed to require commitment proceedings to determine if he/she was still mentally ill and dangerous. In the 1980s, things were tightened up again (after Hinckley), and automatic commitment for an indeterminate period is again possible. (515–516)

11. a. It is difficult for a jury to determine if a person was insane at the time of the crime.
    b. "Insanity" doesn't exist; all behavior is purposeful for the person engaging in it.
    c. Innocent by reason of insanity can lead to an indeterminate stay in a mental institution, which can be worse (longer) than if the defendant were sent to prison. (516–517)

12. They were judged incompetent to stand trial. (517)

13. The difference is a matter of time. Insanity refers to the person's state of mind while the crime was being committed, and competency refers to the person's state of mind at the time of the trial. (517)

14. If a person cannot understand the charges against him/her and respond to his/her lawyer to help build the defense, then the person cannot be put on trial. (517)

15. Either the prosecution or the defense. Sometimes competency is abused as a delay maneuver if either side feels it has a weak case. (517)

16. In the past, he/she could spend years locked up in a mental hospital trying to get his/her legal rights back. Now, since a 1972 Supreme Court decision, he/she cannot be held in limbo forever. He/She must be either officially committed (because he/she is mentally ill and dangerous) or released. (517)

17. By use of antipsychotic medications (517–518)

18. Does medication actually give defendants adequate access to their thinking skills? Are they really as mentally fit with medication as they would be if they were not mentally ill? Antipsychotic medications often make people groggy and passive, which is no way to go to your own trial. Is it fair to make a person look less disturbed than he/she is? Perhaps if the jury saw the defendant without medication, it would leave no doubt that he/she is seriously disturbed. (517–518)

19. In both cases, the person is at risk of losing his/her freedom, whether in prison or in a mental institution. (518)

20. About 55% (518)

21. a. jury
    b. expensive (or time consuming)
    c. time consuming (or expensive)
    d. counsel (or lawyer)
    e. guardian
    f. advocate
    g. guardian
    h. silence
    i. is not (518–519)

22. a. "Beyond a reasonable doubt": 90–95% certain; used in criminal trials
    b. "Preponderance of evidence": 51% certain; civil proceedings
    c. Medical evidence standard: any evidence whatsoever; medical diagnoses (519)

23. a. false positive
    b. false negative (519)

24. Criminal courts want to avoid the false positive—that is, they do not want to send an innocent person to prison. The value judgment behind this is that it is better to let a guilty person go free than to make an innocent person suffer unfairly. (519)

25. Medical doctors want to avoid a false negative—that is, they do not want to miss a disease that is really there. The value judgment here is that scaring you with a false diagnosis is much less of a problem than missing an illness that may kill you if it is not treated. (519)

26. Since someone who is committed loses his/her freedom, we want to be very sure it is necessary—thus a fear of false positives. However, we want to be sure a real problem is properly treated, and so we also want to avoid a false negative. The result is a compromise whereby less certainty is needed than in a criminal trial but more certainty is needed than with a medical diagnosis. (519–521)

27. "Clear and convincing evidence," corresponding to about 75% sure; this is lower than "beyond a reasonable doubt" for criminal judgments and higher than the "when in doubt, diagnose" medical standard. (521)

28. "Mental illness" or "need of treatment" (522)

29. Dangerousness to self, others, or property (522)

30. a. How should dangerousness be defined?
    b. To what extent can future behavior be predicted from past behavior?
    c. How accurately can one anticipate rare events where clearly established odds are not available? (522–525)

31. a. homicide, suicide, physical attack
    b. patient claims voices are telling him/her to burn his/her financial assets.
    c. patient stalks a victim whom he/she believes to be Satan and terrorizes that individual with threats; or a parent locks a child in its room for days at a time trying to keep it away from the evil in this world. (522–525)

32. a. Variability
    b. Differential consequences
    c. Complexity
    d. biases (525)

33. a. grateful
    b. welfare
    c. dangerousness (526)

34. a. 1970s
    b. 1980s
    c. threats
    d. property
    e. stayed about the same
    f. intuition (525)

35. a. false (527)
    b. true (527–528)
    c. false (529–531)
    d. true (527–529)

36. Involuntary patients can be required to submit to "routine" treatment, which may typically be medication. More controversial treatments, such as ECT, require permission from the patient, next-of-kin, or the court. (526)

37. a. dignity
    b. religious worship
    c. meals
    d. privacy, personal belongings
    e. toileting
    f. one's own clothes
    g. telephone
    h. mail
    i. exercise
    j. opposite sex (529–530)

38. "d" (personal belongings); "j" (visitation and telephone communication); "h" (mail) (530)

39. Behavior therapy is reinforcing people for behaving more appropriately. But many of the most ready reinforcers are items on the patients' rights list; that means they cannot be used as earned rewards since they must be provided automatically. (531–532) (See Hint 3.)

40. In extreme cases, electric shock (an aversive stimulus) can be used in extraordinary circumstances to suppress serious self-abusive behaviors. (531) (See Hint 2.)

41. a. There have been some real abuses in the name of behavior therapy that deserve to be exposed and stopped.
    b. Many behavioral techniques are still new and are therefore scrutinized in the same way that other unproven or "experimental" treatments are.
    c. Behavior therapy's specificity and even its very effectiveness create questions about "control" and "manipulation" that less specific insight therapies do not arouse.
    d. Although less intrusive than some medical therapies, behavioral treatments may cause patient distress on the way to producing more productive behavior. (531–532)

42. a. abnormal
    b. institutionalized, or treated
    c. affluent white males
    d. informed consent (532–534)

43. beneficence and nonmaleficence
    fidelity and responsibility
    integrity
    justice
    respect for people's rights and dignity (532)

44. a. Insanity acquittees could be automatically hospitalized until they were no longer dangerous, and if necessary, they could be hospitalized longer than the jail time for the crime for which they were acquitted. (516)
    b. A defendant in a criminal trial cannot be held as "incompetent to stand trial" indefinitely. As soon as the possibility of becoming competent in the foreseeable future is eliminated, the person must be formally committed to a mental institution or released. (517)
    c. The court set a standard of proof at "clear and convincing evidence" (75%) for involuntary commitment decisions. (520)
    d. The court ruled that if a person is locked up because he/she needs treatment, then adequate, individualized treatment in a humane environment must be provided. (529)
    e. The court gave indirect support for right to treatment because it said a person cannot be locked up for custodial care just because of mental illness. (528)
    f. The court subtly shifted emphasis from absolute patient's rights to support for mental health professionals' decisions about what is best for the patient. (528) (See Hint 2.)
    g. The limit on client-therapist confidentiality is when the public welfare is at risk. (523)
    h. The court placed limits on a mentally retarded woman's right to consent to sex. (530)
    i. This is another case in which the court dealt with competency to consent to sex. (530)
    j. This is an instance where patient abuse was being justified as behavioral therapy. (531)

Practice Test (p. 294)

1. a. Just the opposite—if that were true, we would need a *sanity* defense instead.
   b. Right!
   c. No. Mental state at the time of the crime is the only issue.
   d. Incorrect. The insanity defense came first.

2. a. Sorry. This would be the "irresistible impulse" rule.
   b. Correct!
   c. No, this is the Durham test.
   d. Wrong. Mental state at the time of the crime is all that is relevant.

3. a. Incorrect. The jury does not decide when to use the test, only if the accused passes the test.
   b. Not a problem. Insanity defenses are designed to be used rarely.
   c. No. In fact, the "crazier" a person is, the more likely it (or any other test) is to apply.
   d. Right!

4. a. Incorrect. This is the traditional approach.
   b. Yes!
   c. No. Only three states have done that (Idaho, Montana, and Utah).
   d. No. Some states adopted the "guilty, but mentally ill" verdict, but it is controversial.

5. a. This is true, not an exception.
   b. This is sometimes the case.
   c. This is true, but we are looking for an exception here.
   d. Right! No one claims the insanity defense does this.

6. a. You got it!
   b. Nonsense answer with a lot of legal-sounding stuff; all of it irrelevant.
   c. No. Dangerousness is an issue for civil commitment, but not with competence to be tried.
   d. Incorrect. Fit to be released from a hospital does not equate with competence to be tried.

7. a. No. the genuineness of the problem is an issue in both cases.
   b. Incorrect. Both of them have to do with criminal law.
   c. Right!
   d. Sorry. The source of the disorder is not the issue.

8. a. Incorrect. An insanity defense is a defense in a criminal trial.
   b. No. Competency is an issue in a criminal trial.
   c. Correct!
   d. No. The Tarasoff case dealt with confidentiality.

9. a. No, this is a genuine concern.
   b. Sorry, this is a genuine concern.
   c. Incorrect. This is often an issue.
   d. Right! This would be an issue only in a criminal case.

10. a. No. A false positive is to conclude there is something there when there is not.
    b. Incorrect. A *true* anything is not an error at all.
    c. You got it!
    d. No. This is when you do something you should not have done, as opposed to an error of *omission*, when you fail to do something you should have done.

11. a. Incorrect. In the medical standard, *any* chance of being accurate is sufficient.
    b. No. This is just a bit more than half sure.
    c. Sorry. This requires almost complete certainty.
    d. Yes!

12. a. Half right, but criminal is about 95% or so.
    b. Half right, but criminal is "beyond a reasonable doubt."
    c. Correct!
    d. Half right, but in civil commitment it is about 75%.

13. a. No. The Tarasoff case involved confidentiality issues.
    b. Actually, the text says nothing about interjudge reliability here.
    c. Just the opposite. The people making the decision want to err on the safe side.
    d. Yes!

14. a. Right!
    b. No. The "thank-you" proposition is not concerned with patient treatment, but with justification for his/her commitment.
    c. No. The "thank you" is coming from the wrong source here.
    d. Nonsense answer. Of course, we want to treat people well, but this is not the issue.

15. a. This is a reasonable, if difficult question, because it is a judgment about behavior.
    b. You got it! This is a value judgment that only the society can make.
    c. This is a reasonable question for people who deal in treatment, as mental health folks do.
    d. This is a hard one, but it still deals with behavior, not value judgments about behavior.

16. a. Correct!
    b. No. Remember, Ricky Wyatt was not accused of a crime.
    c. No. Ricky Wyatt was not on trial for anything.
    d. No. Ricky Wyatt was already in an institution when the issue came up.

17. a. No, this is too extreme a conclusion.
    b. Incorrect. This is too extreme.
    c. Right!
    d. Incorrect. Remember the concept of "presumptive validity," which says mental health professionals should generally be assumed to know what they are doing.

18. a. Sorry, this is a right of mental patients.
    b. This is a valid right of patients.
    c. Correct! This one goes too far.
    d. No. This is guaranteed as a right.

19. a. No. The legality of extramarital sex was not the issue.
    b. Incorrect. The morality of extramarital sex is no business of a court of law, only the legality of it, and it is not illegal.
    c. No. It may well have been unfair to the husband, but this was not the issue.
    d. Right!

20. a. This is a valid point, but read on.
    b. This is a criticism that has been made, but there are more possibilities.
    c. This is a commonly made point, but look at the other options too.
    d. Correct!